THE BRITISH INVASION FROM THE NORTH

A Da Capo Press Reprint Series

THE ERA OF THE AMERICAN REVOLUTION

General Editor: Leonard W. Levy
Brandeis University

THE BRITISH INVASION FROM THE NORTH

Digby's Journal of the Campaigns of Generals Carleton and Burgoyne from Canada, 1776-1777

Introduction and Notes by
JAMES PHINNEY BAXTER

DA CAPO PRESS • NEW YORK • 1970

A Da Capo Press Reprint Edition

This Da Capo Press edition of
The British Invasion from the North
is an unabridged republication of the
first edition published in Albany, New York, in 1887.

Library of Congress Catalog Card Number 74-114756

SBN 306-71926-6

Published by Da Capo Press
A Division of Plenum Publishing Corporation
227 West 17th Street, New York, N.Y. 10011

Manufactured in the United States of America

THE BRITISH INVASION FROM THE NORTH

LT GEN. BURGOYNE.

THE BRITISH INVASION FROM THE NORTH.

THE CAMPAIGNS

OF

GENERALS CARLETON AND BURGOYNE

FROM CANADA, 1776–1777,

WITH THE JOURNAL OF LIEUT. WILLIAM DIGBY,

OF THE

53D, OR SHROPSHIRE REGIMENT OF FOOT.

ILLUSTRATED WITH HISTORICAL NOTES,

BY

JAMES PHINNEY BAXTER, A. M.

ALBANY, N. Y.:
JOEL MUNSELL'S SONS, 82 STATE STREET.
1887.

TABLE OF CONTENTS.

ILLUSTRATIONS.

DEDICATED

to the

Memory

of

My Revered Father,

Dr. ELIHU BAXTER,

to whom

the Men of the Revolution were the most Heroic,

the most devoted to duty,

and the most

pure in heart of all men, ancient or modern.

INTRODUCTION.

In offering to the public a new addendum to that stirring theme, the British invasion from Canada in the War of the Revolution, a few explanatory words seem proper. While engaged during the fall and winter of 1885-6, in examining manuscripts in English archives relative to America, a Journal in the British Museum, written by William Digby, an officer in the army of invasion, and containing interesting particulars relative to the two campaigns of 1776 and 1777, attracted my attention, and I obtained permission from the Museum authorities to have it copied. Having familiarized myself with the Journal, I became so interested in it, that I laid aside other work in which I was engaged and began collecting materials for annotating it. This work led to a study of the subject, of which the Journal treats but partially, and to complete my task properly, a succinct account of the two campaigns and of questions growing out of them connected with the hero of the final and more important one — General Burgoyne — seemed necessary as introductory to Digby's work; hence my account of the campaigns of Carleton and Burgoyne. In my work I have received favors from many sources, notably from the officials of the British Museum, especially from Mr. Henry Kensington; from the

British War and Admiralty Offices, which have generously furnished me with particulars relative to officers engaged in the two campaigns, and from Douglas Brymner, Esq., of Ottawa, Canadian archivist. Mr. William L. Stone, so well known to all historical students as an authority in matters relating to the Revolutionary period, has been untiring in giving me valuable aid and encouragement; Mr. F. D. Stone, librarian of the Pennsylvania Historical Society, and particularly Mr. John W. Jordan, his able assistant, have rendered me valuable aid, and the same may be said of Mr. A. R. Spofford of the National Library at Washington; Mr. F. Saunders of the Astor Library, New York, and William H. Egle, M. D., of the State Library of Pennsylvania at Harrisburg. Last and not least, I must refer to the admirable, I may say unequaled work of Colonel Horatio Rogers, embodied in Hadden's Journal and Orderly Books, from which I have derived much information. Of the author of the Journal, William Digby, but little can be said. I have been baffled thus far in obtaining particulars concerning his family and early history. He entered the British military service as an ensign in the Fifty-third Regiment of Foot, on February 10, 1770, at which date the regiment was doing garrison duty in Ireland under the command of Colonel John Toovey, an officer of distinction in the British army. In this capacity he served until April 1, 1773, when he was promoted to the rank of lieutenant, which was his rank when hostilities commenced between Great Britain and her North American colonies. On the 4th of April, 1776, Digby embarked from Ireland with his regiment under Major-General Burgoyne for the relief of Quebec, and shared in the perils attendant upon the expulsion of the Americans from Canada during that year; and through the winter which followed was stationed at Chambly. In the spring of 1777, the four flank companies of the Fifty-third Regiment were selected to accompany Burgoyne's expedition to reduce the colonists into submission to the British crown, the eight battalion companies being left behind to protect Canada against another invasion. These companies were subsequently employed by Burgoyne to garrison Ticonderoga; but Digby followed the fortunes of his general through that trying campaign, which ended in the surrender of the British army of invasion to the Americans at Saratoga. Digby was among the paroled officers, but unfortunately has left us no account of his experiences after the surrender. From the time when he signed the parole at Cambridge, he disappears from view until the 10th of August, 1785, — some time after the acknowledgment by Great Britain of American independence — at which date his regiment was still doing garrison duty in Canada, when we find him retiring on half pay, "by exchange receiving the difference," and, on March 1, 1786, he appears, by record of the War Office, under the title of lieutenant, "by exchange, repaying the difference." On the twenty-second of the same month he is recorded as having retired. This is the last glimpse we have of our journalist. Of the Journal itself, I can say but little. It is not an original kept during the campaign, but a compilation made by the author, undoubtedly, as he says, for the partial eye of a friend. My copy was made by a scribe recommended to me at the Museum, and was compared with the original by Mr. Kensington, who pronounced it correct. It has been printed *verbatim et literatim*, except that I have introduced capitals in some instances where they seemed necessary, and have corrected the spelling of two or three words, which I believe have been errors of the scribe growing out of obscure writing, as *Livingstone* for *Levestoe*, and *Ticonderoga* for *Ticonderago*. I have also added to the punctuation and have placed a few words in brackets to clear up apparent ambiguities of meaning. I regret having been unable to correct proof by the original manuscript, as this is the only proper way to secure verbal accuracy, but I trust that no material errors will be found in the work.

James Phinney Baxter.

61 Deering St., Portland, Maine, *November* 1, 1887.

THE CAMPAIGNS OF CARLETON AND BURGOYNE FROM CANADA.

1776 AND 1777.

THE author of the following journal, William Digby, lieutenant of the 53rd Regiment of British Grenadiers, had passed into oblivion and the stream of memory would never have brought us any tidings of him, had not this waif, surviving the vicissitudes and perils to which it must have been exposed for more than a century, brought to hand enough to enable us to mentally outline the man and partially estimate his character. That his was a manly spirit guided by an unswerving instinct of justice; devoted to duty and singularly free from that undue proneness to criticism of those above him so common to men in conditions similar to those in which he found himself during the disastrous campaign of General Burgoyne, all will be ready to admit after perusing his journal, and though we may know nothing of his family tree, of the time or place of his coming or going, or indeed of any subsequent events of his life, we shall regard him with confidence and respect. The regiment of which Digby was lieutenant was organized in 1755,[1] at a time when the French with their savage Indian allies were attacking the American frontier settlements, rendering a war between the mother country and France unavoidable.

At the time of its formation it was called the 55th, but Governor Shirley[2] of Massachusetts, and Sir William Pepperell[3] had each formed a regiment called respectively the 50th and 51st, which after the war were disbanded, and the gap was closed by lowering the numbers of the regiments above them, by which the 55th became the 53rd. At the time when the English colonies in America were demanding from the home government what they conceived to be their rights, the 53rd was garrisoned in Ireland, from whence it was ordered to Canada to take

---

[1] *Vide* Historical Record of the 53rd Regiment (Cannon), London, 1834. The uniform of the regiment was: "Cocked hats; red coats faced with red, lined with yellow and ornamented with yellow lace; red waistcoats and breeches and white gaiters."

[2] William Shirley was governor of Massachusetts from 1741 to 1756, and was prominent in the war with the French.

[3] Sir William Pepperell was a colonel of militia, and distinguished himself at the siege of Louisburg in 1745, for which he received the order of Knighthood. He died in 1759. *Vide* Life of, by Parsons, London, 1856.

part in that momentous drama, the first scene of which had opened in the quiet rural village of Lexington. The troops sailed from Ireland with a knowledge of the successes which the American arms had achieved in Canada, expecting indeed to learn on their arrival that Quebec had fallen into the possession of Montgomery, but with anticipation of a speedy subjugation of their despised antagonists, whose commander the aristocratic supporters of royalty designated as Mister,[4] declining to recognize his title of general, and regarding those who had taken up arms in defense of their rights a lawless rabble, ignorant of civilized warfare.[5] The

---

[4] Lord George Germaine, the British minister, persisted in his correspondence with Howe and others in designating General Washington as "Mr.," and this example of his superior the British commander felt bound to follow. He therefore addressed his first letter to *Mr.* Washington, which the latter declined to receive, and Howe returned it by Colonel Patterson, one of his officers, addressed to George Washington, etc., etc., etc. Washington took no notice of the insult, but stated that he declined to receive "any letter directed to him as a private person when it related to his public station." Colonel Patterson pointed out that "etc., etc., etc." implied all the titles which he might choose to claim, and ended by verbally conveying to him the contents of Howe's letter. This folly was not long persisted in by General Howe, who although he had declared that he would acknowledge "no rank but that conferred by the king," found himself obliged to recognize Washington by his appropriate title if he would hold communication with him. *Vide* Sparks' Life, Appendix No. 1, Vol. IV.

[5] Not only were they characterized as lawless and ignorant, but as full of all iniquity. General Gage wrote on

expedition, consisting of fifty-four transport ships and convoyed by two men of war, sailed from Cork in April, 1776, the troops being under the charge of Lieutenant-Colonel Fraser, who ended his career in the campaign of the next year with so many others of his brave companions. Leaving these troops to pursue their voyage across the Atlantic, we will glance retrospectively at the progress of events during the preceding year. The battles of Lexington and Bunker Hill had disclosed to the king and his ministers the unpleasant fact, that they had been at fault in supposing that Englishmen in America would give way at once upon the appearance of regular troops, a fallacy which they had hitherto indulged, and they began to awaken to the unpleasant prospect of a prolonged conflict, concerning the outcome of which, there was among thoughtful men a diversity of opinion.

What made it the more embarrassing to the British government was the opposition of its people at home to the war. The principle for which

---

July 24, 1775: "A Pamphlet published by the Continental Congress, called a Declaration of the United Colonies, has been sent in from the Rebel Camp, copies of which will no doubt be sent to England from Philadelphia. They pay little regard to facts, for the Contents of it is as replete with Deceit and Falsehood as most of their Publications;" and, again, "Mr. Washington, who commands the Rebel Army, has written to me on the subject of the treatment of the Rebel Prisoners in our custody. I understand they make war like Savages, capitivating women and children." *Vide* Correspondence in Public Records' Office, London.

the colonists had taken arms was a popular one, and a powerful party in England warmly espoused it. When the determination of the government to subjugate the colonists by force of arms became known, the ministry was bombarded with petitions from every part of the kingdom. These petitions set forth all the arguments against the course determined upon which ingenuity could devise. Many even of the first officers in the army threw up their commissions, declaring that they would not serve in such a war against their own countrymen. But the sluggish spirit of George the Third was thoroughly aroused against his unruly subjects, and he was stubbornly deaf to arguments in their favor however reasonable they might be. He was fully bent upon chastising them into submission, and was hotly seconded by his ministers. But the conditions existing in the two countries were quite dissimilar. In the colonies the people freely offered their lives and fortunes to the common cause, and multitudes gathered under the new flag, animated with hope and with a fixed determination never to yield their rights, while in England on the contrary, the unpopularity of the war rendered enlistments on a large scale impossible. Though unusual bounties were offered, enlistments proceeded so slowly that the king found it necessary to look across the channel for aid. He applied to Catherine of Russia to lend him some of her battalions, but was met with a tart refusal;[6] to Holland, which turned an indifferent ear to his appeal, and finally to Germany with better success.

The petty sovereigns of this country to their eternal disgrace, loaned for hire seventeen thousand of their people to the British king, as they doubtless would have loaned them to the colonists had they sought them with a larger price. When it became known in England that the king had hired German troops in order to subjugate their countrymen in America, a considerable portion of the English people raised their voices against the act. They saw in it perhaps, the possibility of an abridgment of their own liberties by similar means. But the king was delighted with the new acquisitions to his forces; indeed, he regarded them with greater complacency than he regarded his own more thoughtful subjects. Their stolid minds were not agitated with

[6] George the Third, when he applied to Catherine of Russia for twenty thousand of her subjects to employ against the colonies, gallantly left her to fix her own compensation; but she refused his application with so much spirit, that the king in a letter to Lord North said, that some of her expressions might "be civil to a Russian ear, but certainly not to more civilized ones." Horace Walpole took delight in ridiculing the king for his correspondence with "Sister Kitty." Schiller thus holds up the German sovereign to public view. After speaking of the objections which some of the soldiers made to being sold for the American war, he continues: "Our gracious sovereign paraded the troops and had the chattering fools shot then and there. We heard the crack of the muskets, we saw their brains sprinkled against the wall, and then the rest shouted, 'Hurrah for America!'"

theories of human rights, and their sympathies would not be with a people whose manners were to them an offense, and whose language a mystery; hence there could be no fear that they would desert to the Americans as some of the English levies might. The employment of these hirelings against the colonists was abhorrent to many of the English people;[7] but the employment of the savage Indian tribes against them was still more so, and this feeling was shared even by the British commanders themselves. But England possessed a monarch incapable of listening to reason where his prejudices were opposed, and a ministry whose incapacity has perhaps never been equaled. The harshest measures were blindly resolved upon, and it was determined to crush out the rebellion before it could gather more strength, or engage the sympathy of France, who was watching the struggle with keen satisfaction, not a satisfaction in which sympathy for the oppressed colonists found a place, as it was but the preposterous struggle of the *canaille* against the *noblesse;* but a satisfaction which would be intensified if, peradventure, both combatants should be so weakened as to make it possible

[7] Chatham, Burke and others denounced the employment of the savages in the most ardent manner. We are told that the vehemence of the latter caused tears of laughter to roll "down the fat cheeks of Lord North at hearing an absent man denounced for measures for which he himself was mainly and directly responsible." *Vide* Fonblanque's Life of Burgoyne, London, 1856, p. 243, n.

for her to again found her imperium in the new world.

How was it with the Americans? Hopeful of success they had assumed the offensive and had made their triumphant way into Canada: Montgomery pushing through the lake region of northern New York, and Arnold through the wilderness of Maine, finally joined their forces together in the heart of the enemy's country. Stronghold after stronghold fell before the invaders, until at last, the British General Carleton fleeing to escape capture in the habiliments of a peasant, took refuge in the fortress of Quebec, under whose walls the victorious Americans encamped, confident of conquering the last remnant of King George's troops left on the soil of Canada. This was the condition of affairs in December, 1775, while the king was drumming up reluctant recruits in England, and negotiating for others with his brother despots on the continent, as before stated. But a Canadian winter was upon Montgomery; disease and exposure were wasting his army, and something had to be done. The darkest and shortest days of winter came, and an attack, one of the most daring in the annals of arms, was made upon Quebec. Montgomery, whose intrepid spirit had never forecast failure, and whose presence alone gave animation to the enterprise, fell with many of his no less brave compatriots, and beaten back, shattered but not disheartened, the Americans sullenly sat down before the walls of the city, repaired as well as they could their sore damage, and laid out new schemes for the discomfiture of their enemies. Arnold was in command, a man perhaps no less daring nor less fruitful in expedients than Montgomery, and as spring advanced, he prepared for a final attack upon Carleton. His batteries commanded the river, his red-hot shot were thrown into the city, but disease was at work in his army to which few recruits found their way. In the beginning of May, Thomas,[8] who had been assigned to the chief command, arrived, and while he was considering the question of raising the siege, the advance ships of the fleet which had sailed from Ireland in April came in sight, and leaving behind every thing which could incumber his retreat, he at once hastened to abandon his position, followed by Carleton with reinforcements from the fleet. Although the Americans stubbornly contested their ground, as may be seen by a perusal of this journal penned by

[8] General John Thomas was from Plymouth, Massachusetts, where his descendants still reside. He, like Montgomery, had seen service in the French and Indian wars. At the beginning of the war, he was one of the first to raise a regiment, with which he joined the Continental army at Roxbury in 1775. He was appointed one of the first brigadier-generals, and commanded a division at the siege of Boston. He was appointed a major-general in March, 1776, and in the following May joined the army before Quebec, but was attacked by the small-pox, which prevailed among the troops, shortly after his arrival in camp, and died at Chambly on the 2d of June. He was a man of ability and greatly esteemed by his soldiers. Washington placed confidence in him, and believed that he would accomplish much for the American cause.

an unfriendly but just spirit, they were forced back by the superior strength of the British with their German and Indian allies. These divided into two parts, one under Carleton, who followed the St. Lawrence to Montreal to attack Arnold, who held that place, and the other under Burgoyne, who pressed on toward Fort St. Johns, forcing back Sullivan[9] to that point.

Here however, Arnold, who had retreated before Carleton, was enabled to form a junction with Sullivan; but the two generals seeing how useless it

---

[9] John Sullivan was of Irish parentage and a native of Berwick, Maine. He was born February 17, 1740, and was reared on a farm, but upon reaching maturity studied law and began the practice of his profession at Durham, New Hampshire. He was a delegate to the first Continental Congress. When the Continental army was organized in 1775, he was appointed a brigadier-general, and the following year was made a major-general. He was assigned to the command left vacant by the death of General Thomas, and shortly after took the place of General Greene on Long Island. In the battle which took place there in August of the same year (1776) he was taken prisoner, but was soon exchanged, when he was assigned to the command of General Charles Lee's division in New Jersey, Lee having been taken prisoner. He participated in the battles of Brandywine and Germantown, and soon after was assigned to the command of the Rhode Island troops. He was engaged, in the summer of 1778, in the unsuccessful siege of Newport, and the next year ended his military career in an expedition against the Indians. Owing to some difficulty with the board of war, he resigned his commission in 1779. He was after this, a member of Congress and president of New Hampshire, and in 1789, received the appointment of district judge, an office which he retained until his death, January 23, 1795.

was to attempt to withstand the onset of forces so much superior to their own, determined to fall back upon Crown Point and there make a final stand. This determination they acted upon, leaving the enemy to pursue them as best they might—a problem difficult of solution. In order to make an attack upon the Americans likely to be attended with success, vessels were requisite, and these must be provided. With commendable energy, Carleton at once set about improvising a navy, and by the 5th of October had constructed and equipped a fleet of one ship, two schooners, one radeau,[10] one gondola,[11] and twenty-two gunboats with eighty-seven guns. Some of these vessels had been transported in pieces from Chambly to Fort St. Johns and there put together. Being now ready, Carleton proceeded with his fleet up the Sorel to Isle aux Noix at the entrance to the lake. He was now in a condition to attack the Americans with a good prospect of success, as he knew the force which they possessed was inferior to his. The fleet to be opposed to him had three more guns but of much lighter caliber

[10] The word *radeau* is equivalent to the English raft. The radeau was the prototype of the modern floating battery, having low but strong bulwarks to protect the men handling the guns, which were usually of heavy caliber. It was a cumbersome craft to manage, but, at the same time, effective.

[11] A gondola was quite unlike its Venetian namesake, being a large flat-bottomed affair with square ends, and having a large capacity for carrying.

and was inferior in other respects. On the morning of the 11th of October, accompanied by a large number of savages in their birchen canoes, some of which were of immense size, capable of carrying thirty men, Carleton moved upon the American fleet which, in command of Benedict Arnold, was drawn up in the form of a crescent between Valcour island and the mainland. A battle ensued, which was contested with spirit on both sides, but the tide of affairs with the Americans was at ebb, and when night fell they found themselves in no condition to continue the fight on the following day; hence in the darkness of the night, they passed unperceived through the British fleet and made all the speed possible to reach Crown Point, hoping that with the guns of that fortress joined with those of the fleet, they might counterbalance the superior force of the enemy. When in the morning, Carleton found that Arnold had eluded him, he followed in pursuit, and succeeded after a fierce battle in destroying and dispersing the American fleet. Nothing now remained for him to do but to push on to Crown Point. This he did as quickly as possible, but the Americans had evacuated their works there and fallen back upon Ticonderoga, which they put into a good condition for defense before he was able to make an attack upon them in their new position. The season was advancing, and perhaps yielding a too ready ear to the dictates of prudence, instead of following up his advantage and risking an attack upon Ticonderoga, which if successful might have changed the issue of the war,[12] he resolved to proceed no farther, but to withdraw his army to winter quarters. Thus closed the campaign of '76, disastrous and disheartening to the American patriots.

General Carleton, having withdrawn his army from Crown Point, and stationed portions of it at Isle aux Noix, St. Johns, Montreal, and other points in the province, went himself to Quebec where his family was domiciled, while General Burgoyne sailed for England to make preparations for the campaign of '77, which would, it was confidently believed by the British generals, terminate the war. The winter passed pleasantly enough with the British troops, who found plenty to amuse them, but with the Americans quite differently. The latter looked forward with anxiety to the coming campaign, and labored to put themselves in a condition to meet it successfully. They suffered privations and hardships innumerable, but having put hand to plow thought not to look back. Doubtless they often longed for the comforts which

---

12 "Lord George Germaine sought in this delay an excuse for venting his rancor against General Carleton, but the king, in spite of the powerful influence which the minister exercised over his mind, defended his officer, for on the 17th November he writes to Lord North, 'Sir Guy Carleton gives sufficient reasons for not earlier attempting to pass the lakes.'" He has been, however, severely criticised by writers for abandoning Crown Point, which would have afforded him an advanced starting point for the next campaign. *Vide* Fonblanque's Life of Burgoyne, n. p. 217 *et seq.*, and General Phillips' Letter, ibid.

they had once enjoyed — the leeks and garlics which they had forsaken to attain freedom — but they had in Washington a Moses in whom they confided, and they repined not over much. So the winter passed. Burgoyne in England with the ministers of the irate king, laid out an elaborate plan for the coming campaign. The New England provinces were to be violently dissevered from the western and southern by two armies, which were to serve as opposite wedges; the northern wedge to be directed by Burgoyne, the southern by Howe, and the two lines of fracture to meet at Albany in the State of New York. It was an excellent plan, and to any but an omniscient eye would have appeared to be almost certain of success. General Burgoyne arrived at Quebec on the 6th of May, and on the 10th, General Carleton, who was to remain in Canada as commander-in-chief of the Canadian department, for which reinforcements were on the way, passed over to him in accordance with orders from England, the command of about seven thousand troops. Germaine had written him under date of Whitehall, the 26th of the preceding March: "With a view of quelling the rebellion as soon as possible, it is become "highly necessary that the most speedy juncture of "the two armies should be effected; and, therefore, "as the security and good government of Canada "absolutely require your command for the defense "and duties of that province, you are to employ the "remainder of your army upon two expeditions; the "one under the command of Lieutenant-General Bur-"goyne, who is to force his way to Albany, and the "other under the command of Lieutenant-Colonel St. "Leger, who is to make a diversion on the Mohawk "river."[13] Upon receiving his command, Burgoyne at once proceeded to Montreal and began putting things in readiness to carry out this plan, so far as it related to the movement from the north which had been intrusted to him, writing to Germaine on the 19th of May: "The only delay in putting the troops in motion is occasioned by the impracticability of the roads, owing to late extraordinary heavy rains, and this difficulty will be speedily removed by exerting the services of the parishes as soon as the weather clears. In the mean time, I am employing every means that water carriage will admit for drawing the troops and stores toward this point. I trust I shall have vessels sufficient to move the army and stores together, and, in that case, will take post at once within sight of Ticonderoga, and only make use of Crown Point for my hospital and magazine. It is consigned to the New England colonies to furnish supplies of men and provision to oppose the progress of my army, and they have undertaken the task, upon condition of being exempt from supplying Mr. Washington's main army."[14]

---

[13] *Vide* A State of the Expedition from Canada. London, 1780 Appendix IV, p. vii.

[14] Ibid., p. xi.

This letter serves as a prelude to that momentous drama, which Burgoyne has himself conveniently divided for us into three acts; a drama which all Europe watched with intense curiosity, and which for a century has been discussed with unflagging interest. The first act of this great drama opens on the 12th of June at St. Johns, on the eve of the embarkation of Burgoyne's army. Nothing which could promote its efficiency in the projected campaign had been neglected. Its equipment, which was lavish, included the most approved artillery of the age, and inspired with the confidence of success it awaited the order of its commander to embark. Carleton, with that amiable generosity which characterized him, had come to St. Johns to bid his old comrades in arms a god-speed: an abundant feast had been prepared, and for the last time Burgoyne, Riedesel, Acland, Fraser, Phillips, Carleton, Balcarres and others of like bravery, who had passed thus far unharmed through many battles, gathered around the social board in joyous good-fellowship. After the repast to which wine and wit gave a keener zest, Carleton bade them an affectionate but enthusiastic good-bye, and with his staff took the return road to his head-quarters at Quebec, while the first brigade of the army soon began its embarkation, their martial ardor being inspired by the stirring strains of the regimental bands, and the awe-inspiring thunder of artillery as they marched to their boats. Both the English troops and their

German allies were trained soldiers in every sense, men who could march up to the cannon's mouth without flinching, and they made a gala occasion of their embarkation on this, the most perilous expedition which they had ever undertaken. Burgoyne had divided his army into brigades, and its progress up the lake was at the rate of about twenty miles a day, every thing being ordered with such exactness, that each brigade occupied at night the camp left by its predecessor at daybreak. Anburey,[15] whose descriptions are so graphic, wrote of the splendid spectacle which Burgoyne's army offered to the beholder as it floated on the placid bosom of the lake: "I cannot forbear portraying to your imagination one of the most pleasing spectacles I ever beheld. When we were in the widest part of the lake, whose beauty and extent I have already described, it was remarkably fine and clear, not a breeze was stirring, when the whole army appeared at one view in such perfect regularity as to form the most complete and splendid regatta you can possibly conceive. In the front the Indians went with their

[15] Thomas Anburey was a volunteer in Burgoyne's army, and was the author of a book entitled Travels through the Interior Parts of America, in a Series of Letters, By an Officer. It was published in London in 1789, and a second edition appeared in 1791. It was translated into German and, in 1793, into French, with annotations by M. Noel, ancien professeur de belles-lettres au College de Louis-le-Grand. Anburey remained a prisoner with the captive army until September, 1781, when he returned to England.

birch bark canoes, containing twenty or thirty each; then the advanced corps in regular line with the gunboats; then followed the *Royal George* and *Inflexible*, towing large booms—which are to be thrown across two points of land—with the two brigs and sloops following; after them Generals Burgoyne, Phillips and Riedesel in their pinnaces; next to them the second battalion followed by the German battalion, and the rear was brought up with the suttlers and followers of the army. Upon the appearance of so formidable a fleet you may imagine they were not a little dismayed at Ticonderoga, for they were apprised of our advance as we every day could see their watch-boats."[16]

At this moment let us pause to take a view of the theatre of action. While Burgoyne is advancing easily toward Crown Point, which Carleton had abandoned the previous autumn, and which the Americans have since neglected, St. Leger, who has been detached from Burgoyne's command with a thousand men which he soon increases to seventeen hundred, is quietly sweeping round by the St. Lawrence, Lakes Ontario and Oneida, toward Fort Schuyler, and after destroying all obstacles which oppose him, is to join his chief at Albany, the objective point of Burgoyne's expedition and that to be sent by Howe from the south to act in concert with it. On the American side, the army under the command of

[16] *Vide* Travels Through the Interior Parts of American London. 1789. Vol. 1, pp. 303-6.

General Schuyler is posted at the several forts about Lake George and along the Hudson and Mohawk rivers: St. Clair is at Ticonderoga; General Gansevoort[17] at Fort Schuyler, and the commander-in-chief himself at Fort Edward, while various bodies of troops more or less important, are at other points not far distant, or drawing toward the expected field of conflict with the Britons from the North. If we look farther away, we shall find Howe and Clinton at New York, the former instead of directing a force up the Hudson to co-operate with Burgoyne at Albany, strangely preparing an expedition against Philadelphia, all of his preparations being jealously watched by Washington, who is planning to baffle him at every point. Without special incident of importance, Burgoyne arrived at Crown Point on the 29th of June, and on the 1st of July his army appeared in front of Ticonderoga. On the 2d, Fraser took possession of a rise of ground which was named Mount Hope, cutting off St. Clair's communication with Lake George, while Phillips and Riedesel advanced, the former taking position on the right and the latter in front of Fort Independence,

[17] Peter Gansevoort was a native of Albany, and born on July 17, 1749. He was a major under Montgomery in the campaign against Canada in 1775, and at the time here mentioned held a colonel's commission. His successful defense of Fort Schuyler when besieged by St. Leger, gained him the thanks of Congress. In 1781 he was commissioned by the State of New York a brigadier-general. He died July 2, 1812, after an honorable and useful life.

which formed a part of that system of defenses to which Ticonderoga belonged. With inexcusable folly, St. Clair had neglected to fortify a hill which overlooked and commanded his position, and when the sun arose on the morning of the 5th of July, his sentinels beheld the British in possession, planting their batteries on its summit and watching curiously his every movement with their glasses.[18] Alarmed at this prospect a council was summoned, and it was resolved to abandon this important post in which so much confidence had been placed. Accordingly, St. Clair on the night of the 6th, fled in haste, not even stopping to destroy his stores which had been collected at infinite pains, but leaving guns, provisions and cattle to strengthen the hands of the enemy.

The story of this disastrous retreat has been related too often to be repeated here; suffice it to say, that the loss of Ticonderoga was a bitter one to the Americans, and by many was looked upon as a vital one, while in England the news of its capture was received with transports of joy. Germaine with great

---

[18] It would appear from Digby's Journal that the occupation of this hill by Burgoyne was disclosed during the night to St. Clair, by fires carelessly built, presumably by his Indian allies. It is remarkable that St. Clair's retreat on the next night was disclosed in a like manner, by a fire set carelessly at the head-quarters of General Roche De Fermoy, his French ally. Commenting on this latter incident, General De Peyster remarks, "that generally whenever the Americans were unsuccessful, a foreigner was mixed up in it." If Digby's presumption is correct, the English had like cause of complaint.

complacency announced the event in Parliament, "as if it had been decisive of the campaign and of the fate of the colonies," and King George when he heard of it was so elated, that he burst into the apartment of the queen exclaiming vociferously, "I have beat them! — beat all the Americans!"[19] Burgoyne was triumphant, and on the 10th, celebrated his victory by a Thanksgiving, and ended the day with a *feu de joie* of artillery at Crown Point, Ticonderoga, Skenesborough and Castleton, and with this dramatic demonstration he closed the first act of his drama.

On the next day he wrote to Germaine. "Your Lordship will pardon me if I a little lament that my orders do not give me the latitude I ventured to propose in my original project for the campaign, to make a real effort instead of a feint upon New England. As things have turned out, were I at liberty to march in force immediately by my left, instead of my right, I should have little doubt of subduing before winter the provinces where the rebellion originated."[20] Feeling however obliged by his orders to force his way to Albany, he applied to Carleton to spare him a sufficient number of troops to garrison Ticonderoga, so that he might not be obliged to weaken his forces by leaving a portion behind for garrison duty; but

---

[19] *Vide* Journal of the Reign of George the Third, (Walpole) London, 1859, vol. 2, p. 131.

[20] *Vide* A State of the Expedition from Canada.

Carleton did not entertain his application favorably, and in spite of his urgent appeal for help, left him to solve the problem of the campaign unaided, as best he might.

Preparations therefore for an advance were actively undertaken, but while they were going forward Schuyler was not idle. Calm and undismayed by his severe losses, he directed every effort toward obstructing the passage of his enemy southward. The keen axes of his skillful woodsmen soon laid the forests, which bordered the road leading from Skenesborough where Burgoyne lay, across the pathway of the advancing Britons. He destroyed bridges; blocked water-courses with boulders; stripped the country of subsistence, and drove the cattle away so as to leave nothing to sustain the invaders on their advance. Thus blocking the way between him and his enemy, he retreated southward and finally encamped his army near the junction of the Mohawk and Hudson. Here with his advanced outposts at Stillwater, he awaited coming events, strengthening by every means in his power his slowly-increasing army. Burgoyne now began to face troubles which he had not calculated upon. The difficulty of getting supplies increased, and the labor required of his soldiers in removing obstructions from their path; building roads and bridges and getting their artillery forward, told upon them severely, so that his progress was slow. His Indian allies, discontented at being checked in their murderous career, began to desert in considerable numbers, and these desertions, added to his losses in battle and by sickness, weakened his army seriously. While these troubles were at their height, a messenger arrived at his camp with news that St. Leger had reached Fort Schuyler, and he at once felt the necessity of a movement forward. He had been informed that the patriots had gathered at Bennington, horses, provisions and other stores of which he was in sore need, and that many loyalists in the vicinity were only awaiting a favorable opportunity to join his army. He therefore sent forward an expedition composed of Germans under General Baum, to attack Bennington and seize the stores there. By accomplishing this purpose he would not only obtain provisions, which he so much needed, and horses, which would enable him to mount his cavalry, but would be in a position to open the way for co-operation with St. Leger. The plan was an unwise one and he paid the penalty of his rashness. Baum's command was destroyed by Stark,[21] and a body of troops under Breymann, sent

[21] John Stark was born of Scotch parents at Londonderry, New Hampshire, August 28, 1728. When twenty-four years of age he was surprised while on a hunting expedition, by a body of St. Francis Indians and carried into captivity, but was ransomed by a friend. He served as a ranger in the French and Indian war, and was made a captain in 1756. He was a conspicuous figure at the battle of Bunker Hill. He was in command at Trenton and Princeton, and after the battle of Bennington, he enlisted a considerable force

to the support of the German commander, was driven back with the loss of guns, baggage, and every thing which could incumber flight. This blow fell heavily upon Burgoyne, who had begun the campaign as though he had an easy task before him, and had made himself somewhat ridiculous by bombastic proclamations, while success inspired the patriots with new hope, and their army grew apace while Burgoyne's constantly decreased. To add to his embarrassments, his Indians who had set out so enthusiastically under St. Luc, disheartened by the affair at Bennington, deserted him; still, his orders were to force a junction with Howe at Albany, and there seemed but one duty before him, and that duty was to push forward. On the 20th of August, four days after the defeat at Bennington, he wrote to Germaine.[22] "The great bulk of the country is undoubtedly with Congress in principle and zeal; and their measures are executed with a secrecy and dispatch that are not to be equaled. Wherever the king's forces point, militia to the amount of three or four thousand assemble in twenty-four hours; they bring with them their subsistence, etc., and the alarm over, they return to their farms. The Hampshire Grants in particular, a country unpeopled and almost

---

and joined Gates, having been raised to the rank of major-general. He served with honor through the war, and, at its close, retired to private life. He died on May 8, 1822, and lies buried at Manchester, in his native State.

[22] *Vide* A State of the Expedition. Appendix IX, p. 25.

unknown in the last war, now abounds in the most active and rebellious race of the continent, and hangs like a gathering storm on my left. In all parts the industry and management in driving cattle and removing corn are indefatigable and certain ; and it becomes impracticable to move without portable magazines. Another most embarrassing circumstance is the want of communication with Sir William Howe. Of the messengers I have sent, I know of two being hanged, and am ignorant whether any of the rest arrived. The same fate has probably attended those dispatched by Sir William Howe, for only one letter is come to hand, informing me that his intention is for Pennsylvania ; that Washington has detached Sullivan with two thousand five hundred men to Albany ; that Putnam is in the Highlands with four thousand men. That after my arrival at Albany, the movements of the enemy must guide mine, but that he wished the enemy might be driven out of the province before any operation took place against the Connecticut ; that Sir Henry Clinton remained in the command in the neighborhood of New York, and would act as occurrences might direct. No operation, my lord, has yet been undertaken in my favor ; the Highlands have not even been threatened. Had I a latitude in my orders, I should think it my duty to wait in this position, or perhaps, as far back as Fort Edward, where my communication with Lake George would be perfectly secure, till some event happened to assist my movement forward; but my orders being positive to 'force a junction with Sir William Howe,' I apprehend I am not at liberty to remain inactive longer than shall be necessary to collect twenty-five days' provision, and to receive the reinforcement of the additional companies, the German drafts and recruits now (and unfortunately only now) on Lake Champlain. The waiting the arrival of this reinforcement is of indispensable necessity, because from the hour I pass the Hudson's river and proceed toward Albany, all safety of communication ceases. I must expect a large body of the enemy from my left will take post behind me. When I wrote more confidently, I little foresaw that I was to be left to pursue my way through such a tract of country, and hosts of foes, without any co-operation from New York; nor did I then think the garrison of Ticonderoga would fall to my share alone, a dangerous experiment would it be to leave that post in weakness, and too heavy a drain it is upon the life blood of my force to give it due strength. I yet do not despond.— Should I succeed in forcing my way to Albany, and find that country in a state to subsist my army, I shall think no more of a retreat, but at the best fortify there and await Sir W. Howe's operations.

"Whatever may be my fate, my lord, I submit my actions to the breast of the king, and to the candid judgment of my profession, when all the motives become public, and I rest in the confidence that whatever decision may be passed upon my conduct, my good intent will not be questioned.

"I cannot close so serious a letter without expressing my fullest satisfaction in the behavior and countenance of the troops, and my complete confidence that in all trials they will do whatever can be expected from men devoted to their king and country."

From this it will be seen that he fully realized the perils of his situation from a military point of view; that when he passed the Hudson his communication would inevitably be cut off, and that he could not depend upon the country for subsistence. He had at least expected that Carleton would relieve him to the extent of forwarding troops to hold Ticonderoga, that he might not be obliged to weaken his force by garrisoning that post; but even in this he was disappointed, and obliged to leave some of his most effective troops behind to hold the forts he had captured. But he had no choice to make. His orders were peremptory to push forward. Misfortunes never come singly it has been said, and Burgoyne soon had reason to realize the truth of the saying, for he had not recovered from the shock of his defeat at Bennington, when he learned of the defeat and flight of St. Leger. Thus was he left alone with his rapidly wasting army to meet the exultant forces of the patriots, and he looked anxiously for help toward the south. Where was Clinton, who was to have been sent by Howe from New York to co-operate with him? He had heard nothing from that direction, and now sent a messenger in disguise to urge Clinton to hasten forward to his relief,[23] at the same time gathering all the provisions possible for his army, and pushing on toward Albany. On the 11th of September his troops received orders to be in readiness to cross the Hudson, which they had reached, but heavy rains prevented them from so doing until the 13th, when they crossed on a bridge of boats. The hazard of thus severing communication with their base of operations was regarded with apprehension by his officers, and we know that Burgoyne himself fully comprehended the responsibility which he took in making the step, but it was a necessary one in the plan laid out for him, and in accordance with the key-note of the campaign — "*This army must not retreat.*" Having crossed the river, he encamped on the heights and plains of Saratoga, where, like the excellent dramatist that he was, he completed the second act of his drama. Burgoyne did not linger in camp. Albany, where he was to meet Clinton, and where he had hoped also to have met St. Leger, had not his plans in connection with that officer gone

[23] Clinton wrote, some days later: "There is a report of a messenger of yours to me having been taken, and the letter discovered in a double wooden canteen." Probably this was the messenger dispatched at this time, and one of the several which suffered death at the hands of their captors. Previous to this he had dispatched at least ten messengers at different times and by different routes to open a communication with Clinton.

awry, was his objective point, and on the 15th, his army in splendid array set out in three columns to the music of fife and drum, with standards fluttering in the breeze, gay uniforms and glittering arms, forming a pageant which was never forgotten by those who witnessed it, and which the imaginative may still depict with approximate accuracy. That night he encamped his army at Dovegat where it remained for two days, while the way was being cleared for the advance of his artillery. Realizing the dangers which surrounded him, his orders were strict. His troops lay upon their arms fully accoutred, and he issued orders that any soldier who passed beyond his advanced sentries should be instantly hung. As though they already felt the shadow of coming disaster, a strange silence suddenly fell upon his camp. It was remarked by the Americans that neither drum beat nor trumpet sounded within the British lines, perhaps because of the constant activity required in opening roads and getting forward baggage and supplies, with the fatigue consequent upon such exertions, or that their position might not be too well defined. General Gates had superseded Schuyler — an officer of superior merit — the loss of Ticonderoga having afforded the enemies of the latter an opportunity for a hearing by Congress, and his army blocked Burgoyne's path to Albany. The Americans had thrown up fortifications from the river bank back to the heights a mile away. On the 19th, Burgoyne having divided his army again into three columns, himself led the center composed of English regiments toward the heights, while Riedesel and Phillips took the road by the river, and Fraser swept round to the west by the Quaker Springs road to join Burgoyne upon a clearing known as Freeman's Farm, near the American left wing, Burgoyne having ascertained by a reconnoissance that the American right occupied a position too strong for him to successfully attack. The march of the British was necessarily slow on account of the difficulties which they encountered, as it was often necessary to halt in order to remove trees and construct bridges over water-courses. Shortly after noon, Morgan began the action by attacking the advancing center, which being reinforced by Fraser compelled him to give way in confusion; but subsequently receiving reinforcements he renewed the conflict. The battle becoming general, Arnold, who had harassed the enemy continually on its advance, now engaged in conjunction with Morgan the combined divisions of Burgoyne and Fraser. Although they fought with desperate energy, the odds were against them, when Gates sent his tardy reinforcements to their support, and they were seemingly upon the point of victory when the artillery of Phillips forced them back toward their lines. The two armies were now face to face upon opposite slopes, and for a short space there was a lull in the storm of battle; but the struggle was soon resumed, and the tide of conflict ebbed and flowed, each side at times seeming near victory, when at a critical juncture for the British, Riedesel came upon the field at double quick and with his well served artillery brought the battle to a close — the exhausted Americans falling back to their camp, carrying with them their wounded and prisoners. At this critical juncture, Fraser and Breymann quickly prepared to follow up the advantage thus gained, and were about to pursue and attack the Americans in their camp, when they were recalled by the prudent Burgoyne, much to their chagrin and that of the troops in their command, who were eager to follow. What the result of such a movement would have been, it is now impossible to calculate,[24] but the failure of Burgoyne to follow up the advantage gained by Riedesel was made one of the many subjects of severe criticism against his management of the campaign. Burgoyne held the field and claimed a victory; but, says an eminent authority:[25] "As the intention of the Americans was not to advance, but to maintain their position, and that of the English not to maintain theirs, but to gain ground, it is easy to see which had the advantage of the day." The British army as it lay upon the field, was kept in constant alarm through the

[24] General Schuyler, in his diary, says: "Had it not been for this order of the British general, the Americans would have been, if not defeated, at least held in such check as to have made it a drawn battle."

[25] Colonel William L. Stone, in Burgoyne's campaign, Albany, 1877, p. 49.

night by parties of skirmishers from the patriot camp, and could get no rest. The irrepressible Arnold, who seemed never so happy as when breasting the infernal billows of carnage, urged Gates with all his eloquence to make a night attack, but was not listened to, and this difference of opinion resulting in angry words, Gates suspended his impulsive subordinate from command, an act which probably ignited that train of passion which finally destroyed the patriotism which had possessed his soul, and made room for the foul spirit of treason to brood in. On the following morning, his sick and wounded having been removed to the river bank in the rear of the army, Burgoyne formed his lines for a forward movement and awaited the lifting of the river fog, which hung like a veil between him and the American camp, when there occurred one of those singular events which apparently insignificant in themselves, are fraught with momentous consequences. General Fraser, who was his most trusted adviser and ever foremost in daring enterprise, suggested to Burgoyne that as the grenadiers who were to lead in the attack were fatigued by the duty of the previous day, it would be well to let them rest until the following morning, when they would be in a condition to advance with greater spirit. To this Burgoyne listened and recalled his orders, permitting his soldiers to return to camp, where they rested as well as they might under the circumstances. By this delay a messenger from Clinton was enabled to reach him, bearing a letter in cypher with the cheering news that the fleet from the south was about to ascend the Hudson for his relief, and that the forts below Albany, which was now but about thirty miles from his camp, would be attacked on the 22d. This information completely changed his plans and perhaps the fate of his army, as he resolved to fortify his camp and to remain where he was until he received further news from Clinton, to whom he immediately sent back his messenger,[26] informing him

[26] Fonblanque tells us that "This communication was deposited in a hollow silver bullet, which the bearer was directed to deliver into the general's own hands. The man succeeded in making his way to Fort Montgomery, on the Hudson, where, in compliance with his inquiries for General Clinton, he was led into the presence, not of Sir Henry Clinton, but of a namesake, General Clinton of the American army, the late governor of New York. On discovering his mistake the unfortunate man swallowed the bullet, but an emetic being administered, the dispatch was discovered, and its bearer hanged as a spy." *Vide* Life of Burgoyne, p. 286 *et seq*. It is hardly probable that two incidents of precisely the same nature could have occurred, yet there may be seen in the rooms of the New York Historical Society a copy of the identical dispatch, in the handwriting of Governor Clinton, which was taken from the silver bullet borne by the messenger who was hung, and this message was not from Burgoyne to Clinton, but from Clinton to Burgoyne, and bears date nearly three weeks later than the date of the message dispatched by Burgoyne. It is as follows:

"FORT MONTGOMERY, *October* 8, 1777.

"Nous y voici, and nothing now between us and Gates. I sincerely hope this little success of ours may facilitate your operations. In answer to your letter of the 28th Sep-of his perilous situation, and urging his co-operation. This delay was of almost vital importance to the

---

tember, by C. C., I shall only say, I cannot presume to order, or even advise, for reasons obvious. I heartily wish you success.

"Faithfully yours,

"Gen. BURGOYNE." "H. CLINTON."

The bearer of this message was Sergeant Daniel Taylor, who, about noon on the 10th of October, rode into the camp of the American General Clinton and inquired for General Clinton, stating that he was a friend and wished to see him. Upon being conducted to his presence he saw his mistake, and hastily swallowed the bullet, which was of an oval form. The movement was noticed, and Dr. Moses Higby sent for, who administered an emetic, which caused him to throw up the bullet. He recovered it and succeeded in swallowing it a second time, and refused to again take an emetic; but Clinton threatened to hang him and find it with the surgeon's knife, when he yielded and again threw it up. On the 12th he was hung upon an apple tree near the church in the village of Kingston, during the conflagration of the village, which had been fired by Sir Henry Clinton's troops who had then reached there. This is substantially the account given by Lossing and others, and can only be reconciled with Fonblanque's account, which is wholly based upon that of Lamb (*vide* Journal of Occurrences, etc., p. 162), by supposing the messenger sent by Burgoyne to Clinton on the night of the 21st of September, to have been Daniel Taylor. Learning subsequently the story of his fatal mistake and death, without knowing the date of its occurrence, Fonblanque supposed his capture to have taken place while he was on his way to Clinton instead of on his return to Burgoyne. We can only account for Taylor's error in mistaking the American for the British camp, by supposing that when Taylor left Sir Henry Clinton at Fort Montgomery, which that general had just captured from his namesake, he understood that Sir Henry was to immediately advance, and that meeting with insurmountable diffi-

Americans, as it enabled them to strengthen their position and to get forward much-needed reinforcements and war material; indeed, Wilkinson, who can never be accused of pessimism, took a rather despondent view of the situation of the American position at this moment of suspense when the patriots, anxiously peering through the fog, were awaiting the expected attack. He says:[27] "We were badly fitted to defend works, or meet the close rencontre; the late hour at which the action closed the day before; the fatigue of officers and men, and the defects of our organization had prevented our left wing from drawing ammunition, and we could not boast of more than a bayonet for every three muskets; the fog obscured every object at the short distance of twenty yards. We passed an hour of awful expectation and suspense, during which, hope, fear and anxiety played on the imagination." But Burgoyne waited in vain. On the 22d and 23d, to make sure that Clinton should receive a knowledge of his situation, he dispatched officers in disguise to him, with an urgent request to hasten to his

---

culties which delayed him, and supposing Sir Henry to have gotten ahead of him, he thought it proper to report in person to the author of the message the particulars of his delay; otherwise it would have been a useless performance for Taylor to have sought Sir Henry Clinton's presence. Unless we adopt such an explanation there would seem to be no reason for the act.

[27] *Vide* Memoirs of My Own Times, Phila., 1816, vol. 1, p. 250.

aid, and on the 27th and 28th sent two other messengers on the same errand.[28] The 5th of October arrived; the season was advancing; his army was on short allowance and some movement must be made. He now convened a council of his officers to consider the situation. Riedesel wisely advised him to fall

---

[28] The dispatch sent on the 23d reached Clinton on the 5th of October. The officer dispatched on the 27th was Captain Thomas Scott of the Fifty-third regiment, who has left a journal recounting the perils through which he passed. After eleven days of travel, he was told by a man whom he met that Sir Henry Clinton was in possession of Fort Montgomery, and he turned his weary steps thitherward, reaching the fort on the 9th, and safely delivering his dispatch to Clinton. On the 10th, he departed northward with the expedition of Clinton to Kingston, reaching it on the 12th, at which time it was fired by the British while the execution of poor Taylor was taking place. From here he started to reach Burgoyne, but after encountering great perils and learning of Burgoyne's surrender, he made his way back and finally reached Clinton in safety. The officer dispatched on the 28th was Captain Alexander Campbell of the Sixty-second regiment, who made his way safely through the American lines and delivered his dispatch to Clinton at Fort Montgomery on the 5th of October, the day upon which the dispatch of the 23d reached its destination. Campbell set out immediately on his return, and eluding the vigilance of the Americans reached Burgoyne's camp on the night of the 16th, after the terms of the surrender had been agreed upon, but before the articles had been signed. It was the cheering news which he bore of Clinton's advance up the Hudson, which for a moment rekindled Burgoyne's waning hope and caused him to reconsider the terms of surrender which he had agreed upon. Captain Campbell was one of the officers who surrendered, and after much service, and passing the intervening grades of rank, became a general in the British army January 1, 1812.

back to Fort Edward and there await the expected aid from the south, but Burgoyne hesitated. His position was daily becoming more critical. An officer whom Gates had allowed to return to his camp, brought news of an attack by the Americans in his rear upon Ticonderoga, an attack, which though unsuccessful, had resulted in the capture of a portion of the Fifty-third regiment with one of his brigs and a bateau; indeed, he realized that he was being cut off from his base of operations. The wolves, attracted by the bodies of the slain exposed by partial burial, made night hideous by continual howlings, which added to the alarms pervading his camp day and night on account of threatened or attempted attacks, destroyed all repose, the loss of which told upon the strength and spirits of his men. He now resolved to make a reconnoissance in force, and if he found the Americans too strong, to fall back as advised. On the 7th of October, selecting fifteen hundred men, with Riedesel, Phillips and Fraser, himself assuming command, he formed this force in line of battle in a field within three-quarters of a mile of the American left wing, intending to test the possibility of forcing a passage, and if he found this to be impracticable, he deemed it probable that his enemy by a vigorous attack could be dislodged, which would greatly favor his retreat. But the Americans were awaiting this movement of their foes with anxious impatience, and Gates was soon made aware of the movement in front, by the drumbeat to arms, which was caught up and repeated until it reached him at his head-quarters in the rear. Wilkinson, his dashing adjutant, then but a mere youth, was at once dispatched to learn the cause of the alarm, and soon returned, reporting the nature of the movement and advising an attack. To this advice Gates replied: "Well, then, order on Morgan to begin the game."[29] Making a detour through the wood, Morgan attained a ridge above Fraser — who with five hundred men was posted so as to be able to attack the American left — from whence he fell upon him with terrible fury, while simultaneously an attack was made by General Poor on the British left, and Learned held the center composed of Germans in check. So impetuous was the onslaught of Morgan, that Fraser's command, composed of the flower of the army, gave way, though Fraser himself was ubiquitous, inspiring his men at every point by word and example. Morgan then, with his usual celerity of movement, fell upon the flank of the British right, causing it to waver, when Dearborn[30] with his New

[29] *Vide* Memoirs of My Own Times, vol. 1, p. 268.

[30] Henry Dearborn was born at Hampton, New Hampshire, March, 1751. He was one of the first to receive a captain's commission in the continental army, and participated in the battle of Bunker Hill in June, 1775. When the expedition for the invasion of Canada was organized, he was one of the foremost to take part in it, and in the assault on Quebec was made prisoner, but in May, 1776, was liberated by the magnanimous Carleton. He was immediately after his liberation promoted to a majority, and subsequently to a

England troops, fell upon the front with such effect as to shatter it to fragments. The Americans now attacked the center with all their force, and for awhile the Germans sustained the brunt of the battle unmoved. Arnold, although deprived of his command by Gates, was a controlling spirit in the conflict and fought on his own account, appearing everywhere at the proper moment to turn the tide in favor of the Americans. Seizing at this moment the command of two brigades, he led them to the assault, and although the Germans stood firm for a while, in the end he succeeded in completely routing them. Fraser, who had been the most conspicuous figure in the conflict, had fallen mortally wounded

---

lieutenant-colonelcy in Scammel's regiment, succeeding that officer in command at his death. He took a prominent part in the battles of Saratoga and Monmouth, and witnessed the surrender of Cornwallis at Yorktown. After the war he removed to the district of Maine, and in 1789, was appointed by President Washington marshal of the district. He served two terms in Congress and was secretary of war under President Jefferson in 1801, which office he retained for eight years, when he received the appointment of collector of customs at the port of Boston. When the War of 1812 with Great Britain broke out, he was created senior major-general, and at once entered active service, capturing York in Upper Canada, and Fort George at the mouth of the Niagara. Subsequently he was in command of the military district of New York. At the close of the war, he resigned his commission and was appointed minister to Portugal, which office he retained for two years when he resigned. On the 6th of June, 1829, he died at Roxbury, Masssachusetts.

by one of Morgan's sharpshooters,[31] and Burgoyne had taken his place, exposing himself recklessly to the fire of the American riflemen. He seemed to see the shadow of coming disaster, and paid little heed to the urgent appeals of his officers not to expose himself unnecessarily. Thus the fight continued, until seeing his troops everywhere giving way, Burgoyne ordered a retreat, and the British fell back within their lines abandoning their artillery. Although Arnold as before stated was without a command, he placed himself at the head of a body of Americans, and under a consuming fire assaulted the works of the enemy from right to left. With the fury of a madman he attacked the great redoubt, and driv-

[31] During the battle Fraser was everywhere, inspiring the troops by word and example. He rode a gray horse and was a conspicuous object. Arnold had noticed him from time to time, and knowing how important a factor he was in the conflict, he approached Morgan and said: "*That officer upon a gray horse is of himself a host, and must be disposed of. Direct the attention of some of the sharpshooters among your riflemen to him.*" Morgan immediately selected several of his best riflemen, among whom was Timothy Murphy, a famous shot, and called their attention to the heroic rider of the gray charger, saying: "*That gallant officer is General Fraser. I admire and respect him, but it is necessary that he should die; take your stations in that wood and do your duty.*" In a moment a bullet severed the crupper of the general's horse, and then another cut through his horse's mane. "*Sir,*" said his aid, "*It is evident that you are marked out for particular aim; would it not be prudent for you to retire from this place?*" "*My duty forbids me to fly from danger,*" replied Fraser, and immediately fell, drooping upon his horse's neck, mortally wounded. The deadly bullet of Tim Murphy had done its cruel work.

ing the infantry of Balcarres from an abattis within, he dashed to the left, regardless of the fiery storm which swept his path, and taking the lead of Learned's brigade attacked the Germans on their right flank, killing General Breymann and taking the key of the British position. As the Germans retreated they fired a parting volley, killing his horse and wounding him severely in the leg. With the approach of darkness the conflict came to an end, and with it Burgoyne's last hope of success. The next morning Fraser, who was the idol of his brother officers as well as of all grades of the army even to the camp followers, died, and Burgoyne who was deeply affected by his loss, remained within his lines during the day. At sunset, in accordance with his friend's request, Burgoyne buried him with the most impressive solemnity on a hill within the great redoubt. A retreat was immediately ordered, and at nine o'clock the British stole away in the darkness, drenched to the skin by one of those cold, driving storms so common to the autumnal season in this latitude. His wounded and sick he left behind, confiding them to the tender mercy of his enemy. Through the darkness and the storm, the beaten but brave army pursued its weary march northward, Burgoyne intending to push it across the Hudson, so as to resume communication at Battenkill with Lake George and Canada. Two hours before daybreak, the almost exhausted troops reached Dovegat, where Burgoyne called a halt against the advice of his officers, who urged him to press on. By this halt he lost valuable time, as the heights of Saratoga which commanded the Fish creek ford was only occupied by a small force of Americans, and he might have reached the place and crossed the Hudson without serious opposition. As it was however, Wilkinson says that when "the front of Burgoyne's army reached Saratoga the rear of our militia was ascending the opposite bank of Hudson's river, where they took post and prevented its passage."[32] After a two hours' halt, Burgoyne moved his army from Dovegat across Fish creek where it encamped on the opposite bank, while he remained on the south side, taking possession of General Schuyler's mansion, in which he passed the night.[33] The next morning

---

[32] *Vide* Memoirs of My Own Times, vol. 1, p. 282.

[33] Every writer upon this subject hitherto, has charged Burgoyne with spending this night in revelry, and even his biographer, Fonblanque, who would present him to us in favorable light, fails to examine critically the evidence upon which this charge rests, and leaves us with the unpleasant impression of Burgoyne's criminal frivolity still upon our minds. The original evidence of this charge appears to be a statement made by Madame Riedesel, a lady who held Burgoyne in condemnation, but whom we must allow to have been above doing an intentional injustice even to one whom she condemned. The halt had been called and Burgoyne had taken possession of Schuyler's deserted house, when General Phillips informed Madame Riedesel somewhat sarcastically, that Burgoyne intended to spend the night there and give them a supper, and she continues, "In this latter achievement, especially, General Burgoyne was very fond of indulging. He spent half of the nights in

Burgoyne became aware that the Americans were in possession of the heights on the opposite side of the river, and finding it impossible to cross in the face of

---

singing and drinking and amusing himself with the wife of a commissary, who was his mistress, and who, as well as he, loved champagne." By this passage, if carefully read, it does not appear that Madame Riedesel alludes to this particular night when they were all in such a distressing situation, but in a general way to numerous nights, and as she was not prepossessed in favor of Burgoyne, she probably made her statement as explicit as an adherence to truth would permit her to make it. In "The German Auxiliaries in America," we find the account as follows: "While the army were suffering from cold and hunger, and every one was looking forward to the immediate future with apprehension, Schuyler's house was illuminated, and rang with singing, laughter, and the jingling of glasses. There Burgoyne was sitting, with some merry companions, at a dainty supper, while the champagne was flowing. Near him sat the beautiful wife of an English commissary, his mistress. Great as the calamity was, the frivolous general still kept up his orgies. Some were of the opinion that he had made that inexcusable stand merely for the sake of passing a merry night." Writers upon this subject have adopted this account, inferring that it is original, when it is only Madame Riedesel's dressed up by a reckless writer. Given Burgoyne's fondness for a merry supper and the commissary's wife, with Phillips' sarcastic remark relative to the halt, which he disapproved of, and we have all the elements of this improbable if not impossible story. That a man situated as Burgoyne then was, would halt his exhausted and half-famished army, and that too in a position which imperiled its very existence, as well as his own, for the express purpose of having a dainty supper and an hour's dalliance with his mistress, is too much to believe without the most explicit statements of a truthful eye-witness, and for the sake of humanity we are glad that no such evidence exists. This however is by no means a singular instance of a fiction growing out of the careless reading of a truthful statement.

such a force, took post on the ground he had occupied on the 13th of September, on the heights of Saratoga. He now resolved to continue his retreat up the west bank of the Hudson, and sent forward a force to clear his way to Fort Edward; but to his dismay, his men came hastily back with the news that it was garrisoned by the Americans. Gates, who had waited for the storm to cease, advanced on the 10th, and late in the afternoon encamped south of Fish creek.

Being misled by the departure of Burgoyne's expedition to clear a way to Fort Edward into the belief that his army was retreating, he ordered an attack to be made early in the morning on what he supposed to be a guard left to protect the baggage, and returned to his head-quarters a mile and a half in the rear. Burgoyne becoming aware of this, prepared a trap which would have resulted disastrously to the Americans had it not been opportunely discovered, greatly to his chagrin, for he afterwards denominated it "One of the most adverse strokes of fortune during the campaign."[34] And where was Clinton?

[34] Wilkinson gives a graphic account of this movement. He says Gates had the night before given the following order: "'*The army will advance at reveille to-morrow morning, Morgan's corps to keep the heights on the left, and the main body to march on the great road near the river.*' I could not approve of this movement, and the general required my objections. I was of opinion 'that he would commit himself to the enemy in their strong position.' He replied 'that they were already on the retreat, and would be miles ahead of us before morning.' I answered, 'that he

He had started on his expedition up the Hudson most grandly; had attacked and taken Forts Montgomery and Clinton,[35] and having removed obstruc

---

had no assurance of this, and that I had just left their guards on post;' and went on to observe, 'that, with submission, I conceived we ought to reconnoiter before the army marched; because, should we, contrary to his calculation, explore our way through a dense fog, and fall in with the enemy posted behind their intrenchments, the consequences might be destructive.' These observations appeared to have weight with the general, and he ordered me to rise early to attend to the movement, and report to him; but he would not give up the opinion that the enemy had retreated, and observed, 'it was natural that they should sacrifice guards to conceal their movements.'" Wilkinson was up, and riding to the front, found Morgan already on the move, and that he had been fired upon by a picket. He hastened to Gates, and was instructed to order Patterson and Learned to support Morgan. Just then he says, the order came from Gates: "'That the troops must immediately cross the creek, or return to their camp.' I felt the critical importance of the movement we were making in the dark, for the fog still continued; I feared the consequences, trembled for my general, and was vexed at his absence. In this tumult of the passions, I returned an hasty answer: 'Tell the general that his own fame and the interests of the cause are at hazard; that his presence is necessary with the troops.'" They had reached the creek, when he continues: "Our horses had halted to drink, and, in leaning down on the neck of my own, I cast my eyes up to the opposite bank, and through the fog discerned a party of men in motion." This led to the discovery that the British army was awaiting them with its artillery ready to pour destruction into their ranks. The discovery was however made in time to prevent the advancing troops from being caught in the dangerous trap which the British general had set for them. *Vide* Memoirs of My Own Times, vol. 1, pp. 285–289.

[35] Forts Clinton and Montgomery were placed on contiguous heights, the former one hundred and eighty feet above

tions, had apparently opened a path to Albany; but after burning Kingston and sacking a few of the stately mansions near the river, he quietly returned to New York leaving Burgoyne to his fate. The position of that general was now desperate, his army being constantly under fire on its flanks, in front and rear. He was even cut off from a supply of water although so near the river, as the sharpshooters prevented his soldiers from getting any by day or night. A council was now called and five propositions laid before it. General Riedesel advised the adoption of the fourth, which was to leave the artillery and baggage, and following the west side of the Hudson, to cross the river four miles above Fort Edward, then garrisoned by the Americans, and to continue the retreat to Ticonderoga leaving Lake George to the right. Burgoyne adopted the proposal of Riedesel, which was a wise one had the way then been open, and he had every thing made ready for the march, when he learned by scouts that the Americans were intrenched opposite the ford which he would have to cross, and that parties were posted along the shore

---

the river, and were constructed in 1775–6. Fort Montgomery was large enough to accommodate eight hundred, and Clinton four hundred men, and both were built of stones and earth. Below them the river was obstructed by a strong boom and massive iron chain, the latter eighteen hundred feet in length, buoyed by spars and timber rafts. These obstructions were the result of a recommendation in a report of a commission to Congress, of which General Knox of Maine was one.

Horatio Gates

Major General in the Army of the United States, after the Original Painting by Stuart.

Eng^{d} by H. B. Hall & Sons, New York.

to watch his every movement. Worn out, without food or shelter, what could be done? A night of suffering and suspense fell upon the devoted army, and under the cover of the darkness, the Americans crossed the river and completely blocked the way before him.

Seeing that all hope was gone, on the 13th, he again called a council of his generals, who unanimously decided to at once open a treaty with General Gates for a surrender. Even while they deliberated, their tent was perforated with rifle balls, and an eighteen-pound shot swept across the table at which they were seated. On the 14th, Burgoyne sent Lieutenant-Colonel Kingston to the camp of Gates with a proposal for a "cessation of arms" pending negotiations for a surrender. This was acceded to, and on the 15th articles of "convention," as Burgoyne desired to call them, were finally agreed to. These articles were to receive his signature on the morning of the 16th, when news reached him of the taking of the forts on the Hudson by Clinton, and of the probability of his presence there at this time with his forces. He at once called a council of his officers to see if he could get their support in breaking the agreement with Gates. They decided that he could not do so with honor. However, he resorted to a pretext, and sent word to Gates that he could not sign the articles unless convinced that the American army outnumbered his own by at least three or four to one, as he had heard that he had sent a part of his army to Albany during the negotiations, which was contrary to good faith. This Gates denied and asserted on his honor that his army had not been divided in order to relieve Albany, and was even stronger than when negotiations were entered into. He moreover drew up his army in order of battle on the dawn of the 17th, and gave Burgoyne to understand that he must sign the articles of convention or prepare for battle. His generals urging him, Burgoyne at nine o'clock on the 17th of October, finally placed his reluctant signature to the important paper, which placed his army as prisoners in the power of a lately despised foe. At eleven o'clock, the splendid army which had left Canada a few months before, now shattered and disheartened, laid down its arms and prepared for its sad march to Boston where it was to embark for England. Burgoyne in full court dress upon which he had bestowed great care, was presented to Gates, who was dressed in a plain blue overcoat, and after the introduction, the captive generals proceeded to the head-quarters of Gates, where they were received by the American generals with proper courtesy. Riedesel immediately sent for his brave and lovely wife, his constant companion in so many trying scenes, who came at once with their children and was taken charge of by General Schuyler, who arranged every thing possible for the comfort of herself and helpless charge. The English and German generals dined in the tent of Gates; compliments were passed and healths drunken in strange contrast to the scenes of a short time before. As the dinner ended, the captive army began its march to Boston, while Burgoyne in the presence of the two armies drew his sword and presented it to Gates, who receiving it with a courteous salute, returned it immediately to his vanquished foe, who thus closed the third act in his picturesque but tragic drama.[36]

But another act must be added, and one fraught with momentous interest to Burgoyne. By the articles of convention which he had just signed, he and his troops were to embark at Boston on transports to be sent there by his government. This was a convenient port for the captive army to reach, and it probably did not occur to either Burgoyne or Gates that it could be other than a convenient one for embarkation. Had Burgoyne objected to it, Gates would probably have yielded to his views, as he had become alarmed at the information which had reached him of Clinton's progress up the Hudson, and desired to bring the negotiations to a speedy conclusion. We shall see that in selecting Boston as his port of embarkation, Burgoyne was most unfortunate. After a tedious march, his troops divided into two columns under guard of a force of Americans reached Boston on November the sixth, where they were quartered in barracks; the Germans on Winter, and the

[36] *Vide* Journal of Occurrences during the Late American War, etc. (Lamb), Dublin, 1809, p. 167; A State of the Expedition, etc., Appendix XV.

British on Prospect Hill, while quarters were provided for the officers in Cambridge and adjoining towns. Wilkinson was dispatched by Gates to convey the good news of the surrender and the articles of convention to Congress, but was delayed on the way by illness, and the news arrived some time before he was able to present them in person.[37] He found that copies of the articles had already preceded him, and that a variety of opinions prevailed respecting them, Gates being openly blamed for the too liberal concessions which had been granted to a foe, who it was claimed, was wholly in his power ; indeed, Wilkinson found it necessary to defend the action of his chief, by showing that he had been obliged to concede many points under the pressure of Clinton's advance, which at the time was threatening. Washington had received news of the surrender, but not from Gates, who only mentioned it to him incidentally in a letter more than two weeks after the fact,[38] and he at once saw that if

[37] *Vide* A State of the Expedition, Appendix XV, XVII.

[38] Lord Mahon remarking upon this inexcusable slight of Washington says, that he "evinced his usual magnanimity. He felt, he could but feel, the slights put upon him at this period, both by his superiors and by his subordinate, by the Congress and by General Gates. But he allowed no word of unworthy complaint to fall from him." His letter to Gates was characteristic. He congratulated him in frank and generous terms, but in closing alluded to the unworthy act of his subordinate in the following manly words: "At the same time, I cannot but regret that a matter of such magnitude, and so interesting to our general operations, should have reached me by report only, or through the channel of letters not bearing that authenticity which the im-

the captive troops were enabled to embark so as to reach England during the winter, nothing in the convention would prevent the British government from assigning them to garrison duty, thereby relieving a corresponding number of troops, who might join in the spring campaign against the colonies. He promptly called attention to this fact, and in reply to Heath's urgent request to facilitate their removal as soon as possible,[39] on account of the great

---

portance of it required, and which it would have received by a line under your signature stating the simple fact." And subsequently to a friend he wrote: "It is to be hoped that all will yet end well. If the cause is advanced, it is indifferent to me where or in what quarter it happens." Shortly after, LaFayette wrote him alluding to the effort which Gates was making to supplant him. "When I was in Europe, I thought that here almost every man was a lover of liberty. You can conceive my astonishment when I saw that Toryism was as apparently professed as Whigism itself. There are open dissensions in Congress; parties who hate one another as much as the common enemy; men who, without knowing any thing about war, undertake to judge you and to make ridiculous comparisons. They are infatuated with Gates, without thinking of the difference of circumstances, and believe that attacking is the only thing necessary to conquer." Fortunately for the cause, the animus of Washington's enemies became apparent and their schemes came to nought. *Vide* History of England by Lord Mahon, London, 1858, vol. 6, p. 193; Sparks' Life of Washington, vol. 5, p. 124 *et seq.;* Letter to Patrick Henry, *ibid.*, p. 147; Marquis de LaFayette, to Washington, Dec. 30, 1777.

[39] Washington's exact words are as follows: "As you have wrote to Congress respecting the difficulty of supplying the prisoners of General Burgoyne's army with quarters, fuel and provisions, I imagine they will give proper directions in the matter. I do not think it to our interest to expedite

burden which they would be to the distressed inhabitants of Boston, he reminded him that it would be impolitic to hasten their departure, going so far indeed as to advise that they should not be furnished with, nor allowed to purchase provisions in the country for their voyage home. He also suggested that Burgoyne would probably apply to have the place of embarkation changed to a port farther south, as the transports would hardly be able to make the port of Boston so late in the season, but this, he said, could not be asked as a matter of right, since

---

the passage of the prisoners to England; for you may depend upon it that they will, immediately upon their arrival there, throw them into different garrisons, and bring out an equal number. Now, if they sail in December, they may arrive time enough to take the places of others who may be out in May, which is as early as a campaign can be well entered upon. I look upon it that their principal difficulty will arise from the want of provisions for the voyage; and, therefore, although I would supply them with every article agreeable to stipulation, I would not furnish an ounce for sea store, nor suffer it to be purchased in the country." In considering this last clause in Washington's letter, one should bear in mind the great scarcity of provisions then prevailing in the country; indeed, the question of the subsistence of his own troops was one which caused him constant anxiety. In this same letter he says: "The present state of the commissary's department gives me great uneasiness," and somewhat later, "the state of the commissary's department has given me more concern of late than any thing else. Unless matters in that line are speedily taken up and put in a better train, the most alarming consequences are to be apprehended." Moreover, it was but proper that provisions for the sea voyage should be furnished from the magazines of General Howe. *Vide* Washington's Letters to Heath, Part I, pp. 77–79.

Boston was the only port agreed upon, and should not be granted as a favor, since it would prove of disadvantage to the American cause.[40] This view of the case was also communicated to Congress, and served as the key-note to all its subsequent action in the premises.

Application was made to change the place of embarkation to Newport, but permission was not granted.

Occasions soon arose to complicate affairs. It had been stipulated that subsistence should be supplied to Burgoyne's men at the same cost as to the American troops in the vicinity. One dollar in specie was at this time equivalent to about three dollars in continental currency, yet Congress gave orders that General Heath should demand payment in specie. This would have been well enough if the price had been estimated at the specie value, but naturally, values were adjusted to the currency of the country. The question was too simple it would seem for discussion, since it depended wholly upon a fact, namely, whether prices were calculated at the currency value or not; and yet Burgoyne whose expenses were $20,000 a week, was asked to pay for his supplies a sum in gold, which changed into the currency of the country would purchase nearly three times the quantity which he received. This was certainly un-

[40] *Vide* Sparks' Life of Washington, vol. 5, pp. 144, 147.

fair, and cannot be adjusted to any system of ethics with which we are conversant. It is but just however to Washington to say, that he protested against this exaction, which he said would "destroy the idea of a cartel."[41] Another question was raised which was reasonable and sufficient. Burgoyne was in arrears for his supplies, since it was no easy matter at this time to get remittances from England, and he was given to understand that he would not be permitted to embark until all indebtedness was canceled, "by an actual deposit of the money."[42] All these obstructions to his plans caused him anxiety and awakened indignation which he did not hesitate to express. Various annoyances arose. Descriptive lists of his officers and men were demanded, that a proper record might be made for future use, a demand which he denominated an insult to his nation, but finally acceded to. An inquiry was also instituted relative to the colors of the regiments, the military chest, etc., which were not found in the return by General Gates of property delivered him by Burgoyne in accordance with the articles of convention. This was a proper inquiry, and it was resolved fairly enough, that the embarkation was not to be delayed on account of it. The inquiry was directed to Gates, who replied that the custom during the last war had been for the mili-

[41] *Vide* Sparks' Life of Washington, vol. 5, p. 307.

[42] *Vide* Washington's Letter to Congress, Dec. 14, 1777, in Sparks' Life, vol. 5, p. 187.

tary chest to be kept in some secure town by the paymaster-general, upon whom warrants were granted, and that "from the best accounts, the enemy's army had been lately cleared off; so that it is not probable there was any military chest." With respect to the colors, he affirmed that General Burgoyne declared upon his honor, that his regimental colors were left in Canada. These last inquiries arose from "suspicions that the convention had not been strictly complied with on the part of General Burgoyne, agreeable to its true spirit, and the intention of the contracting parties." [43] We shall see that these suspicions had a basis in fact. Indeed, General Wilkinson intimates that Gates was cognizant of this in spite of his reply to Congress, as he wished to shield himself from blame as far as possible, on account of his loose dealing in the matter.[44] Madame Riedesel states in her journal, that the colors of the German regiments were secreted in her bed, and were afterward sent in the mattress of an officer to Halifax where her husband subsequently found them.[45] Of the English colors, it is not to be supposed that they were left in Canada. The colors of the Sixty-second regiment were on the field on the 19th of September,[46] and we have an

[43] *Vide* Journals of Congress, Jan. 8, 1778, p. 42.

[44] *Vide* Memoirs of My Own Times, vol. 1, p. 303 *et seq.*

[45] *Vide* Letters and Journals of Madame Riedesel, Albany, 1869 (Stone), p. 143 *et seq.*

[46] *Vide* Memoirs of My Own Times, vol. 1, p. 304.

interesting account of the colors of the Ninth, which were concealed in the baggage of Lieutenant-Colonel Hill, and were by him presented to the king upon his return home.[47] How Burgoyne could have stated that they were left in Canada is inexplicable. Had this concealment of the colors been known at the time, it would have afforded good ground for Congress to declare the convention broken; as it was, it had no proof whatever of the matter, and it was doubtless believed that they had been burnt by those having them in custody, that they might not become trophies to the enemy; hence, the matter of these inquiries relative to the concealment of property, which rightfully should have been delivered to Gates at the surrender, afforded no ground whatever for Congress to detain the convention prisoners. Doubtless an impression prevailed in this season of exaggerated sentiment, when suspicion, jealousy and prejudice necessarily held sway, that if the convention prisoners were allowed to return to England, they would break their paroles and re-enter the service against the colonies, an impression which was unreasonable and unworthy of indulgence. We know, that even Congress did not hesitate to openly charge "former frauds in the conduct of our enemies," which caused Burgoyne to declare his "consternation in finding the British honor in treaties impeached."

---

[47] *Vide* Historical Record of the Ninth Foot (Cannon), p. 32 *et seq.*

Every utterance of the British general was carefully scanned, and a letter which he wrote to General Gates served to strengthen the impression spoken of. In this letter, dated November 14th, complaining of the quarters which had been assigned to his troops and which were undoubtedly quite unfit for them, he used these words: "While I state to you, sir, this very unexpected treatment, I entirely acquit M. Gen. Heath and every gentleman of the military department of any inattention to the publick faith engaged in the convention. They do what they can, but while the supreme powers of the State are unable or unwilling to enforce their authority, and the inhabitants want the hospitality or indeed the common civilization to assist us without it, the publick faith is broke and we are the immediate sufferers."[48] These words, "*the publick*

---

[48] *Vide* Lieutenant-General John Burgoyne and the Convention of Saratoga, p. 35, by Charles Deane, LL. D., Worcester, 1878, to which the reader is referred for an able statement of the subject. The connection of Gates with the efforts being made to evade the obligations of the convention has not heretofore been especially noticed. While his position, being a party to the compact, rendered it proper that he should at least remain neutral, we find that he was active in suggesting pretexts for an evasion of that compact. A letter of his to General Washington under date of November 23d, has been published, in which he says: "If General Burgoyne has any sinister design, what I suggested to Congress in my letter of the 10th instant, a copy of which I conclude your excellency has received, will be a good method of delaying, if not final preventing, the execution of his project." The letter of the 10th of November here alluded to, though often sought for without success, was recently placed in my hands by the kindness of Mr. A. R.

faith is broke," were immediately caught up as a notice from Burgoyne that he considered the terms of the convention broken, and although he denied any such intention, and even offered to re-affirm them by the signatures of his officers if desired so to do, he was not listened to, but Congress resolved that these words indicated his intention and afforded "just grounds of fear," that he would "avail himself of such pretended breach of the convention, in order to disengage himself and the army under him of the obligations they are under to these United States; and that the security which these States have had in his personal honor is hereby destroyed," and they further resolved to suspend the embarkation "till a distinct and explicit ratification of the convention of Saratoga shall be properly notified by the Court of Great Britain."[49] This requirement, Congress must have

---

Spofford, the librarian of Congress, and by it we see what General Gates considered "a good method" of delaying, "if not final preventing" the fulfillment of the terms of the convention. He says "It has occurr'd to me, that should Sir William Howe still Obstinately refuse to settle an equitable Cartel, for the Exchange of Prisoners, that Congress would be Justified, in Ordering the fulfiling the Convention of Saratoga to be delayed, until the United States received Justice in that particular. At any rate, there will be very few of Genl. Burgoyne's soldiers to Embark, as most of the Germans, and a great many of the British, have deserted upon their march towards Boston, and numbers more will yet Desert." This letter was directed to the president of Congress, and the original is in the State department at Washington.

[49] *Vide* Journal of Congress, Jan. 8, 1777, p. 43.

known the British government could not comply with. For it to have ratified the convention formally would have been to recognize the colonies as belligerents, which was tantamount to a recognition of their independence; yet Sir Henry Clinton went so far as to offer by authority of the crown, a renewal of all the obligations of the convention, an offer which was not accepted. It had evidently been determined to detain the captured army as prisoners of war. The severe strain to which Burgoyne had been subjected had seriously impaired his health, and he obtained leave to return to England on parole, agreeing to return whenever Congress demanded it. He took passage home on the Grampus sloop of war from Newport, Rhode Island, on April 20th, 1778, and landed at Portsmouth, England, on May 13th. Before leaving, he paid in specie a large sum for supplies to his troops on their march from Saratoga which General Glover[50] had advanced in Continental cur-

[50] John Glover was born in Salem November 5, 1732. While a young man, he with three brothers removed to Marblehead, where for a while he practiced his trade of shoemaking; but being ambitious to advance his fortunes, he embarked in mercantile business and became one of the leading merchants of the province. He was early in life interested in military affairs, and in 1759, was ensign in Captain Read's company of militia; in 1762, a lieutenant in Captain Orne's company, and in 1773, a captain in Colonel Fowle's regiment. At the beginning of the war he was made colonel of a regiment called Glover's Marblehead regiment, the uniform of which consisted of a blue jacket and trousers adorned with leather buttons. On the 22d of June, 1775, he was ordered with his regiment to Cambridge. On the 1st

rency, and in order to avoid the unfair exactions imposed upon him, of paying in specie for supplies to the troops left behind, he arranged to repay in kind for supplies advanced to them by the American commander. Provisions were to be shipped from the British commissary department on transports, which were to be allowed to enter Boston and depart from it unmolested. A large sum was left in pledge for the performance of this contract, and the provisions were regularly shipped for the maintenance of the troops; but advantage was taken here, and great expense was incurred in handling and storing the supplies after their arrival, payment for which was demanded

---

of January, 1776, Glover's regiment was reorganized as the Fourteenth Continental regiment, and on the 9th of August, joined Sullivan's brigade at New York. After the battle of Long Island, Glover's regiment of sailors and fishermen, succeeded by their skill in transporting the army in vessels and boats safely across the river. "This extraordinary retreat," says Washington Irving, "which, in silence and celerity, equaled the midnight fortifying of Bunker's Hill, was one of the most signal achievements of the war, and redounded greatly to the reputation of Washington. It may be truly said, that by Glover's efforts the army was saved from destruction. On the 23d of February, 1777, Glover was created a brigadier-general, and in the succeeding summer sailed with his brigade to reinforce Schuyler at Saratoga. In the arduous service which followed, Glover's brigade was one of the most efficient, and suffered severe loss. At the battle of October 7th, Glover had three horses shot under him. His brigade formed part of Washington's army at Valley Forge, and in June, 1778, Glover assumed command of Fort Arnold near West Point. From this time he was in active service until July, 1782, when owing to failing health, the result of exposure and

in specie, although General Heath[51] paid the expense in currency, of which at this time it took about four dollars to equal the value of one dollar in gold. General Heath called the attention of Congress to this unfair exaction, but it was promptly resolved to continue it; so that after all, not much was saved by the British government in this attempt to victual the convention prisoners. This condition of affairs, however, could not continue indefinitely, and finding that there was no prospect that the American

---

hardship, he retired on half pay. His death took place January 30, 1797. *Vide* Pictorial Field-Book of the Revolution, New York, 1855, vol. II, pp. 34, 606, 609, 128, *et passim*. History and Traditions of Marblehead, Boston, 1880, pp. 117, *et seq.*, 140–153, 157, *et passim*.

[51] William Heath was born in 1737, in Roxbury, Massachusetts, where his ancestors had settled in 1636. He says of himself that he was "of the fifth generation of the family who have inherited the same real estate (taken up in a state of nature), not large, but fertile and pleasantly situated." From youth he says that he procured and studied attentively "every military treatise in the English language which was attainable." In 1770, he was captain of an artillery company, and was a writer under the *nom de plume* of "A Military Countryman" for the Boston *Gazette*. In these articles he advocated the study of arms, and in one of them used these extraordinary words: "It is more than probable that the salvation of this country, under heaven, will sooner or later depend upon a well-regulated militia." Having been commissioned a captain in the Suffolk regiment, and subsequently superseded by Hutchinson, he was chosen in 1774, captain of the first company of Roxbury, and the same year colonel of the Suffolk regiment. He was a delegate to the Provincial Congresses of 1774 and 1775. In June of the latter year he was made a provincial major-general, and in the August following, the Continental Con-

Congress would allow the convention prisoners to return to England, General Clinton gave notice that he should cease supplying them with subsistence, and that they would have to be provided for as were other prisoners of war. It now being feared that a rescue might be attempted, they were, in November, 1778, a year after their capture, compelled to take up their weary march for Virginia. There, as we know, they remained until the close of the war. Whether the American government, or rather the American Congress, for this was all the government

---

gress conferred upon him the same rank. He was the only general officer at the famous battle of Lexington, and organized and directed the hardy farmers, who on that occasion put the British regulars to flight. Heath commanded a division during the siege of Boston, and was at the head of the eastern department in 1777, and subsequently was assigned to a post on the Hudson. He returned to his farm at the close of the war, and was a delegate to the convention which adopted the Federal Constitution in 1788; was a State senator in 1791–92, and judge of probate for Norfolk county from 1793 until his death, January 24, 1814. Eight years previous to this date he had been chosen lieutenant-governor of his native State, an honor which he declined. He was a great friend of Washington for whom he possessed a remarkable admiration. When Washington parted with him, he gave him a letter testifying to his faithfulness, and this letter he valued beyond price. When Brissot de Warville visited him at his farm in 1788, Heath said: "This letter is a jewel which, in my eyes, surpasses all the eagles and all the ribbons in the world." *Vide* Memoirs of William Heath, Boston, 1798. The Town of Roxbury, Roxbury, 1878, pp. 387–390. New Travels in the United States of America, Dublin, 1792 (J. P. Brissot De Warville), p. 117. Pictorial Field-Book of the Revolution, vol. I, pp. 190, 566. II, pp. 614 *et seq.*

that the United States then possessed, acted justly with regard to the convention, is left for those who are interested in the question to judge. We know from the history of similar assemblies composed of men of various degrees of moral dignity, and in some measure relieved from personal responsibility, that questions possessing elements of a political nature are not apt to receive the same careful treatment, which would be bestowed upon them by a judicial tribunal removed from popular influence and feeling the direct weight of moral responsibility; or indeed from an individual occupying a like position; hence we ought not to be over surprised at the action of our first Congress[52] in this matter of the Saratoga convention. That convention was entered into in good faith by the contracting parties, and should have been justly carried out in letter and

[52] In all great struggles in which imperfect men engage, there are those who ally themselves to the cause of right, and who acquit themselves valiantly, yet are dominated in all they undertake by selfishness. It was so in our great struggle for freedom, and it is painful to contemplate the fact, that many of the men who donned the spotless armor of patriotism and won thereby the admiration of their fellows, were self-seekers in the worst sense of the term. Even Washington justly used the following terms in speaking of some of his contemporaries, who were apparently ardent supporters of the noble cause for which he and a few other pure patriots like himself were willing to sacrifice their lives and all they held dear. "Such a dearth of public [spirit] and want of virtue; such stock-jobbing and fertility in all the low arts to obtain advantages of some kind or another in this great charge of military management, I never saw before, and pray God I may never be witness to

spirit by the American Congress. It seems to have failed from considerations of policy so to act, just as any similarly composed body of men in any other portion of the globe might at that time have failed to act, and while we may not excuse, we may perhaps in some measure mitigate our chagrin with this consideration, though we should have rejoiced had it taken higher ground than any other government in the world would have been likely to take at that period. Burgoyne sailed for home, feeling keenly the injustice which he deemed had been practiced upon him by the American government; but if that government treated him unjustly, his own subsequently treated him with still greater injustice.

The disaster to Burgoyne's army had not been unexpected in England. When the rumor of Howe's erratic expedition against Philadelphia and apparent abandonment of the plan of co-operation with Burgoyne reached England, several weeks before the latter's surrender, although the public mind was in a state of elation at his success at Ticonderoga, it was thrown into consternation, and predictions of defeat were in the air. Even Germaine admitted to one of his noble friends, that Howe had ruined his plans by not operating in conjunction with Burgoyne, and the ministers hastened to send orders to

---

again." Letter of Washington to Joseph Reed, February 10, 1776. Happily for the cause of human progress, there was after all enough of public spirit and virtue to overbalance the self-seeking and vicious spirit which prevailed, and the right triumphed, as it ever must triumph, in the long run.

the latter not to attempt to advance beyond Albany until he could bring about concerted action with Howe. So much apprehension respecting Burgoyne's position was felt in London, that a statesman of the day, in a letter to a friend as early as November 2d, said: "I believe it is also true that a very great man said within these few days, that he expected accounts of a general defeat very soon,"[53] and Chatham, two weeks before the news reached England, spoke of "the sufferings, perhaps the total loss of the northern army." Tidings of the disaster reached England on the 2d of December, and on the next day Colonel Barré called upon Germaine, "to declare upon his honour what was become of General Burgoyne and his troops. Lord North admitted, in reply, that very disastrous information had reached him from Canada. A fierce outburst against the ministry followed. Motions were made in both houses of Parliament for papers. They were, however, successfully resisted on the ground that no official information had been received,"[54] and the ministry succeeded in adjourning Parliament. Said Shelburne, "talk to them about truth. Like Pilate they waived the question and adjourned the court." Burgoyne's dispatches announcing his surrender reached the ministry on the 12th, and excited the ridicule of his enemies by its

[53] The Duke of Richmond to Lord Rockingham.

[54] *Vide* Life of William, Earl of Shelburne, London, 1876, vol. III, p. 10 *et seq.*

sonorous character,[55] although the passage most ridiculed was strictly true. This was to the effect that he had "dictated the terms of surrender." The news of the disaster fired the popular spirit, and subscriptions were at once started throughout the kingdom to raise and equip regiments. The ministry was bitterly assailed, and especially Germaine, who resorted to every means in his power to shield himself by throwing the responsibility of the disaster upon Burgoyne. Germaine himself was suggestively reticent; but his friends and supporters were alert and blatant. This was the condition of affairs which Burgoyne, broken in health and spirits, met upon reaching London. Apparently without realizing the situation, he at once waited upon Germaine, who received him with marks of friendship and drew upon his confidence, thus gaining facts of importance. It was agreed between them to arrange an inquiry, an order for which had already been prepared and was then in the pocket of Germaine. At this juncture, Burgoyne discovered that he was to submit to the "*etiquette*" of not appearing at court, by which means he was to be kept from seeing the king[56] and impressing

---

[55] "The style charmed every reader; but he had better have beaten the enemy and misspelt every word of his dispatch, for so, probably, the great Duke of Marlborough would have done, both by one and the other." Mrs. Inchbald in Preface to the Heiress.

[56] *Vide* a letter from Lieutenant-General Burgoyne to his constituents upon his late resignation, etc., London, 1779.

him with a knowledge of the true state of the case. This, Burgoyne, whose eyes were now open to the artifice of the minister, refused to accede to, and an open war between him and Germaine followed. Burgoyne demanded a court-martial, which was denied him on the ground that he was then a prisoner of war, a novel position to assume but one not without plausible features, and he then decided to appeal to the country. Upon claiming his seat in the Commons, to which he was entitled as the representative of Preston, he was met with the objection which had before proved potent, that he was a prisoner of war, and therefore not entitled to a seat in Parliament; but happily this objection failed to be sustained, and on the 21st day of May he took his seat and asked for an investigation of his conduct. A day was assigned for him to make his statement, which was to the effect that no discretionary powers had been granted to him by the ministry in carrying out his instructions; but that they were "positive, peremptory and indispensable." Burgoyne seconded a motion to inquire into his conduct of the campaign, but Germaine, who dreaded an investigation, succeeded in defeating the motion. This unfair treatment gained him friends and revived the popular interest in him, and his opponents becoming alarmed, it was determined to get him out of the way; hence the king was persuaded to order him back to America as a prisoner of war, although no demand had been made for his return by the

American government. This was an extraordinary proceeding and revealed the desperate straits to which the ministry was reduced. Against this injustice Burgoyne remonstrated so forcibly,[57] that the king was compelled to suspend his order, and the persecuted general proceeded to publish an address to his constituents on the conduct of the campaign in America, which brought to the attention of the English people, for the first time, the full history of the matters at issue; at the same time he applied himself assiduously to obtain a ratification of the Saratoga convention, that his captive army might be liberated. To counteract the influence of his statements, which were gaining him many adherents, he was vilified and abused by his opponents without stint. He was accused of employing savages and sanctioning their barbarities; of artfully supplanting Carleton, and maliciously destroying property on his march toward Albany, all of which charges he fairly refuted at the first opportunity.[58] At the next session of Parliament, Burgoyne renewed his efforts to obtain a vindication of his conduct, openly charging the ministry with double dealing,[59] and he so far suc-

[57] In a letter to the war office, June 5, 1779, he asserted that his health was such that to expose his constitution to another American winter would, in all probability, doom him to the grave. *Vide ibid.*, pp. 22, 26.

[58] *Vide* Speech on a Motion made by Mr. Vyner in the Parliament, May 26, 1778.

[59] *Vide* Speech on the Review of the Evidence in the House of Commons; also, Speech of December 14, and April 22, 1779.

ceeded as to gain permission to present his case, which he prepared most elaborately, supporting his position in a convincing manner by documentary evidence and the testimony of Sir Guy Carleton and officers in his command; but the ministry becoming alarmed at the damaging nature of his revelations, brought matters to a summary conclusion by a sudden prorogation of Parliament, and he again received the royal command to return to America. This he refused to do, and resigned all his valuable appointments except that of lieutenant-general. He was stranded, but not disheartened; for he put the printing press into requisition, and under the title of the "State of the Expedition from Canada," a book which he dedicated to his captive army, he presented to justice-loving Englishmen a full account of the proceedings. In vain was he assailed by anonymous pamphlets, one of which was attributed to Germaine;[60] the sentiment of unprejudiced

[60] This pamphlet is entitled "*A Reply to Lieutenant-General Burgoyne's Letter to his Constituents*," and bears for a motto the words, "*Expende Hannibalem.*" It strikes at the outset the key-note of Germaine's attempt to get him out of the way. "Men of honour," it says, "were at a loss to comprehend upon what principle you could justify your absence from your captive army, whose calamities they considered it your duty to share." His bravery and zeal are extolled, and the cause of difference between him and Germaine pointed out, and his course in defending his conduct and refusing to obey the mandate of the king to return to and give himself up to the Americans, severely criticised. *Vide* pp. 1, 5–7. Another is entitled "*An Essay on Modern Martyrs*," and is conceived in a harsher spirit of censure. The writer most

men was in his favor, and the incapacity of Germaine became so conspicuous, that he was obliged, upon the surrender of Cornwallis, to retire from office, though his influence with the king was so great that he effected his retirement "under the cover of a peerage."[61] Burgoyne was in some measure compensated for his almost unexampled trials, but as a popular idol was never restored to his niche. What was often asserted and quite widely believed at the time, that Burgoyne's army was sacrificed to a blunder of Germaine, is now known from documents left by a contemporary. Germaine, it would appear, was a peculiar man, and one of his peculiarities was an over-nicety with regard to the clerical work of his office. He had arranged to take a vacation in the country, and on the morning of his departure, called at his office to examine the orders to Burgoyne and Howe which were to be dispatched upon that day to America. Upon examining Howe's orders, he was displeased because they were not "fair copied," and angrily ordered them to be recopied. He then went into the country and forgot all about the matter. The result was, that Bur-

---

sarcastically criticises Burgoyne's unfortunate use of the word "*dictated*," as applied to the terms of surrender, which he claimed were of his own dictation, and remarks with much force: "It is not probable, therefore, that he (Gates) would have opposed your wishes, had you (instead of leaving it to his choice) assigned Quebec as the place of embarkation, by which means you might immediately have conducted the whole army out of the provinces in rebellion." *Vide* p. 45.

[61] *Vide* Life of William, Earl of Shelburne, vol. I, p. 359.

goyne's orders were dispatched to him, but Howe's were pigeon-holed, hence the ruin of the elaborate plan to subjugate the colonies.[62] It cannot be denied however, that Howe understood the plan of the campaign. He says in his narrative, "On the 5th of June I received a copy of the secretary of State's letter to Sir Guy Carleton, dated the 26th of March, 1777, wherein he communicates to him the plan of the northern expedition, and adds 'that he will write to Sir William Howe by the first packet.'" It can only be plead in his defense that he had no "positive, peremptory and indispensable orders" to co-operate with Burgoyne. This plea he makes for himself, in the letter under consideration, in these words: "I must observe, that this copy of a letter to Sir Guy Carleton, though transmitted to me, was not accompanied with any instructions whatsoever; and that the letter intended to have been written to me by the first packet, and which was probably to have contained some instructions, was never sent."[63] That the plan of the campaign was generally understood we well know, and moreover that Howe's failure to co-operate with Burgoyne was a puzzle to Washington. On the 4th of July he wrote General Heath: "General Howe evacuated Amboy on Sunday last. From present appearance, Hudson's river seems to be the object of his attention;" and on the 19th:

[62] *Vide ibid.*, p. 358 *et seq.*

[63] *Vide* Narrative of Lieutenant-General Sir William Howe, London, 1780.

"General Howe still lays entirely quiet on board the fleet at Staten Island. Very few troops remain on shore, and the destination [is] a profound secret. Whatever were his intentions before this unlucky blow to the northward,"— referring to the fall of Ticonderoga,—"he certainly ought now, in good policy, to endeavor to co-operate with General Burgoyne. I am so fully of opinion that this will be his plan, that I have advanced the army thus far to support our party at Peekskill, should the enemy move up the river."[64] This leads us to inquire into the motives which influenced Howe at this juncture, and a careful study of the man and his environments may enable us to reach an approximate comprehension of them. Howe, who through an illegitimate source had descended from royalty, was a man enervated by patronage and pampered with flattery; such a man as would, upon sufficient occasion, almost unconsciously permit his *amour propre* to overrule his *amor patriæ.* Burgoyne, a man of singularly popular qualities and rapidly rising in public esteem, had been cast for the principal part in the drama about to be enacted,—was to play the heroic roll, so to speak,— and influenced by that common sentiment of dislike to a subordinate part,—a sentiment especially active with men engaged in public affairs — Howe was disposed quite naturally to view the scheme of the ministry with languid indifference. Although he knew well what the plan

[64] *Vide* Washington's Letters to Heath, Part I, pp. 64, 66 *et seq.*

of the ministry was, the blunder of Germaine in not giving him peremptory orders to enact the part assigned him was a sufficient pretext for him to select a role more congenial to his tastes, one indeed in which he would enact the part of hero; hence his brilliant, but impracticable scheme of a southern campaign, the fruit of a confidence rooted in the rank soil of a hitherto successful experience. This scheme once conceived, would continue to grow more and more attractive in his imagination, and to delude him with visions of a fame to which his ambition yearningly reached; nor were the obstacles in the way of success seemingly great. In common with his fellow officers at this time, he still under-estimated his opponents and failed to comprehend the character of the war in which the British government was engaged; hence it is not strange that he should formulate the scheme of a southern campaign, nor that he should pursue it with confidence. The climax so disastrous to British hopes, and which an eminent writer, classifying it with the decisive battles of the world,[65] has declared to have been "more fruitful of results than those conflicts in which hundreds of thousands of men have been engaged, and tens of thousands have fallen,"

[65] *Vide* History of England, by Lord Mahon, vol. VI, p. 285. Another writer has said: "This war, which rent away the North American colonies of England, is of all subjects in history the most painful for an Englishman to dwell on. It was conceived and carried on by the British ministry in iniquity and folly, and it was concluded in disaster and shame. But the contemplation of it cannot be evaded by the his-

we have witnessed. That Burgoyne was unfairly treated by his own government cannot now be gainsaid, nor that hitherto our own people have too lightly regarded his conduct of the campaign from Canada. In estimating his character we meet with difficulties, possessing as it does qualities of almost kaleidoscopic variety.

We cannot reconcile the warm terms of friendship which he used in addressing Lee, an old companion in arms then in the American service, with the unfriendly epithets of "late half-pay major, and incendiary in the king's service — major-general and demagogue in the rebel army," which he applied to that friend shortly after in correspondence with Lord North, when he was anxious to excuse himself for holding communication with a rebel;[66] nor his statements regarding his regimental colors, with what we now know to be facts; nor yet again can we understand, how, after the direful disasters which had befallen his faithful army, at the moment too in

---

torian, however much it may be abhorred. Nor can any military event be said to have exercised more important influence on the future fortunes of mankind, than the complete defeat of Burgoyne's expedition in 1777, a defeat which rescued the revolted colonies from certain subjection, and which, by inducing the courts of France and Spain to attack England in their behalf, insured the independence of the United States and the formation of that trans-Atlantic power which not only America but both Europe and Asia now see and feel." *Vide* Fifteen Decisive Battles of the World, etc., by Sir Edward Creasy, London, 1873, p. 292.

[66] *Vide* Political and Military Episodes, etc., London, 1876, pp. 169–175.

which he was to deliver his worn-out and almost heart-broken soldiers into captivity, he could bedeck himself in the gorgeous habiliments of the court. These are beyond our comprehension. At the same time, we must admit that he was a man of noble parts, a scholar, a statesman of no mean ability and a thoroughly brave and capable officer. The army which he led has probably never been excelled in soldierly qualities. No one capable of appreciating character can make the individual accquaintance of the men, both British and German who comprised it, and whose biographies have come down to us, without feeling an admiration for and a friendly interest in them. "*Opinionum commenta delet dies naturæ judicia confirmat.*"

REGIMENTAL COLOURS,
53d Regiment.

SOME ACCOUNT

OF

THE AMERICAN WAR

BETWEEN

GREAT BRITAIN

AND HER

COLONIES.

WILLIAM DIGBY, LIEUTENANT 53D REGIMENT.

1776.

PREFACE.

My chief design in committing the following passages to paper was with a view of hereafter bringing to my memory, (when a dull hour presented itself), some incidents which have happened in the course of the Campaigns 1776 and 1777. I have wished to confine such, as much as possible, to the partial eye of a particular friend, one who will make many allowances for their numerous defects, from the degree of friendship subsisting between us. The only merit, (if it can deserve such an appellation), I can claim, is a strict adherence to truth inserted without exaggeration, and facts set down plainly as they happened, not but in some places oversights may have been committed from the inattention to which at times all mankind are liable. I cannot pass over mentioning that during a campaign, the many requisites for bringing such an undertaking to the smallest degree of perfection are impossible to be attained, & even time, one of the first and most necessary ingredients, is often stinted from the frequent calls of duty. It would exceed the bounds I at first prescribed, to enter into the grand causes which actuate a General in the manœuvres and movements of an army; the impossibility of such an attempt must appear evident to every person from the variety of intelligence he must often receive through private channels, together with his orders for acting, neither of which could be communicated to every individual; from the above reasons I have confined myself to simple occurrences, such as were publicly known to the army in general, as it would be the greatest presumption in me to insinuate a knowledge of more. As digressions are often tedious and tiresome, I have put in as few sentiments of my own as possible, being well assured that in such passages where they may be wanting, the reader can supply their place more advantageously than I could pretend to do. To conclude, I have not attempted to apologize or even to enumerate the many faults contained in the following pages. In place of the former, I have depended entirely on the friendship already wished for, & mentioning the latter were to doubt the discernment of the reader, who, if he takes the trouble of venturing on them, will soon, I fear, discover enough to prevent his going through. If on the contrary, his good nature induces him to lean lightly on what cannot merit his approbation, and with a friendly eye pass over their numerous unconnected passages put down without regularity or order, he will cause me to feel for their want of merit only, as they are deficient in affording him amusement or entertainment in return.

CAMPAIGN OF 1776.

BY AN OFFICER IN THE NORTHERN ARMY,

UNDER THE COMMAND OF HIS EXCELLENCY

GENERAL GUY CARLETON.

FIRST CAMPAIGN,

1776.

1776 April

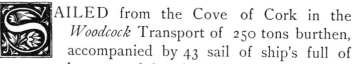

SAILED from the Cove of Cork in the *Woodcock* Transport of 250 tons burthen, accompanied by 43 sail of ship's full of troops and convoyed by the *Caresford* and *Pearl* ships of war, supposed to be destined for Quebec in Canada,— the troops commanded by Lieu^t. Col^o Frazier [67] 24th Regiment until their arrival in America,

---

[97] "Simeon Fraser," says Fonblanque, "was born in 1729, had entered the army at an early age, and attained the command of the Twenty-fourth Regiment of Foot before the war with America broke out," and Colonel Rogers traces through many intricacies his advancement in the army as follows: Lieutenant Seventy-eighth Foot, January 5, 1757; captain lieutenant, September 27, 1758; captain, April 22, 1759; major in the army, March 15, 1761; major in the Twenty-fourth Foot, February 8, 1762; lieutenant-colonel, July 14, 1768; brigadier-general, June 10, 1776. He received the rank of colonel in the army July 22, 1777. He had fought shoulder to shoulder with New England troops at Louisbourg and Quebec. He was an officer of great ability and beloved by the entire army. *Vide* Political and Military Episodes, 241; Hadden's Journal and Orderly Books, p. 455.

when Gen[l]. Carlton,[68] Governor of Canada, was to take the command, and, under him, Lieu[t]. Gen[l].

[68] Guy Carleton was of Irish birth, being born at Strabane, Ireland, September 3, 1724. His soldierly qualities brought him promotion, and in 1757 we find him holding the rank of chief lieutenant in the First Foot. He took part in 1758 in the successful siege against Louisbourg, and for his signal services in that campaign was made lieutenant-colonel of the Seventy-second Foot. His ability attracted the attention of General Wolfe, who selected him as his quartermaster general, and in the great battle on the heights of Abraham he was severely wounded by a musket ball in the head. On September 24, 1766, he was made lieutenant-governor, and October 26, 1768, governor of Quebec. He had known Montgomery in the French war, and when the latter invaded Canada, realized that he had no ordinary foe to combat. With all the material at his command, he endeavored to hold back the enthusiastic invaders, but without success, and barely escaped capture at Trois Rivieres, which he left in disguise just as the victorious Montgomery entered the town. Carleton did not remain in America through the war, but returned to England, July 29, 1778, where he was warmly received. In the spring of 1782 he superseded Sir Henry Clinton as commander-in-chief of the forces in America, and won much popularity by his liberal and just administration of the affairs of his department. A recent historian thus speaks of him: "By his tenderness and humanity, he gained the affection of those Americans who fell into his hands. His conduct in this respect affords a striking and happy contrast to that of nearly all the British officers who served in this country during the Revolution." While we are glad to admit that he showed great kindness to the prisoners who fell into his hands, we must remember The Cedars and his reply to Washington's request for an exchange of prisoners, accompanied by a copy of the Declaration of Independence. While he was not responsible for the barbarity committed upon our soldiers at The Cedars, this reply suggests the spirit which inspired his subordinate in that affair. In the reply alluded to occur the following indecent words:

Burgoyne. We soon lost sight of Ireland, having a fair wind. We had on board two companies

---

"His Excellency General Carlton orders that

The commanding Officers of Corps will take especial care that every one under their command be informed, that *Letters*, or *messages* from *Rebels*, *Traitors* in Arms against the *King*, *Rioters*, *disturbers* of the *public Peace*, *Plunderers*, *Robbers*, *Assassins*, or *Murderers*, are on no occasion to be admitted: That shou'd emmissaries from such lawless Men again presume to approach the Army, whether under the name of Flag of Truce Men or Ambassadors except when they come to implore the King's mercy, their persons shall be immediately seized and committed to close confinement to be proceeded against as the Law directs: Their Papers & Letters, for whomsoever directed (even this Com'r in Chief) are to be deliver'd to the Provost Martial, that unread and unopen'd they may be burned by the hands of the common Hangman."

These are not the words of a philanthropist or even of a calm and generous mind, but rather those of a tyrant, who, if he possessed the power, would use it most cruelly. We know what Garneau says of his treatment of the Canadians after his return from the campaign of '76, namely, that he "sent detachments to pick up straggling enemies, arrest colonists who had joined the Americans and fire their houses; for the British, who spared from destruction the property of insurgents in the Anglo-American colonies, followed their ancient practice with respect to Canada and its foreign-derived race. *As in* 1759, *they now marched torch in hand.*" We know how Washington received this intemperate reply. He simply said, with calmness and dignity, to Hancock: "I shall not trouble Congress with my strictures upon this performance so highly unbecoming the character of a soldier and a gentleman." This was all the notice he took of the matter. In a note referring to this extraordinary reply of General Carleton, Sparks seems almost inclined to doubt its genuineness, but the recent publication of Hadden's Journal sets the matter at rest, as the document is there published in

of the 53^d Regiment, Major, Earl of Balcarres[69] and the Grenadiers to whom I had the honour

---

full. Carleton was, at the time of penning it, laboring under great excitement caused by the shooting of General Gordon by the scout, Whitcomb, a most cruel act, but no more cruel than others which were perpetrated by individuals on both sides, for which neither government was responsible. Carleton seems to have felt ashamed of this performance himself, for, perhaps feeling its effect upon his troops in exciting them to unnecessary cruelty, he issued soon after an order admonishing them not to return evil for evil, nor to forget that "the Englishman, always brave, is accustomed to act magnanimously and philanthropically," and that it behooved "the troops of the king to spare the blood of his subjects." On account of his services in America, he was created Baron of Dorchester, August 21, 1786. He had the same year already been appointed governor of the British possessions in North America, which office he held for a period of ten years. He died in his own home in Berkshire, November 10, 1808. *Vide* Collin's Peerage, vol. 8, pp. 112–117; British Army Lists, *in loco;* Journal of the Principal Occurrences During the Siege of Quebec (W. T. Shortt), p. 42; Garneau's History of Canada, Montreal, 1862, vol. 2, pp. 135, 151; Burke's Peerage and Baronetage, *in loco;* History of Connecticut (Hollister), vol. 2, p. 294, *et seq.;* Annual Register for 1808, p. 162; Life of Washington (Sparks), vol. 3, p. 268; Ibid., vol. 4, pp. 55–57; Hadden's Journal and Orderly Books, pp. 7–10.

[69] Alexander Lindsay, sixth Earl of Balcarres, was of Scotch descent, and at this time but twenty four years of age, having been born January 18, 1752. He was commissioned an ensign in the Fifty-fifth Foot, July 15, 1767, and after two years' experience at Gibralter, and as long a period in study at Göttingen, he returned to England and was commissioned a captain in the Forty second Foot, January 28, 1771. He became by purchase major of the Fifty-third Foot, December 9, 1775, and upon his arrival in Canada, was appointed by Carleton to the command of the light infantry. At the battle of Hubbardton he was wounded, and had many nar-

to belong. The wind continued fair for us till the 19th, when we were becalmed. About noon, we perceived from the main top mast head, a fleet to

row escapes; after the death of Fraser he succeeded that officer in command, and was commissioned lieutenant-colonel of the Twenty-fourth Foot, October 8, 1777.

Finding after the capture of Burgoyne's army, that a general exchange of prisoners was not to take place, he refused to accept his liberty, and returning to Cambridge, shared the captivity of his men until the latter part of 1778, when he returned home on parole. An interesting anecdote is related of a meeting which he had with Arnold while the latter was having an audience with the king. As Balcarres entered the royal presence, the king introduced Arnold to him, but with an action expressive of disgust, Balcarres drew back, exclaiming, "*what, sire, the traitor Arnold?*" A challenge from Arnold was the result. At the signal to fire Arnold discharged his pistol without effect, and Balcarres cooly turning upon his heel was walking away, when Arnold cried out, "*why don't you fire, my lord?*" To this, Balcarres looking over his shoulder, replied, "*sir, I leave you to the executioner.*" He was appointed lieutenant-colonel in command of the second division of the Seventy-first Highlanders, February 13, 1782, and colonel in the army November 20th, of the same year. He was in Parliament as a peer of Scotland in 1784 and for several successive years, and became colonel of the Sixty-third Foot, August 27, 1789. He was made a major-general October 12, 1793, and the next year assumed military and civil command at Jamaica. After seven years of continued and most successful warfare, he resigned his position and returned to England. He had been commissioned a lieutenant-general January 1, 1798, and September 25, 1803, he was made a general in the army. After his return to England he devoted himself to the care of his estates until his death, which occurred at Haight Hall, in Lancashire, March 27, 1825. *Vide* British Army Lists, *in loco;* Burke's Peerage and Baronetage, *in loco;* Foster's Peerage and Orders of Knighthood, *in loco;* Three Years in North America (Stuart), vol. 1, p. 462.

windward bearing down to us with all the sail they could set. On their approaching nearer, we found they were the fleet from Plymouth,[70] mostly Germans. General Burgoyne was on board one of their frigates, who, after giving some orders, separated from us about the 21st, as winds were turned rather foul for us at that time.

May 4th. Discovered at a distance numerous islands of ice, some three times higher than our main top mast head and formed in the most romantic shapes, appearing like large castles, when the sun shone on them, all on fire. The sailors from this imagined we could not be a great distance from Newfoundland, it being about the season for the quantities of ice that surround that part during the winter to break up, they obliged us to steer with great caution, as were a vessel to strike on such a solid body, she must inevitably be dashed to pieces.

5th. Prepared lines to fish on the banks but found no success, though many of our fleet killed some. The banks are properly a mountain hid under water, with various depths of water from 25 to 60 fathom. During our stay upon this kingdom of cod fish, we found it very unpleasant, as the sun scarce ever shews himself, and the greatest part of the time thick and cold fogs; but there are none of these fish which

[70] "The fleet from Plymouth" consisted of thirty sail, and had on board General Riedesel and his German troops. Riedesel, in a letter to his wife, gives an entertaining account of his life on board ship, for which reference may be had to "Letters and Journals of Mrs. Riedesel," p. 22.

require warmer seas. There are also on the banks of Newfoundland great numbers of whales, spouting fish, porpoises, sword fish, &c. The sword fish is as thick as a cow, seven or eight feet long, gradually lessening towards the tail; it takes its name from its weapon, a kind of sword three feet long and about four inches wide: It is fixed above its nose and has six rows of teeth on each side, an inch long, at an equal distance from each other; this fish is excellent eating. The whale and the sword fish never meet without fighting; the latter, they say, is always the aggressor. Sometimes two sword fish join against a whale, and then it is not an equal match. The whale has neither weapon offensive nor defensive, but his tail: To make use of it against his enemy, he plunges his head under water, and, if he can strike his enemy, he kills him with a blow of his tail; but he is very dexterous to shun it, and instantly falls upon the whale and runs his weapon in his back; most commonly it pierces not to the bottom of the fat, and so does no great injury. When the whale can see the sword fish dart to strike him, he plunges, but the sword fish pursues him in the water and obliges him to appear again; then the fight begins again and lasts till the sword fish loses sight of the whale, which fights always retreating and swims best on the surface of the water. It is said, with what truth I cannot say,[71] that the cod can turn itself inside out

[71] Cf. Malte Brun, vol. 5, p. 19.

like a pocket, and that the fish frees itself from any thing that troubles it by this means. I wont vouch for the truth of this.[72]

6th. Fell in with a French fishing vessel. We had mostly got over our sea sickness; though I was but little troubled in that way after the second or third day. Our Capn Richardson was a good seaman and an agreeable companion, which does not always follow. The ship was stout but often missed stays in tacking, not answering the helm well, and, of course not a pleasant vessel to sail with a large fleet.

7th. About 11 at night our captain seemed very uneasy at not hearing a signal from the man of war; it blew fresh against us; we were going on the wind and the night dark and hazy, which is generally the case on the banks. Our grog being out, we prepared for rest, when he came down and told us if the signal

---

[72] This is a prudent disclaimer of our author, who was but repeating the popular belief with regard to this fish (morhua vulgaris), which is extremely voracious, devouring indiscriminately, says Herriot, "every substance which it is capable of gorging; even glass and iron have been found in the stomach of this fish, *which by inverting itself has the power of becoming disburdened of its indigestible contents.*" *Vide* Travels through Canada, p. 30. It is certain that the cod is a great collector of deep-sea objects, and naturalists are indebted to it for specimens of rare and new shells otherwise unattainable. The Basques were fishing as early as 1504 along the Newfoundland shores, to which they applied the name of Baccalaos or Codlands, and although for nearly four centuries the business has been constantly increasing, such is the rapid multiplication of the cod that its numbers have not decreased.

was not made (which was firing two guns from the *Caresford*) by 12 o'clock, he would put the ship about, as by his reckoning, we must be very near Cape Race, no pleasing circumstance at that time of night He had scarce spoke when the sailors on deck cried out, we were most on shore, and we could easily perceive the breakers at a small distance, on which the vessel was put about with the greatest dispatch, and all our guns fired as signals for the rest of the fleet to keep off. Some we saw much nearer land and feared they would be lost, in short, it was a scene of the greatest confusion, every ship getting from shore as well as possible. Cape Race is the south east point of the island of Newfoundland; it lies in 46 degrees 30 minutes north latitude, and the coast runs from thence 100 leagues to the west and terminates at Cape Ray, about 47 degrees, and nearly half way is the great bay of Placentia, one of the finest ports in America.

8th. At day break discovered Cape Ray, and soon after passed close to the little island of St. Paul; tried to count our fleet and found two transports, the *Henry* and *Sisters*, missing with 3 companies of our regiment, and the *Lithy* with one company of the 31st regiment. A vessel, whom we spoke with, informed us she saw them among the rocks and feared they were lost, the night being dark and the shore not the best.— We still continued our course into the gulph of St. Lawrence, which is 80 leagues long, and went through it in about 30 hours with a good wind.

Near half way we fell in with the Bird islands.[73] They are very near each other and covered with birds and nests. They have been often visited, and boats have been entirely loaded with eggs of all sorts. Surely it is wonderful in such millions of nests, every bird should find its own, and had we fired a gun, it is reported the air would be darkened two or three leagues round. Near this we fell in with a fishing vessel; but she could give us no intelligence, whether Quebec was in our hands or our enemies—the latter we had the greatest reason to believe.

9th. We were almost becalmed, so prepared for fishing and had very good success. We hoped soon to double Cape Rosiers, which is at the entrance of the river St. Lawrence. Newfoundland that we had so lately left behind us, and the first land we meet with coming to Canada, "It could never be known," a French writer observes, "for certainty whether it had any native inhabitants." Its barrenness, supposing it every where as real as it is thought to be, is not a sufficient proof that it has had no native inhabitants; for fishing

[73] On Deny's map of 1672, these islands are called "Les isles aux Oyseaux." They were subsequently called the Magdalen islands, and reference is here made to the northernmost of the group. They were formerly owned by Sir Isaac Coffin, a distinguished naval officer, and a native of Nantucket on the coast of Massachusetts, where many of the family name still reside. One of these islands is called Coffin's island from its former proprietor. *Vide* Canada, Nova Scotia, etc., Buckingham, London, 1843, p. 314.

and hunting are sufficient to maintain savages. This is certain, that here was never seen any but Eskimaux who are not natives of this country. Their real home is Labrador or New Britain. It is there at least they pass the greatest part of the year; for it would be profaning the name of the native country to apply it to wandering barbarians who, having no affection for any country, travel over a vast extent of land. In fact, besides the coasts of Newfoundland which the Esquimaux range over in the summer, in all the vast continent which is between the river St Lawrence and Canada and the North Sea, there has never been seen any other people than the Eskimaux. They have been met with also a good way up the river Bourbon, which runs into Hudson's Bay, coming from the West. The original name of these people is not certain, however it is very probable that it comes from the Abenaqui word, Esquimantsic, which signifies an eater of raw flesh.[74] The Eskimaux are, in fact, the only savages known that eat raw flesh, though they have also the custom of dressing it or drying it in the sun. It is also certain, that of all the people known in America, there are none who come nearer than these to complete the first idea which Europeans had of savages. They are almost

[74] This shows our author to have been a careful student. These Indians called themselves *Innuits*, but the name Esquimaux, the proper signification of which is here given, was applied to them by the Algonquins, of which family the Abenaquis were the eastern representatives.

the only people where the men have any beard, and they have it so thick up to their eyes that it is difficult to distinguish any features of the face; they have besides something hideous in their look; little eyes looking wild, large teeth and very foul. Their hair is commonly black, but sometimes light, much in disorder, and their whole outward appearance very rough. Their manners and their character do not disagree with their ill look. They are fierce, surly, mistrustful, uneasy, always inclined to do an injury to strangers, who ought therefore, to be upon their guard against them. As to their wit and understanding, we have had so little commerce with this people that we can say nothing concerning them, but they are, however, cunning enough to do mischief. They have often been seen to go in the night to cut the cables of ships that were at anchor that they might be wrecked upon the coast, and they make no scruple of attacking them openly in the day when they know they are weakly mann'd. It was never possible to render them more tractable, and we cannot yet treat with them, but at the end of a long pole. They not only refuse to approach the Europeans, but they will eat nothing that comes from them. They are tall and pretty well shaped; their skin is as white as snow, which proceeds, without doubt, from their never going naked in the hottest weather; their hair, their beards, the whiteness of their skin, the little resemblance and commerce they have with their nearest neighbours, leave no room to doubt that they have a different origin from other Americans, but the opinion, that which makes them descended from the Biscayners,[75] seems to me to have a little foundation, especially if it is true, as I have been assured, that their language is entirely different. For the rest, their alliance would do no great honour to any nation, for, if there was no country on the face of the earth less fit to be inhabited by men than Newfoundland and Labrador,[76] there is perhaps no people which deserve more to be confined here than the Eskimaux. For my part, I am persuaded they came originally from Greenland, These savages are covered in such a manner, that you can hardly see any part of their face [or] the ends of their fingers. Upon a kind of shirt made of bladders or the guts of fish cut in slips and pretty well sowed together, they have a coat made of bear

---

[75] Biscayners or natives of Biscay, one of the Basque provinces of Spain, are supposed by some ethnologists to be the aboriginal inhabitants of Europe. Traces of them have been found in England, France, Germany, Denmark and Sweden as well as in Spain. These consist of implements of peculiar construction, burial places and kitchen middens. Pickering in Races of Men, p. 19, agrees with our journalist that they are a distinct race from our so-called aboriginal inhabitants.

[76] Gaspar Cortereal visiting this coast in the year 1500, seized fifty-seven of the natives of the country and carried them home for slaves. On account of the anticipated traffic in the inhabitants of this region, the name of Tierra Laborador or the Land of Laborers was bestowed upon it according to one authority, while according to another, it was to distinguish it from Greenland, which was barren, while this would yield to the labor of man.

or deer skins, and sometimes of birds skins. A capuchin of the same stuff, and which is fastened to it covers their head, on the top of which there comes out a tuft of hair which hangs over their forehead. The shirt comes no lower than their waist; their coat hangs behind down to their thighs, and terminates before in a point something below the waist; but the women wear them both before and behind to the middle of the leg, and bound with a girdle, from which hang little bones. The men have breeches of skins with the hair inwards, and which are often covered on the outside with the skins of ermine or such like. They wear also socks with the hair inwards, and over this, a boot furred in like manner on the inside, then a second sock and second boots, and they say, that these coverings for the feet are sometimes three or four fold, which does not, however, hinder these savages from being very nimble. Their arrows, which are the only arms they use, are armed with points made of the teeth of the sea cow, and they sometimes make them of iron when they can get it. It appears that in summer they keep in the open air night and day; but in the winter, they lodge under ground in a sort of cave where they all lie one upon another: but to return,—the island of Anticosty[77] lies at the entrance of the river St. Law·

---

[77]*Anticosti.* This wild island is still uninhabited except by a few fishermen and Indians, who make it their home for a brief season in the summer. It has no harbor in which ships can take refuge anywhere along its coast. The soil

rence. It is about 40 leagues long and but very little breadth, poorly wooded and a wretched barren spot.—

20th. About 10 at night a melancholy accident happened to us. In a gale of wind, the *Providence* transport ran foul of our vessel, which, as there was a great swell of sea at the time, was attended with some danger. One of our grenadiers, I suppose thinking our ship going down, run from his berth below, (where some said he had been asleep), and attempted to get on board her, but in the trial fell between and was instantly crushed to pieces.— Soon after we got clear of her, she being a much larger ship than ours, though neither of us suffered any thing to speak of. I dont think any thing can be more alarming than 2 large ships running foul of

---

thus far has not tempted man to cultivate it. As its situation renders it dangerous to navigation, two relief stations have been established at different points upon it, supplied with provisions for the benefit of those who may be so unfortunate as to be cast upon its inhospitable shores, and guide boards are placed here and there to direct them to these stations. When it was discovered by Jacques Cartier on the day of the Festival of the Assumption, that pious navigator named it *l'yle de l'Assumption*, but quite properly, its old Indian name as given by Champlain, or perhaps a corruption of it, as early writers differ in their orthography, has stuck to it. Thus, Thevet calls it Naticousti, and De Laet, Natiscotes, but Champlain may, after all, have given us in his orthography the sound of the Indian word more nearly than they have done. *Vide* Charlevoix, tom. I, p. 16; *Brief Rècit*, p. 9; Hakluyt, vol. 3, p. 292; Champlain's Voyages, vol. 2, p. 233; Bonchetti, vol. 1, p. 169.

each other in a gale of wind, though I should imagine it worse in a dead calm and great swell of sea, as then there must be a difficulty in getting clear of each other; and, yet, this is often the case in large fleets, where all transports are kept as regular as possible in their stations by the men of war, who often fire on them for attempting to go ahead, and make them pay much for the first shot, doubling it till they become obedient.—On our sailing from Cork harbour, all the masters of transports received sealed instructions, which were not to be opened until by stress of weather, or any other cause, their ship was separated from the fleet 24 hours, after which, these instructions were to be opened, and by them they were ordered to make the best of their way to the island of Coudres[78] 15 leagues below Quebec, that being the place appointed to rendezvous at, as I believe, on our leaving Ireland, it was not well known whether Quebec was in our hands or the enemies. As the weather was still very foggy and hazy, we were obliged to steer with great caution, constantly ringing our bells to prevent other vessels from coming too near. I shall not attempt to entertain the reader with a storm, (so often done by fresh water sailors), where the sea was swelled into billows mountains high, on the top of which our vessel

[78] Isle aux Coudres, *i. e.*—Filbert Island—the name which it still bears, and which was bestowed upon it by Jacques Cartier on account of the abundance of hazel nuts or filberts which he found upon it nearly two and a half centuries before Digby saw it.

hung, and was in danger of being precipitated to the abyss beneath, as, in general, the weather was as favourable for us as we could have wished, and our passage rendered shorter than it is commonly performed with a fleet, where the whole are often obliged to slacken sail for one heavy sailing ship.

21st. Found our mizzen mast had sprung near the deck, so dare not crowd much sail on it; our exactness in keeping proper order in our stations while under way, and obeying of signals from the convoys, was a pleasing sight to one not used to such a scene.—

24th. Had the pleasure of seeing a small vessel a head of us coming from Quebec with the agreeable news of that place being still in our possession; though the enemy had lain before it most part of the winter and made an attempt to storm it on the 31st December under the command of General MtGomery, who fell with many others in the attempt, tho' their numbers were treble ours.[79] I shall here insert his

[79] Richard Montgomery was born at Raphoe, Ireland, December 2, 1736, and fell in the attack on Quebec, December 31, 1775. He was commissioned in the British army in 1754, and participated in the siege of Louisburg in 1758, and after service in the West Indies, returned to England in 1763. He emigrated to New York in 1772, when he married a daughter of Robert Livingston and settled in Rhinebeck. He was representative to the Provincial Congress in 1775, and appointed a brigadier-general early in the same year. On December 9th, while before Quebec, he received his appointment as brigadier-general. While leading the assault against the upper town, having captured the first barrier, he was killed, and his troops seeing him fall fell

orders to his troops the day before the storm, as it will serve to show, how sure he was of success, and the poor opinion he had of our garrison.

GENERAL ORDERS 30TH DECr, 1775.

The general having in vain offered the most favourable terms of accommodation to the governor, and having taken every possible step to prevail on the inhabitants to desist from seconding him, in the wild scheme of vigorous measures for the speedy reduction of the only hold possessed by the ministerial troops in the province, flushed with continual

back in disorder. Montgomery was buried on the 3rd of January, and Henry who was present and witnessed it, thus describes his funeral: "It was on this day that my heart was ready to burst with grief, at viewing the funeral of our beloved general. Carleton had in our former days with the French, been the friend and fellow soldier of Montgomery. Though political opinion, perhaps ambition or interest, had thrown these worthies on different sides of the great question, yet the former could but honor the remains of his quondam friend. About noon the procession passed our quarters. It was most solemn. The coffin covered with a pall, surmounted with transverse swords, was borne by men. The regular troops, particularly that fine body of men, the Seventh Regiment, with reversed arms, and scarfs on the left elbow, accompanied the corpse to the grave. From many of us it drew tears of affection for the defunct, and speaking for myself, tears of greeting and thankfulness toward General Carleton. The soldiery and inhabitants appeared affected by the loss of this invaluable man, though he was their enemy." Other writers mention the peculiar affection borne toward the brave general by those opposed to him. In the British Parliament the most illustrious men of the time eulogized him. It was certainly a strange sight. It is said that "Colonel Barre was particularly remarked for the noble

success and confident of the justice of their cause, and relying on that Providence which has uniformly protected them, the troops will advance to the attack of works incapable of being defended by the wretched garrison posted behind them, consisting of sailors unacquainted with the use of arms, of citizens incapable of soldier's duty, and a few miserable emigrants. The general is confident a vigorous and spirited attack will be attended with success. The troops shall have the effects of the governor, garrison and such as have been active in misleading the inhabitants and distressing the friends of liberty, equally divided

---

pathos of the regrets he consecrated to the death of his gallant enemy. Burke and Fox endeavored to surpass this eulogium in their speeches; Fox especially, who, as yet very young, already discovered the man he was afterward to be. Lord North reprehended them sharply, exclaiming that it was indecent to lavish so many praises upon a rebel. He admitted that Montgomery was brave, able, humane and generous, but still he was only a brave, able, humane and generous rebel. He cited this verse of Addison in Cato: 'Curse on his virtues, they've undone his country.' Fox answered him immediately, with warmth, that 'the term 'rebel,' applied to that excellent person, was no certain mark of disgrace, and therefore he was the less earnest to clear him of the imputation, for that all the great asserters of liberty, the saviours of their country, the benefactors of mankind, in all ages, had been called rebels; that they even owed the constitution, which enabled them to sit in that house, to a rebellion.' He added this passage from the prince of Latin poets, 'Sunt hic etiam sua prœmia laudi, sunt lachrymœ rerum, et mentum mortalia tangunt.'" *Vide* Account of Arnold's Campaign Against Quebec (Henry), Albany, 1877, p. 134; Ramsay's American Revolution, Phila., 1789, vol. 1, p. 244; Botta's History War of Independence, 1820, vol. 2, p. 66.

among them. The one hundredth share of the whole shall be at the disposal of the gen[l], and given to such soldiers as distinguish themselves by their activity and bravery, and sold at public auction. The whole to be regulated as soon as the city is in our hands and the inhabitants disarmed.—

During the whole, General Carlton behaved with the utmost coolness and good conduct, and deserves the greatest credit for keeping the place with such a wretched garrison as M[r] M[t]Gomery was pleased to call them.

26th. Anchored off the Island of Coudres, which is remarkable for a mountain being rooted up in the year 1663 and thrown upon this island, which was made one half larger than before, and in place of the mountain, there appeared a gulph which is not safe to approach.[80]

---

[80] These are almost the exact words of Charlevoix, who says: "In 1663 an earthquake rooted up a mountain and threw it upon the Isle aux Coudres which made it one half larger than before." This earthquake, according to a manuscript in the Jesuits' College at Quebec, began on the 5th of February, 1663, at about half-past five o'clock in the afternoon. It extended, as we know, throughout the northern part of America. The first shock, and the most violent one, lasted for half an hour, but it is said the earthquake continued at intervals for a period of six months with inconceivable violence. Forests were uprooted, mountains precipitated into valleys, rivers diverted from their courses and often swallowed up altogether, and even the mighty waters of the St. Lawrence were lashed to sudden whiteness by subterranean commotion, while showers of volcanic ashes darkened the air in some places, but the country being so lightly inhabited, of course no great damage was done.

29th. Got a pilot to conduct us as quick as possible to Quebec.

30th. Being one of the first ships in the fleet, we were met near the island of Orleans,[81] (a beautiful island about 14 leagues in compass and many inhabitants), by the *Hope* ship going express to England. A lieutenant of a man of war came on board us, and very politely offered to take charge of any letters we might wish to forward to our friends the other side the Atlantic. He informed us General Carlton had made a sally on the enemy, tho. greatly superiour to him in numbers, and drove them with the 29th & 47th regiments, to a strong post they had up the river,[82] where he was obliged to halt till our

---

From the accounts which have come down to us, it was far more violent than any which has occurred in southern Europe within the historic period. *Vide* Letters to the Duchesse de Lesdeguieres, London, 1763, p. 15; Josselyn's Two Voyages, Boston, 1865, p. 205; Conquest of Canada, London, 1849, Appendix XXI.

[81] The Indian name for this island was *Minigo*, but Cartier who discovered it in 1535, gave it the name Isle of Bacchus, on account of the wild grapes found growing there. "Lorsque Jacques Carthier decouvrit cette ile il la trouva toute remplie de vignes, et la nomina l'Ile de Bacchus. Ce navigateur était Bréton, apres lui sont venus de Normands qui ont arraché les vignes et à Bacchus ont substitué Pomme et Cérès." *Vide* Journal Historique, p. 102; Brief Recit., etc., faite en MDXXXV, Paris, 1863, p. 14.

[82] This was at Fort Sorel, which took its name from its builder, M. de Sorel, whose name also attached itself to the river, at the mouth of which the fort was placed. It was first named by Champlain, The River of the Iroquois, and subsequently received the name of the Richelieu from the famous Cardinal of that name.

arrival, they being strongly entrenched. He then proceeded on his voyage. About 12 at night, we came to an anchor before Quebec; Lord Balcarres, our major, and I went on shore. This is the only city in the world that can boast of a port in fresh water 120 leagues from the sea and capable of containing 100 ships of the line, situated on the most navigable river in the world, in latitude 47.56. We then went on board the *Isis*, a 50 gun ship, commodore Douglas[83] commanding, and from him received orders to proceed directly, (the wind being fair), up the river, and ordered another pilot to con-

[83] Sir Charles Douglas, "a very good, a very brave and a very honest man," was a descendant of the Earl of Morton, and was appointed a lieutenant in the British navy, December 4, 1753. He was a man of great energy and of a fearless spirit. Finding the ice obstructing his course to Quebec, and being anxious to relieve the besieged forces there, he put his ship before the wind during a gale and ran her with full force against a block of ice twelve feet thick, crumbling it in pieces by the shock. He said in his dispatches: "We now thought it an enterprise worthy of an English ship of the line in our king and country's sacred cause, and an effort due to the gallant defense of Quebec, to make the attempt of pressing her, by force of sail, through the thick, broad and closely connected fields of ice (as formidable as the Gulf of St. Lawrence ever exhibited), to which we saw no bounds." His arrival on the 6th of May before Quebec caused the besiegers to abandon their post. After a life zealously devoted to his country's welfare, he died March 10, 1789, at Musselburgh, formerly Eskmouth, Scotland. *Vide* Gentleman's Magazine, vol. 2, p. 506; Burke's Peerage and Baronetage, *in loco;* American Archives, vol. 6, p. 456; British Family Antiquity (Playfair), London, 1811, vol. 7, pp. lxxxix–xcv.

duct our ship. It was on the arrival of this man of war the enemy flew, she appearing before Quebec the sixth of May, which was one of the earliest ships that ever made that place before, on account of the ice, and she was near lost, being almost froze in. The great joy expressed by the inhabitants on our informing them what a large body of troops we had coming to their relief is not to be described, after all they had suffered during the winter.

31st. Came to an anchor at Port Neuf 12 leagues above Quebec. The wind not continueing fair, we went on shore and got great plenty of vegetables, &c from the Canadians. The weather was lovely. The country is only cleared about half a mile from the river, and behind such woods,—in all appearance as old as the world itself,—as were not planted by the hands of men. Nothing is more magnificent to the sight; the trees lose themselves in the clouds, and there is such a prodigious variety of species, that even among those persons who have taken most pains to know them, there is not one, perhaps, that knows half the number. Many of our fleet were a small way in our stern waiting for the breeze.

June 1st. Received orders to disembark, (the wind still against us or rather a calm), and march up on shore towards the enemy. We were about 500 men — and more, we hoped, not far in our rear — all in great spirits on leaving the ships. Our camp equipage and other baggage were left on board, to come up when the wind would serve. After easy marches, we came to Trois Riviere[84] a neat village and one of the oldest in the colony half way from Quebec to Montreal, the whole being sixty leagues, the river being navigable 100 leagues from the sea for large vessels. Troops were joining us fast. I suppose we might then have about 1,000 with some field pieces & many of our ships off the town. We posted strong guards, the enemy being so very near, and intended to halt there till the coming up of the rest of the army.

7th. More of our troops came up by water.

8th. About 4 in the morning an alarm was given by an out picquet, of the approach of a strong body of the enemy. The greatest part of the troops still remained on board as they had arrived late the night before. Soon after the alarm was given, a few shots were heard from one of our armed vessels that was stationed a small way above the village, who fired on part of the enemy advancing between the skirts of the wood and the river. In the mean time, the troops on shore were ordered

---

[84] Trois Rivieres is situated at the confluence of the rivers St. Maurice and St. Lawrence, and was thus named on account of an island so dividing the waters as to give the appearance of three rivers. The town was founded in 1618, and at the time Digby saw it, contained about two hundred and fifty houses and twelve hundred inhabitants. At the present time it contains nearly ten thousand inhabitants and is increasing in prosperity.

to line every avenue from the village to the wood, and take post in the best manner possible. Those on board were ordered to land with the greatest dispatch. About 5 o'clock, strong advanced parties were sent towards the wood, where they discovered the enemy marching down in three columns, who immediately began a heavy fire with small arms, which was instantly returned. In the meantime, a strong reinforcement of our troops with some field pieces arrived, which soon swept the woods and broke their columns, the remains of which were pursued by us as far as was prudent. The enemy from that time did nothing regular; but broken and dispersed, fired a few scattered shots which did little execution. A strong detachment of 1200 men under the command of Lieu^t Colonel Frazier, marched up the river to try, if possible, to get between [them] & their battows (boats flat bottomed) but the attempt did not succeed thro. their hasty flight. We took 280 prisoners with their general Thompson,[85] who commanded the

[85] William Thompson, of whom says Henry, "this is a man," was a native of Ireland, and had served as a captain in the seven years' war. The year before, he had been made colonel of the Pennsylvanian battalion. It had been proposed to give him the command in Virginia, but Washington, although Thompson had served with him at Cambridge and won his esteem, fearing that it would create jealousy, opposed the appointment. Congress, however, soon after raised him to the rank of brigadier-general and assigned him to service in Canada. During the battle, Thompson with Colonel Irvine and a small body of men, were cut off from the main body, and becoming entangled in swamps for twenty-four hours wandered about till exhausted. "We concluded,"

expedition, and six other officers. Upwards of 50 were found killed in the woods, and it was supposed many others, wounded and straglers, must have perished there, for they themselves acknowledge on that day to have lost 630 men. Ours was 5 killed and 14 wounded; no officer was hurt.[86]

---

said Irvine, "it would be better to deliver ourselves up to British officers than to run the risk of being murdered in the woods by the Canadians; accordingly we went up to a house where we saw a guard and surrendered ourselves, prisoners at discretion." He complained of the treatment of Colonel Nesbit, the officer in command, who hurried them with a crowd of prisoners on a forced march to headquarters, six miles distant, but said that upon their arrival there they found Generals Carleton and Burgoyne, who treated them very politely and ordered for them refreshments, which General Burgoyne himself served. General Riedesel, however, seems to have regarded the captives with contempt, as he alludes to General Thompson as "a certain Thompson who represents a so-called general." He remained a prisoner for two years, when he was exchanged. In a letter to General Heath, Washington wrote, referring to a proposed exchange of Generals Thompson and Hamilton: "If you cannot succeed in that, they" (the Board of War) "desire you to feel the pulse of the two other brigadiers, either of whom we would willingly exchange for General Thompson." He lived but three years after his exchange, and died September 4, 1781, at Carlisle, Pennsylvania. *Vide* Account of Arnold's Campaign Against Quebec, p. 175; Sparks' Washington, vol. 3, pp. 101, 309, 315, *et passim*, vol. 5, 358; Ramsay's American Revolution, vol. 1, p. 273; Hadden's Journal and Orderly Books, *n.*, p. 176; Memoirs of Major-General Riedesel, Albany, 1868, vol. 1, p. 289.

[86] After the death of General Thomas, who was withdrawing his forces towards the south in order to place them in as strong and safe positions as possible, the command devolved upon Sullivan, who, from his dispatches, appears to

9th. About 6 in the evening we came into the village, after leaving strong guards &c out. The transports, supposed to have gone on shore the night of the 7 May, arrived to our great joy; but this was considerably damped by the account of the death of poor Charles Haughton,[87] a lieutenant in our regiment and my particular friend. He was killed by a fall from a rock, in the island of Coudres, the chape of his sword running into his temple. His premature death was lamented by all who knew him. The different brigades were then formed, and our corps, consisting of all the light infantry and grenadiers of the army, (viz 9th. 20th. 21st. 24th. 29th. 31st. 34th. 47th. 53d. & 62nd regiments, with the 24th regiment under the command of Brigadier general Frazier, lieutenant colonel of the 24th regiment, and called the advanced corps,

---

have been elated at finding himself in possession of the chief command, and he conceived, without knowing the strength of the enemy, the possibility of "recovering," as he expressed it, with his shattered and starving forces, "that ground which former troops have so shamefully lost." In pursuance of this impracticable scheme, for which it is but fair to say he was but partially responsible, since Congress pressed him to it, he pushed the Pennsylvania troops back against the overwhelming forces of the enemy, and thereby sacrificed them, a blunder almost inexcusable under the circumstances.

[87] Charles Houghton, Digby's friend, has left no record of his death save in this journal of his companion in arms. A search of the army lists reveals that he was commissioned an ensign in the Fifty-third Foot on November 6, 1769, and a lieutenant on July 3, 1772. He was, it appears, succeeded by William McFarlane, July 10, 1776, but no mention is made of his death. *Vide* British Army Lists, *in loco.*

the rest of the army consisting of the British regiments above named, and German troops under the command of General Reidezel,[88] were formed into brigades & brigadier generals commanding them, by which we took leave of our respective regiments till the closing of the campaign. Lord Balcarres, major to the 53d regiment, was appointed major to the light

---

[88] Frederick Adolphus Riedesel was born June 3, 1738, at Lauterbach in Rhinehesse, and was in command of the Brunswickers. He entered college at the age of fifteen, but, having his military ardor awakened by witnessing the evolutions of the troops at Marburg, he left the law school there and joined a regiment. He served during the seven years' war with distinction, and was made major-general of the Brunswick troops, which George the Third hired to aid in quelling the rebellion of his American subjects. He was not exchanged until late in the autumn of 1780. After his exchange, he was put in command at Long Island, but in the summer of 1781 resumed his command in Canada. Here he remained until 1783, when he was ordered home. His devoted wife with her children accompanied him through the war, and often shared his perils. Her letters home, giving a graphic account of the scenes witnessed by her during the war, are extremely interesting, and show her to have been a remarkable woman. The Americans were greatly incensed at the employment of foreign troops against them by the British monarch, and exclaimed: "He employs the borrowed tools of the most detestable tyrants of Europe to subvert American liberty and to erect on its ruins the same despotic power of which they are the instruments and guardians in their own native land." The detestation in which these foreign hirelings were held, doubtless caused their acts to be greatly exaggerated. In their own country they were regarded as noble men and brave soldiers, and their martial deeds were embalmed in song. It is well to see how they were received on their return home after their campaign in America, that the scene may be contrasted with the pictures of

infantry; and major Ackland,[89] major 20th regiment, to the battallion of grenadiers. I suppose the army at this period about 9,000.—

10th. Received orders to embark except the above 1200 under the command of brigadier general Frazier,

---

them by American writers. Says Madame Riedesel, writing a few days after her return home: "I had the great satisfaction of seeing my husband, with his own troops, pass through the city. Yes! these very streets, in which eight and a half years before, I had lost my joy and happiness, were the ones where I now saw this beautiful and soul-stirring spectacle. But it is beyond my power to describe my emotions at beholding my beloved, upright husband, who the whole time had lived solely for his duty, and who had constantly been so unwearied in helping and assisting, as far as possible, those who had been intrusted to him, often, too, out of his own purse, never receiving any return for the expenditure — standing, with tears of joy in his eyes, in the midst of his soldiers, who in turn were surrounded by a joyous and sorrowful crowd of fathers, mothers, wives, children, sisters and friends — all pressing around him to see again their loved ones." This was in the autumn of 1783. General Riedesel lived for seventeen years after this, dying January 6, 1800. *Vide* Letters and Journal of Madame Riedesel, pp. 2–7; Memoirs of Major-General Riedesel, pp. 2–6; Graham's History of the United States, vol. 6, p. 420.

[89] John Dyke Acland was a native of Tetton, Somersetshire, and was born February 21, 1747. He was commissioned an ensign in the Thirty-third Foot, March 23, 1774. He became a captain in the same regiment March 23rd, and a major of the Twentieth Foot, December 16, 1775, by purchase. He commanded the grenadiers, both in the campaign of '76 and that of '77. His bravery and carelessness of exposing himself in battle caused him to be twice wounded in the latter campaign, at Hubbardton through the thighs, and at Bemus Heights through the legs. While lying on the field wounded and partially supported by a fence he would have been murdered by a young barbarian, who was

who had not then taken the command of the advanced corps but was expected hourly.

---

upon the point of shooting him when arrested in his cruel design by Major Wilkinson, who protected him. One of the many patriotic poets of the period referred to him and the lamented Fraser in this manner:

> "Bleeding and lost the captured Acland lies,
> While leaden slumbers seal his Fraser's eyes;
> Fraser! whose deeds unfailing glories claim,
> Endear'd by virtue and adorn'd by fame."

His wife, the Lady Harriet Acland, accompanied him through the terrible campaign of '77, and by her beauty, refinement and devotion to her husband, has been made the theme of many pens, and gained the admiration of all lovers of exalted virtue. During his brief captivity, he made many friends among the Americans, and on his return to England defended them against unfair criticism. He had recently entered Parliament, when he was suddenly cut short in a most promising career, dying at Pixton, in Somersetshire, November 22, 1778, but a few months after his return from America. Many conflicting accounts have been given of the cause of his death, one making him the victim of a duel growing out of his defense of the Americans. He had indeed, on the morning of his fatal attack, had a harmless duel, when having returned to breakfast he was suddenly seized with apoplexy, and died four days after. Conflicting stories have also been related of his wife's subsequent marriage. Fonblanque and other writers have declared that after her husband's death, she married the chaplain who accompanied her after the battle of Bemus Heights through storm and darkness to the American camp to seek her wounded husband, but Mr. Wm. L. Stone has furnished undoubted proof that she died the widow of Major Acland, July 21, 1815. *Vide* Burke's Peerage and Baronetage, and British Army Lists, *in loco;* A State of the Expedition, p. 127; Memoirs of My Own Times, vol. 1, pp. 269–271, 377; Political and Military Episodes, p. 301, *et seq.;* W. L. Stone in Magazine of American History, for January, 1880; Hadden's Journal and Orderly Books, pp. lii–lvi, 88.

11th & 12th. Were becalmed.

13th. Sailed up the river with a fair wind as far as lake St. Piere[90] where the wind failed us.

14th. About one in the morning, his excellency, general Carlton, came up and immediately ordered the fleet to get under way; the wind then turning fair, but soon after an express arriving and some shots being heard fired on shore [he] ordered them to anchor. The appearance of such a fleet so great a distance from the sea, was well worth seeing, also the beauty of the river, many villages being scattered on its banks, with the mildness of the weather and the verdure of the country, (the trees being then all in bloom), formed a most romantic and charming prospect, particularly after being so many weeks at sea. In less than an hour, the general's ship got under way, [and] sailed ahead towards the frigate, when the whole fleet weighed, and at day light, were ordered to form a line of battle as near as the channel would admit. On our opening [upon] the fort Sorrel, the troops got orders to be in readiness to land on the shortest notice, the signal being a blue ensign at the frigate's mizzen picue. Soon after we received orders for the light infantry and grenadiers of the army, with the first brigade only, to land, and about 9 in the evening, reached the shore under the command of

[90] This lake was so named by Champlain who entered it June 29th, St. Peter's day. *Vide* Champlain's Voyages, vol. 1, p. 259.

brigadier general Nesbit,[91] lieutenant colonel of 47th regiment.—

We found the enemy had deserted their lines, and about 10 o'clock the troops took post and lay all night on their arms.

15th. At day break, lieutenant general Burgoyne[92] landed with the 9th & 31st Battallions, with six six-

---

[91] William Nesbit had been stationed in Massachusetts and was the Lieutenant-Colonel Nesbit who took part in the battles of Lexington and Bunker Hill and participated in the burning of Charlestown. He had at this time been in the king's service twenty-five years, having entered the Thirty-sixth Foot as an ensign, April 20, 1751, and been advanced to a lieutenancy October 15, 1754, and a captaincy in the second battalion of the Thirty-first Foot, September 2, 1756, which became subsequently the Seventieth Foot. Of this regiment he was made Major May 1, 1760, and November 24, 1762, was raised to the lieutenant-colonelcy of the Fourth Foot. This was his rank in the Forty-seventh Foot at the battles of Lexington and Bunker Hill. His regiment was ordered to Canada in the spring of '76, and Nesbit became brigadier-general of the First Brigade. He was a strict disciplinarian, and was accused by the Americans of harshness and cruelty. He was taken suddenly sick during the campaign of '76, and returned to Quebec, where after an illness of a few weeks, he died. *Vide* British Army Lists, *in loco;* History of the Siege of Boston (Frothingham), p. 200; American Archives, series 5, vol. 3, p. 1089.

[92] John Burgoyne was the descendant of an old and noted family of Sutton. In 1387 it is said that John of Gaunt granted to the family the extensive manors of Sutton and Potton by the following curious deed:

"I, John of Gaunt
Do give and do graunt
Unto Roger Burgoyne
And the heirs of his loyne
All Sutton and Potton
Until the world's rotten."

pounders, as he was appointed to command the expedition against fort Chamble and fort St

---

He was born February 4, 1722–3. The question of his paternity has been discussed by many writers, most ably by Colonel Horatio Rogers, to whose article the reader is referred. He was educated at Westminster, and in 1744 held a commission in the Thirteenth Dragoons. At the age of twenty-one he eloped with Lady Charlotte, the daughter of the Earl of Derby. Four years later he retired from the army and resided on the continent until June 14, 1756, when he re-entered the army with a captain's commission in the Eleventh Dragoons and served under the great Duke of Marlborough in the attacks on Cherbourg and St. Malo in 1758, and on May 10th, of the same year, he was appointed captain-lieutenant in the Second Foot Guards with the army rank of lieutenant-colonel. On August 4, 1759, he was appointed lieutenant-colonel in command of the Sixteenth Dragoons, which achieved fame as "Burgoyne's Light Horse." In 1762, with the rank of colonel in the army and of brigadier-general for the campaign, he served with honor in Spain and returned to England the next year with a brilliant reputation. He had been elected to represent the borough of Midhurst in Parliament in 1762, and served as a representative of this borough for six years, when he was elected to represent Preston, which position he continued to hold through life. He was now at the height of his fame, rich and courted, with a marked reputation as a statesman and literary man. Among other honors conferred upon him, was that of being raised to the rank of major-general in the army May 25, 1772. When the war with America broke out, Burgoyne was one of the first to whom the king turned, and with Clinton and Howe was assigned to service there. The frigate upon which they embarked April 20, 1775, and which reached Boston May 20th, bore the suggestive name of the *Cerberus*, which inspired the following humorous lines :

> "Behold the Cerberus the Atlantic plough,
> Her precious cargo, Burgoyne, Clinton, Howe,
> Bow, wow, wow."

Johns,[93] the latter on the banks of lake Champlain and the former 12 leagues nearer Quebec; and at 9 o'clock, the army in number about 4000, received orders to march. That night we reached St Denis, about 50

He witnessed the battle of Bunker Hill, but took no part in it, and in November returned to England. The remainder of his military career may be traced here in the journal of Digby. Burgoyne's wife died June 7, 1776, while he was engaged in the campaign of that year. Some time after his return from his disastrous campaign in America, he became connected with a public singer with whom he reared out of wedlock, four children, one of whom became the noted field marshal, Sir John Burgoyne. Some of his dramatic compositions attained great popularity and ran through many editions. A complete collection of his works are to be found in the British Museum. He died August 4, 1792, and was buried in Westminster Abbey. *Vide* Burke's Peerage and Baronetage; British Army Lists, and Chronological Register of Parliament, *in loco;* Political and Military Episodes, pp. 4-9, 15, 27, 54, *et passim;* Remembrancer of Public Events, London, 1775, vol. 1, p. 16; Registers of Westminster Abbey, p. 250; British Family Antiquity, vol. 6, p. 314.

[93] Chambly. This fort as well as the town situated at the foot of the rapids of the river Richelieu or Sorel, twelve miles east, south-east of Montreal, took its title from a Frenchman of that name. It occupied the site of a wooden structure called Fort St. Louis, erected in 1764 to protect the inhabitants from the hostile Iroquois. Chambly was captured by the Americans, October 20, 1775, and had been held by them to this time. Fort St. Johns, about twenty-eight miles south-east of Montreal on the same river, had been taken by Montgomery in November, he having passed it in the night and captured Chambly below, which was not so well garrisoned, as the British supposed that St. Johns would be the object of attack. The works here had been first erected by Montcalm, and subsequently enlarged and strengthened by the British. It was about one hundred and fifteen miles north of Ticonderoga, the American stronghold.

miles, which, notwithstanding the great heat of the day and the fatigue the men underwent the night before, they executed with the greatest cheerfulness. We heard the enemy were flying before us in the greatest terror. The Canadian voluntiers took one prisoner and shot another who was in liquor and refused to surrender.[94]

16th. The army halted greatly fatigued, owing chiefly to their being so long confined on ship board.

---

[94] Jones, on the other side, gives graphic pictures of this retreat. He says that the troops "Had barely quitted one end of Chamblee when the advance-guard of the column under Burgoyne entered it at the other. The sick had been sent on ahead from St. Johns to Isle-aux-Noix. But two men could be spared from those fit for duty to row each boatload of them, and these pulled wearily all night long, with their helpless burdens, against the current of the river, for the distance of twelve miles. They reached Isle-aux-Noix just before day. What more distressing situation can be imagined? The greater number of the sick were utterly helpless, some died on the way, others were dying, — all crying out for relief which could not be furnished them. 'It broke my heart,' wrote Dr. Meyrick, a surgeon who was with them on the Isle-aux-Noix, 'and I wept till I had no more power to weep.'" And another writer speaking of the troops which reached Crown Point: "The broken fragments of the army of Canada presented one of the most distressing sights witnessed during the whole war. Of the five thousand two hundred men collected at Crown Point, two thousand eight hundred were so sick as to require the attention of the hospital, while those reported fit for duty were half naked, emaciated and entirely broken down in strength, spirits and discipline." *Vide* Campaign for the Conquest of Canada, Philadelphia, 1882, p. 88; History of Lake Champlain, (Palmer) Albany, 1866, p. 115.

17th. The whole moved in the evening and reached Belloeille, eight leagues.

18th. Marched at 2 o'clock in the morning for fort Chamble, which we reached about 9 the same day, 13 miles, and found the fort burned, the enemy having retreated to St Johns. We found 4 battows and took 2 prisoners. 'Tis remarkable they did not burn or destroy any bridges from Sorrel; had they done so, it must have delayed us greatly, but between the forts of Chamble and St John's, about 12 miles, they destroyed all the bridges, which in such a wild country are not a few, for every rivulet must have something like a bridge to render it passable, and this detained us some hours. About 12 at noon, the line was ordered to move [on] the enemy, who were not then 5 hours before us. The army marched in the greatest regularity, as from intelligence received, the general had no doubt but he should be attacked on his march, our road leading thro. thick woods. When we got within about a league of St Johns, the general was informed that a party which had been taken for an advance guard of theirs coming out to meet us, was their rear guard, covering their retreat, on which three companies of light infantry were ordered on, which they did on a trot, and reached the fort about dark, finding it abandoned and on fire. The army came up about half an hour after and lay on their arms all night.

Following are the general orders from Burgoyne to the army.—

GENERAL ORDERS.

"The expedition on which Lieut Gen. Burgoyne has had the honour to be employed being finished by the precipitate flight of the rebels, he shall think it his duty to make a faithful report to his excellency the commander in chief, of the zeal and activity shewn in the officers and men under his command, to surmount the difficulties of the march and come to action. Those are principles that cannot fail to produce the most glorious effects whenever the enemy shall acquire boldness enough to put them to the proof.—"

Thus was Canada saved with much less trouble than was expected on our embarking from Great Britain. How to pursue them over Lake Champlain, was our next thought, and the tediousness that threatened our operations necessary for so great an expedition was far from pleasing. We had every thing to build, battows to convey the troops over, and armed schooners and sloops to oppose theirs, most of which were taken from us at the breaking out of the affair. It was thought that every thing would be ready in 7 or 8 weeks, but the undertaking was a great one, and, I must say, persevered in with the greatest dispatch possible. Carpenters from all the ships were ordered up with artificers from the different regiments. Most of the Canadians thro. the province were employed in making roads through the woods, bringing up cannons, provisions and all other kind of stores requisite for such an undertaking. The disaffected Canadians were obliged to work in irons. Our fleet at that time was got up to Montreal, where, I believe, they before never saw such a one. The island of Montreal is ten leagues long from east to west and near four leagues in breadth. A mountain rises in the middle about half a league from the town, which is a long square situated on the bank of the river. Boats from all the ships were sent round by the river Sorrel, (which runs into the St Lawrence at that town,) with every article wanting at fort St Johns. There was a carrying place of 6 or 7 miles between that place and fort Chamble, where all boats and battows were drawn over by rollers, with a great number of horses. Two sloops of war carrying 12 guns each, then lying at Chamble, were attempted to be so brought up, but found not practicable, on which their guns were taken out, the vessels taken to pieces and rebuilt at St Johns, during which time, other hands were busyily employed in building the *Carlton*, a 12 gun schooner, and the *Inflexible*, a 28 gun frigate, also a floating battery of great strength, carrying mortars, shells &c and 24 pounders; during which the army was encamped as contiguously to the lake as possible.

July 5th. We were joined by a nation of savages, many more were shortly expected at our camp, and I must say their appearance came fully up [to] or even surpassed the idea I had conceived of them. They were much encouraged by Gen Carlton, as useful to the army in many particulars, but their cruel and barbarous custom of scalping[95] must be shocking to an European; though practised on our enemies. They walked freely thro. our camp and came into our tents without the least ceremony, wanting brandy or rum, for which they would do anything, as their greatest pleasure is in getting beastly intoxicated. Their manner of dancing the war dance is curious and shocking, being naked and painted in a most frightful manner. When they give the war whoop or yell, (which is a signal for engaging) they appear more like infernals, than of the human kind; but more of them hereafter. The weather was then intensely hot, scarce bearable in a

[95] We are told that the torture of prisoners had its origin with the Iroquois, and was adopted by other Indian tribes throughout America; but the practice was world-wide before America was discovered. The fearful accounts in the relations of the Jesuits of the tortures inflicted upon their captives by the savages, find an almost exact parallel in Maccabees, where Antiochus not only mutilates and burns, but scalps his victims. Scalping was also common among the Scythians. "The modern scalping-knife," says Catlin, "is of civilized manufacture, made expressly for Indian use, and carried into the Indian country by thousands. His untutored mind has not been ingenious enough to design or execute any thing so savage or destructive as these civilized refinements in Indian barbarity. If I should ever cross the Atlantic with my collection, a curious enigma would be solved for the English people who may inquire for a scalping-knife, when they find that every one in my collection bears on its blade the impress G. R." *Vide* 2 Maccabees 7, pp. 3–20; Moeurs des Sauvages (Lafitau), vol. 2, p. 287; American Indians (Catlin), vol. 1, p. 236.

camp, where the tents rather increased than diminished it, and the great number of men in so small a space made it very disagreeable, though we all went as thinly clothed as possible, wearing large loose trousers to prevent the bite of the moscheto, a small fly which was then very troublesome. Our men in general were healthy, and not much troubled with fevers and fluxes, so common when encamped in a warm climate, and lying nights on the ground under heavy dew. The tree spruce, which grows there in great plenty, as indeed in most parts of America, is an excellent antiscorbutic, and when made into beer is far from a disagreeable flavour. The Canadians in general are a very happy set of people. They possess all the vivacity of their ancestors, the French, and in the country appear on an equal footing; their noblesse choosing mostly to reside in Montreal or Quebec, both good towns and many English settled there. It would be the greatest presumption in me to attempt a description of the customs, manners, curiosities, trade &c of Canada. For such I must refer the reader to many abler hands who have more fully expatiated on them than I could pretend to do

22d. Lieut Frazier[96] 9 regt and lieut Scott[97] 24 regt were sent on a party of observation by gen Frazier

[96] Alexander Fraser was a nephew of General Simon Fraser, and had served in the Ninth Regiment of Infantry

[97] Thomas Scott was commissioned an ensign in the Twenty-fourth Foot May 20, 1761, and served in Germany

to discover if possible what the enemy were about on the lake. They had 12 regulars and about 30 Indians in cannoes. The bark cannoes are the best and will paddle very swift. They are made in

---

for ten years, having been commissioned a lieutenant October 25, 1766. He was made a captain-lieutenant May 13, 1776, on which date General Carleton, in an order, directed him to report to General Burgoyne, "in order to receive his commands relative to the assembling of the Indians," and it appears that he was placed in command of a body of these blood-thirsty savages, whom he found it no easy matter to control. We are told that on a certain occasion, having friends to dine, the Indians of his command unceremoniously came into the room where he was entertaining his guests and insisted upon drinking with them. He at first prevailed upon them to retire by giving them a bottle of rum, but they soon returned, under pretense of having business with him, and grew so troublesome that he was obliged to break up his entertainment. Having been dispatched to Canada before the surrender of Burgoyne, he escaped captivity with his fellow soldiers. He was transferred to the Thirty-fourth Foot November 11, 1776; was made major in the army November 18, 1790; lieutenant-colonel March 1, 1794, and of the Forty-fifth Foot, September 1, 1795, and shortly after disappears from the army lists. *Vide* British Army Lists, *in loco;* Letters of Sir Guy Carleton, 1776–78, vol. 1, p. 482; Travels Through the Interior Parts of America, vol. 1, pp. 214–19.

---

the following year, and later at Gibraltar. He was advanced to a lieutenancy June 7, 1765. He served through this and the subsequent campaign with distinction, and was made a captain-lieutenant July 14, 1777. He was intrusted by Burgoyne, after the terrible battle at Freeman's Farm, with the dangerous service of conveying dispatches through the American lines to General Clinton, which would subject him to certain death if discovered. He has left a journal of his adventures upon this occasion. After eleven days, in

the following manner: the bark which is very thin, they lay on flat ribs mostly made of cedar. These ribs are confined their whole length by small cross bars which separate the seats of the cannoe. Two main pieces of the same wood, to which these little

---

which he encountered hardship and peril, he reached Clinton just after he had captured Fort Montgomery, and delivered his dispatches. On the next day he set out on his return to the imperiled army of Burgoyne, and, after several days, making his way through woods and marshes, he heard rumors of Burgoyne's capitulation, and found it impossible to get through the American lines. He therefore turned back and was fortunate enough to reach Clinton's fleet in safety. He shortly after found his way to Canada, and on October 8th was appointed captain in the Fifty-third Regiment, a portion of which had been left by Burgoyne to garrison Ticonderoga. He served with marked ability in Canada, returning to England in 1788. After severe service on the continent, in which he participated in many battles, he was promoted to the rank of major November 13, 1793, and on the 27th of October, 1794, lieutenant-colonel of the Ninety-fourth Regiment by purchase, and, in 1796, was adjutant-general to the forces at the Cape of Good Hope. During the year 1799 he was in command of a native brigade in India, and participated in the taking of Seringapatam. On January 1, 1801, having returned to England the previous year broken in health by severe and almost constant service for forty years, he was made colonel by brevet, and assigned to the recruiting service. On August 10, 1804, he was promoted to the rank of brigadier-general, and April 25, 1808, major-general on the North Britain staff, in which position he served until June 4, 1813, when he received his last appointment of lieutenant-general in the army, a position which he had earned by service of the most arduous kind performed with unusual judgment and zeal. He died in 1814. *Vide* British Army Lists, *in loco;* Captain Scott's Journal, quoted by Fonblanque, pp. 287-90; Burgoyne's Orderly Book, pp. 53-55.

bars are sewed, strengthen the whole machine. Between the ribs and the bark they thrust little pieces of cedar which are thinner still than the ribs, and which help to strengthen the cannoe, the two ends of which rise by degrees and insensibly end in sharp points that turn inwards. These two ends are exactly alike, so that to change their course and turn back, the canoemen need only change hands. He who is behind, steers with his oar, working continually, and the greatest occupation of him who is forward, is to take care that the cannoe touches nothing to burst it. They sit or kneel on the bottom, and their oars are paddles of 5 or 6 feet long, commonly of maple; but when they go against a current that is pretty strong, they must use a pole and stand upright. One must have a good deal of practice to preserve a ballance in this exercise, for nothing is lighter and, of consequence, easier to overset than these cannoes, the greatest of which, with their loading does not draw more than half a foot of water, and will carry 12 men, two upon a seat, and 4000 pounds weight. The smallest of these will carry a sail, and with a good wind can make 20 leagues in a day. Without sails they must be good canoemen to make 12 leagues in a dead water.—About 20 miles from St John's near the Isle aux-Noix—island of nuts—they fell in with a party of the enemy, and, after some fireing, brought them to us prisoners, with the loss only of one Indian and a few wounded. The captains name was

Wilson,[98] who informed us they were very strong at Crown Point[99] and Ticonderoga,[100] both places

---

[98] James Armstrong Wilson, son of Thomas Wilson and Jean Armstrong, was born in 1752 in the Cumberland valley, and came from warlike stock, some of his ancestors having served as officers in the French and Indian wars. When the Revolution opened, he raised a company of which he was commissioned captain January 9, 1776. This company was included as number five in Colonel William Irvine's, or the Sixth Pennsylvania Regiment. He had command of a party of thirty men, and was on a reconnoissance, when without exercising sufficient prudence, he penetrated to the river Sorel, where he encountered the British and Indians, under the command of Captain Craig. Wilson's men fought so well as to excite the admiration of their foes. Two men on each side lost their lives; one of the British infantry being mortally wounded, and one of their Indian allies killed; and on the American side, likewise, one man was killed and another mortally wounded. After his release from captivity he returned to his home near Carlisle, Pennsylvania, where he remained until his exchange was effected. He was subsequently commissioned a major in one of the regiments of the Pennsylvania line, then being organized, but owing to disability caused by exposure in the Canadian campaign he was compelled to retire from service. He continued in failing health until March 17, 1783, when he died, in the thirty-

---

[99] Crown Point is on the western shore of Lake Champlain, about ninety miles north of Albany. On the peninsula, which is nearly a mile in width, the French built a fort in 1731, which they named Fort St. Frederic, in honor of Frederic Maurepas, the secretary of state at that time.

---

[100] Ticonderoga, or Cheonderoga (brawling waters) as the Indians called it, a promontory at the outlet of Lake George, has been the scene of many battles, and its soil has been often enriched with human blood. There can be but little doubt that on this historic spot occurred the battle which Champlain so graphically describes as having taken place

of great strength by nature, and neither men nor cannon wanting to make them more so; also their force on the lake was great and much superior,

---

sixth year of his age. The Carlisle *Gazette* thus spoke of him: "The many virtues of this good and amiable man endeared him in a particular manner to all who knew him. In him his country has lost a disinterested and inflexible patriot." Major Wilson married Margaret, daughter of Captain Robert Miller of the Revolution, who, with several children, survived him.

I am indebted for important facts in this note to the kindness of Dr. W. H. Egle, of Harrisburg, State Librarian of the Commonwealth of Pennsylvania.

In 1759 this fort was captured by the British and Provincials, under General Amherst, and was taken from them by the Americans, under command of Colonel Seth Warner, in May, 1775, there being at this time a garrison of but twelve men in the fort.

---

between the Iroquois and the Hurons, in which he took part so unwarrantably in the summer of 1609. From immemorial time it had served as the gateway between the vast tribal regions of the south and those of the north. Here, so well suited was the place for a defensive post, Montcalm, in 1756, built his fort, and, with "the poet's tongue of baptismal flame," called it *Carillon*, on account of the music of the waterfall near by, which reminded him of a chime of bells. But the sweet voice of the waterfall was drowned by the harsh din of battle in 1758, between the English and French. In this battle, the English under Abercrombie were defeated. The next year Amherst laid siege to and captured it. For sixteen years it remained in the possession of the English, when Ethan Allen, in 1775, took it from the English, who retook it in 1777, but were soon forced to part with it. In 1778 it was again taken by General Haldeman, but was soon abandoned to the Americans. *Vide* Champlain's Voyages, Prince Society, vol. 2, p. 223; Hinton's Hist. U. S., vol. 1, pp. 172, 174, 231 *et passim.*

he believed, to any we could bring against them that year. The fort of St Johns, at the time it was attacked by the enemy, was garrisoned by a few companies of the 26th regmt. They stood out some days but were obliged to surrender to superior numbers. The remainder of the regiment, with part of the 7th were at Chamble, where they made but a very short stand ; less than even the enemy imagined. There they took a great store of powder which might have been easily destroyed, and turned out the means of their rapid movement toward Quebec, the capital.—[101]

25th. As brig. gen Gordon,[102] who commanded the first brigade of British, was rideing from St Johns

---

[101] The following account of the capture of Fort St. John is from Hadden's Journal, pp. 2 and 3: "The *Fort* at *Chamblee* or rather the *Shell* of a large square House *loop holed*, is an ancient structure raised about 50 Feet, totaly of Masonry and intended as a defence against the sudden attack of the Savages. It was surrender'd by *Major Stopford* (last year) to the *Rebels* (who brought 1 Gun & a Horse load of powder against it) after firing a few Shot: and he neglected to destroy a large quantity of powder then in the *Fort*, they were enabled to return and attack Fort St. Johns. The powder might have been thrown into the *Rapids* as the Fort is immediately above them. There was also a *Well* in the Fort. *Timidity* and *Folly* in this instance seem to have been the cause of all the succeeding misfortunes in Canada. I did not learn that any Men were *Killed* or wounded in the Fort, and it certainly might have held out long enough for the Enemy to have expended *all their* ammunition, in which case they must have abandoned their enterprise. On the contrary with the above supplies they besieged and took St. Johns in about Six weeks."

[102] Patrick Gordon was commissioned in the First Foot as captain, or first lieutenant, January 22, 1755, and promoted

to Lapraire, (about 4 leagues) he was shot by a scouting party of the enemy from the wood; two balls took place in his shoulder, of which he died the following day, and in a general order to the

---

to the captaincy of the second battalion of the same regiment, February 16, 1756, and major of the One Hundred and Eighth Foot, October 17, 1761. He was raised to the lieutenant-colonelcy of the Twenty-ninth Foot previous to the departure of the troops from Ireland, and soon after his arrival in Canada was further rewarded by having bestowed upon him a brigadier-general's commission. He died on the first of August, and was buried at Montreal on the third. Hadden says: "About the 2nd of August Brigadier Gen'l Gordon was wounded and died. Lord Petersham narrowly escaped the same fate. The distance between *St. Johns* and *Montreal*, passing by *Chamblee*, is about 30 miles; on this Road the Army lay encamped or Canton'd, but there was a shorter *route* by *La Prairie*, and this tho. unguarded, was thought secure from the distance & panic of the Enemy, and Officers constantly travell'd it without escorts. The *Rebels* having information of this circumstance and wishing for intelligence, detached one *Whitcomb*, with four others to waylay this Road, and they succeeded but too well. *Whitcomb* shot Gen'l *Gordon* when he might have taken him Prisoner. The day following he seized & carried off, the Qr. Master of the 29th Reg't and a Noncommissioned Officer, who knew nothing of the late accident. *Whitcomb* returned by the edge of Lake Champlain and got safe into *Tyconderoga* with his Prisoners tho. pursued by the Savages." Whitcomb's own account of this transaction is as follows: "Twenty third, early in the morning, I returned to my former place of abode, stood there the whole day, saw twenty three carts laden with barrels and tents going to St. Johns. Twenty fourth, staid at the same place till about twelve o'clock then fired on an officer, and moved immediately into Chambly road; being discovered, retreated back into the woods and staid till night; then taking the road and passing the guards till I came below Chambly, finding myself discovered, was obliged to conceal

army from his excellency, general Carlton, after having expatiated on such a cowardly and cruel manner of carrying on the war; he describes the dress, person &c of the scout, their captain, called

---

myself in the brush till dark." The next day he completed his escape. Anburey gives an interesting account of the affair, and says that after being wounded, "The General immediately rode as fast as he could to the camp at St. Johns, which he had but just reached, when with the loss of blood and fatigue, he fell from his horse; some soldiers took him up and carried him to the hospital, where, after his wound was dressed, and he was a little at ease, he related the circumstance, which being immediately made known to General Carleton, a party of Indians were sent out to scour the woods, and search for Whitcomb, but in vain, as he hastened back to Ticonderoga. General Carleton, however, imagining he might be lurking about the woods, or secreted in the house of some disaffected Canadian, issued out a proclamation among the inhabitants, offering a reward of fifty guineas to any one that would bring Whitcomb, alive or dead, to the camp. A few days after this, General Gordon died of his wound, in whose death we sincerely lamented the loss of a brave and experienced officer. When Whitcomb returned to Ticonderoga, and informed the General who commanded there, that although he could not take an officer prisoner, he believed he had mortally wounded one, the General expressed his disapprobation in the highest terms, and was so much displeased at the transaction, that Whitcomb, in order to effect a reconciliation, offered his services to go again, professing he would forfeit his life, if he did not return with a prisoner." We shall see how well he performed this promise. General James Wilkinson calls Whitcomb an assassin, and doubtless states correctly that the shooting of Gordon was looked upon by the Americans as a criminal act. *Vide* British Army Lists, *in loco;* Hadden's Journal, pp. 4–6; American Archives, Fifth Series, vol. 1, p. 828; Travels Through the Interior Parts of America, vol. 1, p. 256; Memoirs of My Own Times, vol. 1, p. 69.

Whitcomb,[103] a famous ranger from Connecticut, wishing, should he be taken, he might be spared for the hands of the hangman, a soldier's death being too honourable for such a wretch.

---

[103] Lieutenant Benjamin Whitcomb was one of the most active and daring scouts on the American side. For his services he was, shortly after this date, made a major. After shooting General Gordon and narrowly escaping capture by the troops and Indians sent in pursuit of him, which would have resulted in his immediate execution, being stung by the reproaches of some of his companions in arms, who regarded the shooting of Gordon a criminal act, he immediately returned to the place where the shooting took place, though it seemed certain death for him so to do, avowing it as his purpose to capture an officer or lose his life in the attempt. The result was the capture by him of the quartermaster, Alexander Saunders, and a non-commissioned officer, both of whom he carried prisoners safely to Ticonderoga. Anburey relates the particulars of the affair: "The regiment of which our friend S[aunders] is Quarter-master, having occasion for some stores from Montreal, he was going from the camp at St. John's to procure them; he was advised not to go this road, but by way of Chamblee, on account of the late accident; but you know him to be a man of great bravery and personal courage, joined with uncommon strength; resolving not to go so many miles out of his road for any Whitcomb whatever, he jocosely added that he should be very glad to meet with him, as he was sure he should get the reward; in this, however, he was greatly mistaken, his reward being no other than that of being taken prisoner himself. Previous to his setting out he took every precaution, having not only loaded his fusee, but charged a brace of pistols; when he came near to the woods I have already described, he was very cautious, but in an instant Whitcomb and the two men he had with him sprung from behind a thick brush and seized him before he could make the least resistance; they then took from him his fusee and pistols, tied his arms behind him with ropes,

29th. By a flag of truce, the general sent all the prisoners taken at Trois Rivieres on parole to their respective homes, relying on their word of not bearing arms till duly exchanged; how they attended to their parole I am not a judge, though many were of

---

and blindfolded him. It was three days before they reached the canoe that had been concealed, during which time they had but very scanty fare; a few hard biscuits served to allay their hunger, while the fruit of the woods was a luxury! When Whitcomb had marched him to such a distance as he thought he could not make his escape, were he at liberty, through fear of losing himself, for the greater ease on his own part and to facilitate their march, they untied his hands and took the cloth from his eyes.—At night, when they had partaken of their scanty pittance, two out of the three used to sleep whilst the other kept watch. The first night he slept through fatigue; on the second, as you may naturally suppose, from his great anxiety of mind, he could not close his eyes, in the middle of which an opportunity occurred whereby he could have effected his escape, for the man whose watch it was, fell fast asleep. He has since told me how his mind wavered for a length of time, what measures to pursue; he could not bear the idea of putting them to death, though justified by the rules of war; if he escaped from them, they might in all probability retake and ill-treat him. The great hazard of all, which determined him to abide by his fate, was, that by being so many miles in a tract of wood, where he could not tell what direction to take (having been blindfolded when he entered it), he might possibly wander up and down till he perished with hunger. In this restless state he remained till daybreak, when they resumed their march, and in the evening came to the creek where the canoe was concealed." The next morning Whitcomb reached Ticonderoga with his prisoners. The shooting of Gordon stirred up much bitterness of feeling against the Americans, and when a flag of truce was sent by them to the British the day after Gordon's death, General Carleton issued the following proclamation:

opinion it would soon be forgot on their getting clear from Canada.[104]

HEAD QUARTERS, QUEBEC, *Augt. 4th*, 1776.

"The commanding Officers of Corps will take especial care that every one under their command be informed, that *Letters*, or *messages* from *Rebels*, *Traitors* in Arms against the *King*, *Rioters*, disturbers of the *public Peace*, *Plunderers*, *Robbers*, *Assassins*, or *Murderers*, are on no occasion to be admitted: That shou'd emmissaries from such lawless Men again presume to approach the Army, whether under the name of Flag of Truce Men or Ambassadors except when they come to implore the King's mercy, their persons shall be immediately seized and committed to close confinement to be proceeded against as the Law directs: Their Papers & Letters for whomsoever directed (even this Com'r in Chief) are to be deliver'd to the Provost Martial, that unread and unopen'd they may be burnt by the hands of the common Hangman."

The following is extracted from an order of General Phillips, issued from Chamblee the 26th of July. After speaking of the shooting of General Gordon, he says:

"The Person who commanded the Party which attacked General Gordon is Whitcomb of Connecticut calling himself Lieutenant. He is between 30 and 40 years of Age, to appearance near 6 feet high, rather thin than otherwise, light brown Hair tied behind, rough Face, not sure whether occasioned by the small Pox or not. He wears a kind of under Jacket without Sleeves, slash Pockets, leather Breeches, grey woolen or yarn Stockings, and Shoes. Hat

[104] The kindness of General Carleton to his prisoners was never forgotten by them. Henry, one of those released prisoners whom Digby here alludes to, calls him the "Amiable, it might be said, admirable Major Carleton." After their parole, a copy of which may be seen in Henry's account, he says: "Captain Prentis procured me permission from government with a few friends to traverse the city. An officer of the garrison attended us. Our first desire was

August 14th. Our corps moved up to the Isle Aux Noix,[105] in such battows as were ready, by which the first brigade took up our ground at St John's, and was, of course, a general movement to the army. The island is about one mile long and half a one in breadth, mostly covered with wood, which in a short time we cleared for our camp, which was badly situated, being in a swamp, and much troubled with

---

flapped, a gold Cord tied round it. He had a Forelock, Blanket, Pouch and Powder Horn.

"Should he, or any of his Party, of the same nature, come within reach of our Men, it is hoped they will not honor them with Soldier's Deaths if they can possibly avoid it, but reserve them for due Punishment, which can only be effected by the Hangman." *Vide* Hadden's Journal and Orderly Books, pp. 7, 8, 237; Travels Through the Interior Parts of America, vol. 1, pp. 258–263.

---

to see the grave of our general and those of his aids, as well as those of the beloved Hendricks and Humphreys. The graves were within a small place of interment, neatly walled with stone. The coffins of Montgomery, Cheeseman and McPherson were well arranged side by side. Those of Hendricks, Humphreys, Cooper, etc., were arranged in the south side of the inclosure; but, as the burials of these heroes took place in a dreary winter, and the earth impenetrable, there was but little soil on the coffins, the snow and ice, which had been the principal covering, being now dissolved. The foot of the general's coffin was exposed to the air and view. The coffin was well formed of fir plank. Captain Prentis assured me that the graves should be deepened and the bodies duly deposited, for he also knew Montgomery as a fellow soldier and lamented his untimely fate. *Vide* Arnold's Campaign Against Quebec, p. 170.

---

[105] Isle-aux-Noix, situated at the northern extremity of Lake Champlain and commanding the entrance to the

snakes &c The old lines thrown, up by the French, [in the] last war, when they expected General Amherst[106] from Crown Point, were mostly out of repair and cost us some fatigue to put them in a state of defence, as also to throw up others towards the enemy. I cannot here omit inserting an epitaph wrote by the enemy on the grave of a captain, lieutenant and two privates, who were, a few days before their main body sailed from the island, and a little after our arrival at St Johns, scalped by some of our Indians, after having surprised them, though the most positive orders to the contrary were given by General Burgoyne, with a reward offered for prison-

---

Richelieu or Sorel, was so named by Champlain on account of the abundance of nut trees found growing there by him. In the campaign alluded to by Digby, the fortification of the island by the French is described by Sismondi, and seems to be of sufficient interest to reproduce here. He says: "Ils durent évaçuer encore la position de Fort Frédéric (Crown Point). Toutefois leur commandant, Burlamanque, se fortifia à l'Ile-aux-Noix, à l'extremité du Lac Champlain; et comme il avoit encore sous ses ordres trois mille cinq cents hommes, il réussit a fermer le chemin de Quebec au Général Amherst, et à l'empêcher de seconder l'attaque du Général contre cette ville." *Vide* Histoire des Français, vol. 29, ch. 54.

[106] I. Jeffery Amherst was born in Kent, January 29, 1717, and entered the army at the early age of fourteen years. He saw active service on the continent under General Legineu, upon whose staff he served, and by his ability rose rapidly in rank. In 1758 he was a major-general, and in that year engaged in the conquest of Canada, aided by New England troops, who entered into the contest with enthusiasm; indeed, it was in this war that the men who were now

ers to prevent scalping. The following was wrote on an old board at the head of the grave, which is no bad ruff production, and I wish with all my heart there had been no occasion to have shewn the author's talents on such a melancholy subject. I shall not speak of the horrid cruelty of such a custom being well assured the reader's heart must detest such barbarity, and be roused against the cruel savages who inflicted [it], though on our enemies, who still are our fellow creatures, on whom the rules of war even among the most uncivilized nations do not justify the exertion of such a scene of torture.

Beneath this humble sod
Lie
Cap^n Adams, Lieu^t Culbertson & 2 privates of
the 2^d Pensilvanian regiment.
Not Hirelings but Patriots
Who fell ——— not in battle,
but unarmed,
Who were barbarously murdered and inhumanly
scalped by the emissaries of the once just but
now abandoned Kingdom of Britain.
Sons of America rest in quiet here,
Britannia blush, Burgoyne let fall a tear,
And tremble Europe's Sons with savage race
Death and revenge await you with disgrace.[107]

---

opposing the British troops in their attempt to subjugate them were trained in arms. For his success in wresting Canada from the French, he received the order of the Bath. In 1763 he was made governor of Virginia, and in 1770 of the Isle of Guernsey. In 1772 he was made commander-in-chief of the army, and in 1776 was created a baron. He

---

[107] Very few particulars of this distressing occurrence have come down to us. Robert Adams was the son of Thomas

The Burial Place of Adams and Culbertson.

The main land was but a small distance from us, it scarce there deserves the name of a lake, it being

---

died, after a most brilliant career, August 3, 1787. *Vide* British Army Lists, *in loco;* The Conquest of Canada, pp. 230-277, *et passim;* History of the United States (Hinton), Boston, 1834, vol. 1, Book 2; History of Nova Scotia (Haliburton), Halifax, 1829, vol. 1, pp. 199-229.

---

and Katherine Adams, and was born in 1745 in what was subsequently Toboyne township, in Cumberland county, Pennsylvania. He was a soldier in the Bouquet expedition to the westward in 1764, and when the Revolution opened he raised a company of "Associators," which formed the second company of Colonel William Irvine's regiment, of which he was commissioned captain, January 9, 1776. Joseph Culbertson was the son of Alexander and Margaret Culbertson, and was born in 1753 in the Cumberland Valley. His ancestors came from the North of Ireland about the year 1730, subsequently locating about seven miles from what is now Chambersburg. Owing to several contiguous farms being owned by different members of the family, the place was known as "Culbertson's Row." Joseph was an early "Associator," and received his commission as ensign in Captain Wilson's company, January 9th, the same day that Adams received his. He had two brothers in the Pennsylvania line, Robert and Samuel, both officers. It would appear that Adams and Culbertson, in company with several other officers and men, on the 21st of June, crossed from their camp at Isle-aux-Noix to the western shore of the lake for the purpose of fishing, and not supposing any enemy to be in the vicinity, took no arms with them. Near the shore was the house of a Frenchman who sold spruce beer to the soldiers, a beverage which was not only refreshing, but supposed to possess medicinal virtues and very popular at this time. A small band of Indians, in which were two Canadians, were in ambush on the shore of the lake watching their movements, and surprised them while they were stopping at the Frenchman's house to drink, killing Adams and Culbertson and two of their companions,

not very broad, but the shore is such a swamp and so thick with wood, that you can scarce land, and those unbounded forests quite uninhabited, except by Indians and other savage beasts.

30th. For some days past we had the most severe and constant rain; it poured through all our tents and almost flooded the island; yet the days were very hot with violent bursts of thunder, attended with frequent flashes of lightening. The idea of service to those who have not had an opportunity of seeing any, may induce them to believe the only hardship a soldier endures on a campaign is the danger attending an action, but there are many others, perhaps not so dangerous, yet, in my opinion, very near as disagreeable,—remaining out whole nights under rain and almost frozen with cold, with very little covering, perhaps without being able to light a fire; fearing the enemy's discovering the post, and

---

and, with the exception of two who escaped, carrying the others into captivity. The men thus cruelly murdered, for they had no arms and were therefore incapable of defense, were scalped and mutilated in the usual barbarous manner of the Indians. As soon as Colonels Wayne and Hartley heard of the affair, they started in pursuit of the murderers, but failed to capture them. They, however, destroyed the house and mill of a Tory named McDonald, who was supposed to have furnished information to the savages. This "accident" Wilkinson suggests, caused General Sullivan to evacuate his position at Isle-aux-Noix. *Vide* A Letter from Crown Point, American Archives, vol. 6, pp. 1253, 1270; Memoirs of My Own Times, vol. 1, p. 61. I am indebted for several important particulars in this note to Dr. Wm. H. Egle of Harrisburg, librarian of the Commonwealth of Pennsylvania.

not knowing the moment of an attack; but always in expectation of one; not that I would be thought to insinuate from this a preference to the former, excepting when the nature of the service .equired it, and visible advantages were likely to flow from it. We had a guard about 4 miles above the island, on the main land, where there were great flocks of wolves. During the night we could hear them after a deer through the woods, and then cry something like a pack of hounds in full chase. They often came near our out centries, but they being loaded, did not much mind them.

Sep 2^d^. I went on duty to St Johns, and was present at the launching of the *Carlton* schooner. She was compleat in guns &^c^. &^c^. and the command of her given to lieut. Decars[108] of the navy.—

---

[108] James Richard Dacres, who was now put in command of the *Carleton*, was born in February, 1749, and entered the navy at the early age of thirteen years. He was a lieutenant on the ship which bore Burgoyne to Quebec. In the battle which followed his appointment to the command of the *Carleton*, he was severely wounded and supposed to be dead; indeed, he was about to be consigned to the waters of the lake, when a brother officer interfered and his life was thereby saved. He recovered sufficiently from his wounds to be the bearer of dispatches to England announcing the particulars of the engagement. In these dispatches his gallantry was highly commended by Capt. Pringle, and he was soon put in command of the sloop-of-war *Ceres*, which was subsequently captured by the French frigate *Iphigenie*. He was made a post-captain September 13, 1780, and was engaged in many brilliant naval achievements during the next few years. For his important services to the crown he was made a rear-admiral of the Blue, February 14, 1799, of the

3rd. About 10 o'clock at night an alarm was given by a cannoe full of Indians, that the enemy were bearing down upon the island (the wind being fair for them) with 6 or 7 schooners & sloops, and many battows full of men, on which General Frazier desired we might stand to our arms without the least noise or beating of drums & there wait their arrival. Our works were not near finished, but what cannon we had were immediately drawn up to the embrasures to play on them while landing. Our advanced corps, which was all the force we had on the island, consisted of about 1400 men all in good health and spirits and well prepared to give them a warm reception. An express was directly sent down in a cannoe to Genl Carlton at St Johns, acquainting him with the above particulars and stateing the strength of the island, &c. &c. I shall here insert general Frazier's orders to us, as it may be the cause of the reader's having some idea of the island.

BRIGADE ORDERS.

In case of an alarm, the Battallion of Grenadiers to form behind the lines directly in their front. The

White, January 1, 1801, and of the Red, April 23, 1804, and in the latter year was put in command of the Jamaica station, where he remained until 1808, being promoted to the rank of vice-admiral of the White, November 9, 1805. He died in England, January 6, 1801. *Vide* Royal Naval Biography (Marshall), part 1, vol. 2, p. 29; Universal Magazine, London, vol. 59, pp. 270–2; Ibid., vol. 62, p. 274; London Chronicle, vol. 48, p. 282; Ibid., vol. 49, pp. 40, 214; Allen's Battles British Navy, vol. 1, pp. 391, 415; Annual Register for 1799, 1801, 1804.

light infantry will man the lines in their front, their left towards their own quarter guard, and the 24th regiment to form on the right of the light Infantry. The officer commanding the Grenadiers to detach a subaltern and 40 privates to assist in working the long 12 pounders and howitzers placed to guard the west passage of the river. The officer commanding the Light Infantry to send one captain, one subaltern and 60 privates to the 4 gun battery which guards the East passage. The officer commanding the 24th regiment will send a subaltern and 40 men to the bastion in which the 4 six pounders are; these detachments to be made immediately on hearing an alarm. The whole to strike their tents and leave them on the ground. The men are to get under arms without the beating of drums or making the least noise; they are to be particularly careful not to throw away their ammunition by fireing at too great a distance. Officers will be very attentive that the men are well covered by the works from the fire of shipping. All guards without the lines, to retire to the inside on the appearance of shipping. The guards at the landing place to remain, and to take care that no person takes a battow without permission. The serjeant of that guard will likewise take charge of all the wooden cannon, and to be under the charge of the centry. A non commissioned officer of the Artillery to be at the store for the purpose of delivering ammunition, the surjions to take post there. The women and children to go immediately to the northern extremity of the island, where the bullocks are to be drove. The general will take post at the 4 gun battery in front of the light Infantry. An orderly officer from each Battallion to attend him to carry orders. The Canadian labourers to be divided in three parts, and a division to be placed in the rear of each battallion with spades, pick axes and hand barrows. Artificers, convalescents, and every person in the least able to serve to take arms. Captain Monning's[109] company of Canadians to retire to Scot's farm, and the guard behind Blury river[110] to advance to Livingston's house; these posts to be defended to the last extremity.

During the night we rested on our arms expecting them every minute.

4th. About 6 in the morning, we very distinctly heard 13 or 14 cannon shot, and imagined they were fireing on a small guard of ours up the river. Capn Frazier and a few Indians were sent out to try, if possible, to take a prisoner. All hands were ordered out to throw up more works, and the Enemies delay surprised us, as they well knew the

---

[109] Monin commanded an irregular company of Canadians, and was engaged with the reckless McKay in expeditions against the Americans, small parties of whom he surprised and either killed or captured. These men, on account of their cruelty, were warmly hated by the Patriots, who repaid them in their own coin whenever occasion offered. Monin was killed in the battle of Freeman's Farm September 19, 1777.

[110] The Bleurie river is opposite Isle-aux-Noix and empties into Jackson's creek.

more time we had to repair our works, the stronger the island would be. We continued very impatient for a prisoner to acquaint us with their intentions, not judging what their aim could be by bringing so large a force so very near and yet not attacking us.

5. Captain Frazier returned without any intelligence, except counting their vessels. On being perceived, they gave chase, but he being in a birch cannoe soon got clear of them.

6th. Lieutenant Scott went up towards the enemy who were still cruising off the island Amott,[111] about 30 miles from us. He had a cannoe full of Indians, and was if possible not to return without a prisoner. When night came on, he paddled his birch cannoe through their fleet. This the reader will think rather improbable; but the Indians have a method of putting the paddle in the water and taking it up again without the smallest noise, and the night being very dark favoured him. He thus got through their fleet undiscovered, and at day break covered himself and party in some bushes on [the] shore side, where he did not long remain until a battow of theirs came on purpose to cut wood

[111] Isle la Motte is an island about six miles long in the northern part of the lake. The sieur la Mothe, a French officer, erected on the west side of this island and near the water's edge, in 1665, a wooden fort or redoubt, to which he gave the name of Fort St. Anne. This fort was subsequently called Fort la Mothe, and the Frenchman's name was also bestowed upon the island. When Kalm passed through the lake in 1749, he says that the fort had entirely disappeared, though he was shown the spot where it stood.

for fuel; they not dreaming of danger left their arms in the boat on going ashore. The first who landed, an Indian starting from his ambush caught him by his pouch-belt, but the fellow by a sudden exertion, and being greatly frighted, disengaged himself, the belt breaking, and ran with all his speed to alarm his comrades in the battow; who, before they could make use of their arms, received a heavy fire from the Indians, which did great execution among them, and left but a very few to row back the battow. Scott findeing he would soon be discovered, was obliged to take into the woods, where the Indians in some time brought him opposite our island.[112]

18. Our Indians destroyed another battow of the enemy, but could not take a prisoner. We then gave over all thoughts of their comeing down to attack us, and the building of our vessels went on with great dispatch at St Johns.

---

[112] This is the American account of this affair; "On the same day (6th) the boats were ordered on shore to cut fascines to fix the bows and sides of the gondolas, to prevent the enemy from boarding them and to keep off small shot. A boat's crew of the sloop *Enterprise* went on shore without a covering party. They had been out on the same duty the two preceding days with covering parties and returned unmolested, but upon this occasion they neglected that precaution, when they were attacked by a party of the Forty-seventh Regiment and savages, under Lieutenant Scott of the light infantry of the Twenty-fourth Regiment, who pursued them into the water. They all reached the boat, but before they could row off, three of them were killed, and six others were wounded." *Vide* The Campaign for the Conquest of Canada, p. 145, *et seq.*

25. An officer of theirs gave himself up to us.[113] The manner it happened was as follows. He was sent with two men from them to reconnoitre our situation &c. &c. They had seven days provisions given them on setting out, and came undiscovered opposite our island, where he took an exact view of our camp works &c. &c. and sent one man back with the intelligence. He and the other then proceeded through the woods down to St Johns, where he saw the *Carlton* and *Maria*[114] near finished and other vessels on the stocks. His seven days provisions being then almost finished, he returned back, still undiscovered by our Indians, which was surprising, as they were generally on scouting parties through the woods. On comeing opposite to where their fleet lay when he left them, he perceived they had quit that station, as the preceding day, from a gale of wind, they were obliged to take shelter under the Isle-of-Mott. He was then greatly at a loss what course to take, his provisions being all gone, and after liveing a day or two on nuts and whatever he could pick up in the woods, he was obliged to surrender himself to one of our out posts and was immediately conveyed to General Frazier, who from his

[113] This was probably Ensign McCoy, who was dispatched by Arnold down the west side of the Sorel with a squad of three men to obtain intelligence of the enemy. Lieutenant Whitcomb was also dispatched with a like squad down the east side of the river for the same purpose, but we have an account of his return, while no mention is made of McCoy's.

[114] She was so named in honor of the Lady Maria Howard, the wife of Sir Guy Carleton.

sullen manner did not much depend on the intelligence he gave. He informed that they had no intention of coming down to attack us by land, well knowing the great superiority they must have over our forces on the lake, their fleet being much superior, he was convinced, to any we could bring against them that year. That Col Arnold [115]

---

[115] Benedict Arnold was born at Norwich, Connecticut, January 3, 1741. His father was a man of character, and of his mother it was said by one who knew her intimately, that she "was a saint on earth and is now a saint in heaven." A letter from her to Benedict while at school, is worthy of reproduction here, as showing the character of his early training:

"NORWICH, *April* 12, 1754.

"DEAR CHILD: I received yours of the 1st instant and was glad to hear that you was well; pray, my dear, let your first concern be to make your peace with God, as it is of all concerns of the greatest importance.

"Keep a steady watch over your thoughts, words and actions. Be dutiful to superiors, obliging to equals, and affable to inferiors, if any such there be. Always choose that your companions be your betters, that by their good examples you may learn.

"From your affectionate mother,

"HANNAH ARNOLD.

"P. S.—I have sent you 50s. Your father put in 20 more. Use it prudently, as you are accountable to God and your father. Your father and aunt join with me in love and service to Mr. Cogswell and lady, and yourself. Your sister is from home."

In spite of his excellent training, he grew to be a man ostentatious in manner, insincere and thoroughly selfish. That he possessed military ability of a high order, was ever

was Commodore on the lake, and commanded on board the *Royal Savage* of great force. He also said that there were 20,000 men at Crown Point and Ticonderoga well supplied with cannon provisions &^{c}. &^{c}.

26th. We had a violent storm of rain, wind, thunder, and great flashes of lightening during the night. I often thought the tent would take fire. Next morning I mounted an advanced guard four miles above the island, the storm still continueing, and passed a most disagreeable day and night with scarce any shelter from the constant heavy rain. We could there hear their evening gun very plain, and it was

---

alert and thoroughly brave, no one can doubt. Many of the men who engaged with him in the war for independence were governed by no higher motives than those which actuated him: possessed, indeed, a desire for self-aggrandizement as inordinate as his, and never realized the moral splendor of the cause for which they contended. When the news of the battle of Lexington reached him at New Haven, where he was keeping a druggist's shop, he at once seized his sword and hastened to Boston to offer his services to his country. He suffered severe hardships in the war which followed, and did not shrink from making any personal sacrifice to attain success. He rendered valuable service to the cause of liberty; but smarting under the sting of disappointed ambition, he rushed in a fit of passion to the commission of an act wholly inexcusable. That he has been painted in darker colors than he deserved is now known. After his treason, he went to England and died at Brampton June 20, 1801. Though treated with consideration by the king, he suffered indignities from men, who perhaps, made the occasion of his treason serve to enable them to show their inborn contempt of a New England colonist who was naturally disliked at this time in England.

proposed in a few days to move up to Riviere-la-Cole,[116] seven miles nearer them.

27th. Had the pleasure of seeing two of our schooners, the *Maria* & *Carlton*, come up to us from St Johns. Captain Pringle[117] was appointed Commodore of the Lake Champlain and to command on board the *Maria*, so called after lady Maria Carlton. In the evening I was seized with a violent shivering and lightness in my head, which was attributed to cold, I must have got the preceeding night on guard. About 10 o clock I was quite delireous and out of my senses, after which I

[116] Riviere la Colle, nine miles southerly from Point au Fer, on the western side of the lake. According to Hadden, there was a small settlement there at this time.

[117] Thomas Pringle was of Scotch birth, and this was the beginning of a notable career. After his success on Lake Champlain, he returned to England as bearer of dispatches, and was made a post-captain November 25th. In January, 1777, he was assigned to the command of the *Ariadne* and joined the West India fleet, attaining distinction in several naval engagements. On April 4, 1794, he was made colonel of the Marine Forces, and on June 4th, in reward for his brilliant services in the victory over the French fleet of Admiral Villaret, he was created a rear-admiral of the Blue, and June 1, 1795, rear-admiral of the Red. He subsequently took command at the Cape of Good Hope, and February 14, 1799, was made vice-admiral of the White, and January 1, 1801, vice-admiral of the Red. His death took place at Edinburgh December 8, 1803. *Vide* Political Index to Histories Great Britain, etc. (Beatson), vol. 2, p. 47; London Chronicle, vol. 41, p. 406, vol. 43, p. 186, vol. 44, p. 458, vol. 45, p. 286, vol. 48, p. 58; Universal Magazine, London, vol. 62, pp. 140, 274; Military Memoirs (Beatson), vol. 6, pp. 160, 270; Annual Register, 1794, 1795, 1799, 1801; Naval History of Great Britain (Brenton), vol. 2, pp. 42, 169, *et seq.*

cannot tell what happened. I was blistered on my back, and all the next day continued in the same distracted situation. Indeed, I believe my friends thought it was all over with me, but it pleased God to spare me, and on the 30th I returned to my senses, but so weak and faint, as scarce able to turn in my bed, and what made it more disagreeable was our corps of Grenadiers moveing up to Riviere-la-Cole the day I fell ill. My tent could not be struck on account of my situation, so [I] was left almost alone on the island, but did not remain long in that situation, as the First Brigade landed from St Johns, the 31st regiment composing part of it, when my brother in law, Capt. Pilot,[118] gave me every assistance in his power,— got

---

[118] Henry Pilot, the brother-in-law of Digby, was commissioned a lieutenant in the Thirty-first Foot, July 18, 1764, and shortly after embarked for Pensacola, the capital of West Florida, which country had the previous year been ceded to Great Britain by Spain. At this time the yellow fever prevailed there, and upon its arrival the regiment suffered severe mortality. It continued here however, until the breaking out of the Carib war. On the eve of the campaign against the Caribs — September 23, 1772 — Pilot was promoted to a captaincy, and served in that capacity during the arduous and destructive campaign of the following two years. At the conclusion of the Carib war, he returned to England, where he was stationed at the time of the breaking out of the war in America. He participated in the campaign of '76, but was performing garrison duty when Burgoyne's army surrendered; hence he escaped the captivity which befel a portion of his regiment. As his name disappears from the army list in 1782, it is reasonable to suppose that he left his regiment in Canada, where it was

me a good physician and had me removed into his tent which had a stove, where I recovered fast. The few days I continued ill, there was heavy rain and the island almost flooded; but, fortunately, my tent had stood it out pretty well. We were all provided for the cold weather — we then soon expected in crossing the lake,— with warm clothing, such as under waistcoats, leggings, socks &c. &c., and smokeing tobacco was counted a preservative of the health against dews, which arose from the many swamps and marshy, drowned lands that surrounded the island.

October 5th. Went up to our corps at Riviere-la-Cole, after remaining with my friends of the 31st regiment till I recovered sufficient strength. I sailed up in a raddoux vessel carrying six 9 pounders, commanded by captain Longcroft,[119] who

---

then and for several years afterward stationed, and returned home, perhaps with Digby, who retired at the same time. From this period we lose sight of him until June 14, 1800, when he was appointed town major of Dublin. Of his subsequent career we have no particulars. *Vide* British Army Lists, *in loco;* Historical Record of the Thirty-first Foot, pp. 33–42.

[119] Edward Longcroft's name does not appear in the subsequent operations of Burgoyne's Army. After his return to England he was commissioned a commander in the British service, April 23, 1782, a position which he continued to hold for a number of years. *Vide* Court and City Register for 1789 and 1794. Edward Longcroft entered the British naval service as a midshipman on board the *Arrogant*, October 3, 1769, and served on this ship until he joined the *Namur*, December 26, 1770. On April 18, 1771, he joined the *Princess Amelia* of eighty guns, then under the orders of Admiral Rodney, who had recently been appointed to the

showed me every civility in his power. The floating Battery, *Maria* and *Carlton*, sailed with us, and our little voyage was pleasant, the day being fine and the lake now running very broad. General Burgoyne was on board the *Maria*, who ran aground on a bank, but was towed off without any damage. The vessels were all cleared and ready for action, waiting only for the *Inflexible*, our largest vessel, which was shortly expected up.[120]

Jamaica station, and served until July 14, 1772, when he received his discharge. We see no more of him until we find him in command of the *Loyal Convert* on Lake Champlain. It is probable that he was on the fleet that sailed from Cork, in the spring of 1776, for the relief of Quebec, and that he was acting as a volunteer, since his name does not appear on the Admiralty record during this period. At what time he returned to England we are not informed; but he was promoted to the rank of first lieutenant on the *Grafton*, February 13, 1781. He was placed on half pay September 11, 1781; but on May 1, 1782, was put in command of the *Zebra*, one of the squadron under command of Commodore Dacres, who has been mentioned elsewhere. On April 15, 1783, he went on half pay and remained out of the service until April 15, 1805, when he was put in command of the *Sea Fencibles* between Kidwelly and Cardigan. On March 1, 1810, he again went on half pay, and died August 16, 1812. I am indebted to the courtesy of the Lords Commissioners of the Admiralty for materials of this note.

[120] The *Inflexible* was a three-masted vessel, and the *Maria* and *Carleton* were schooners. After trying in vain to drag these vessels around the Chambly rapids on rollers, they had been taken to pieces and so transported to a convenient place from which they could be launched. After laying the keel, the *Inflexible* was ready to enter the water in twenty-eight days, but Carleton was obliged to float her below the

6th. The fleet went up a little higher with a fair wind. The enemies were cruising off Cumberland Bay, about 20 miles above ours.

7th. The First Brigade moved up to our post at Riviere-la-Cole, and ours went up to point-au-Faire,[121] seven miles higher. The order for our proceeding on the Lake was as follows. Three small boats in front of all as a party of observation, our schooners and armed vessels in line of battle following: Gun

---

Isle-aux-Noix, where the water had a sufficient depth, in order that she might receive her guns, which consisted of eighteen twelve-pounders. The "raddoux vessel" which Digby was on, was the *Loyal Convert*, and had been captured from the Americans when they abandoned Quebec. The entire fleet was as follows:

Ship *Inflexible*, Lieutenant Schank, 18 12-pound guns.

Schooner *Maria*, Lieutenant Starke, 14 6-pound guns.

Schooner *Carleton*, Lieutenant Dacres, 12 6-pound guns.

Radeau *Thunderer*, Lieutenant Scott, 6 24-pound guns, 6 12-pound guns, 2 howitzer guns.

Gondola *Loyal Convert*, Lieutenant Longcroft, 7 9-pound guns.

Twenty gunboats, each having a brass field-piece of from 9 to 24 pounds each, some carrying howitzers.

Four tenders, or long boats, carrying field-pieces.

Twenty-four long boats carrying provisions.

The entire fleet comprised twenty-nine vessels armed with eighty-nine guns and manned with six hundred and seventy thoroughly trained and disciplined men, all under the command of Pringle, who on all occasions showed himself to be a most daring and efficient officer. Both Pringle and Dacres rose subsequently by their ability to the highest rank in the British navy.

[121] Point au Fer is a headland on the eastern shore of the lake. Burgoyne considered it of sufficient importance to fortify it with a block-house.

boats carrying 24 or 12 pounders in their bow and maned by the Artillery. The battallion of Grenadiers in flat bottomed boats, and in their rear, the remainder of the army in battows. One gun fired from a gun boat, was a signal to form 8 boats a breast; and two guns, a signal to form a line of boats. This had a pretty effect, as our men were all expert at rowing, having been ordered to practice frequently. This was the first intention of our crossing, but afterwards, found not to answer so well as our armed vessels and gun boats engageing theirs separately, leaving the troops on land to wait the decision, as were any accident to happen to the armed vessels, the troops must be in a most hazardous situation, and little able to defend themselves with small arms against the cannon of the enemy.

At Point-au Faire, the lake turns quite a sea, forming a most beautiful prospect, being intersperced with numerous islands, mostly thick with trees, which at that time of the year (the trees changing their colour) added still to the scene. This place is thickly covered with wood, under which we pitched our tents, waiting for the *Inflexible;* she being obliged from want of water to have her guns brought up in boats, after which a ship of the line would have water sufficient; and it certainly was a noble sight to see such a vessel on a fresh water lake in the very heart of the Continent of America & so great a distance from the sea

8th. It blew fresh and a good deal damaged our battows by strikeing against each other, on which we anchored our flat bottom boats off the shore, and brought the battows round a point to a small creek under some shelter from the land. There were many deer in the woods about, some of which we shot, also great flocks of wild pidgeons, which, as our fresh provisions (sheep &c we brought from St Johns and Isle-aux-Noix) were almost finished, helped out his majesties allowance of beef and pork very well. The wood was so thick round us, that some of our men were near losing themselves on straggling a small distance from camp, against which there were particular orders. It is surprising, with what a degree of certainty an Indian will make his way from one country to another through the thickest woods, allowing the sun to be constantly hid from his sight by clouds, where a person, not used to such a country, would soon be lost, and the more attempts made to extricate himself, perhaps, would only serve to entangle him the deeper.

9. We had 3 men killed on the spot by a tree that was cut down near their tent, and unfortunately fell on them while asleep. To prevent such a melancholy accident happening again, an order was given for no tree to be felled, within 100 yards of the camp. About 12 o'clock we heard the enemy very distinctly scaleing the guns[122] on board their fleet, and soon hoped to make [them] exercise them in a

[122] Scaling a gun is, in military parlance, to cleanse it of scales occasioned by rust, which is accomplished by exploding in the gun small charges of powder.

different manner. The bad intelligence, the army received of General Howes[123] opperations to the southward, was not a little surprising, our expectations being sanguine from that quarter, he having the command of so great an army, and so fine a fleet

---

[123] Sir William Howe was a grandson of George the First by his mistress, the Baroness Kilmansegge. He was born August 10, 1729, and entered the army at the age of eighteen. He was made lieutenant, September 21, 1747, and captain of the Twentieth Foot, June 1, 1750, major of the Sixtieth Foot, January 4, 1756, and lieutenant-colonel, December 17, 1757. He took part in the siege of Louisbourg, in 1758, and participated as commander of the light infantry in the capture of Quebec under General Wolfe. He was in command of a brigade against the French in 1761, and, in 1762, acted as adjutant-general in the operations against Havana. He was commissioned a colonel in the army, February 19, 1762, colonel of the Forty-sixth Foot, November 21, 1764, and lieutenant-governor of the Isle of Wight in 1768. He was created a major-general, May 25, 1772, and, when the war broke out in America, formed one of the noted trio to whom was assigned the task of subjugating the refractory colonists. With his associates, Clinton and Burgoyne, he reached Boston, May 25, 1775, and led the assault on Bunker Hill. He succeeded General Gage in the command of the British forces in America in the following October. He was in great favor with the government, which seems to have placed full confidence in his ability. He led a luxurious life in Boston, frequenting, it is said, the faro table, the ball-room and the theatre, and carrying on an *affaire d'amour* with a popular belle of the day, which caused a writer to say that "as Cleopatra of old lost Mark Antony the world, so did this illustrious courtesan lose Sir William Howe the honor, the laurels, and the glory of putting an end to one of the most obstinate rebellions that ever existed." He was created lieutenant-general in the army, August 29, 1777. He was relieved from his command in America in May, 1778, and returned to England. He represented Nottingham in Par-

under his brother lord Howe,[124] we could expect no accounts by land, that being in possession of the enemy, but the sea was open, and, had he performed any capital stroke, it should not be kept a secret from the army. General Carlton, some imagined, might have received intelligence, which it was said he could not divulge were they ever so favourable. Certainly he is one of the most distant, reserved men in the world; he has a rigid strictness in his manner, very unpleasing, and which he observes even to his most particular friends and acquaintance, at the same time he is a very able General and brave officer; has seen a

---

liament during the sessions of 1778, '79 and '80, and became lieutenant-general of ordnance, April 23, 1782, member of the Privy Council June 21st of the same year, colonel of the Nineteenth Light Dragoons, April 21, 1786, general in the army, October 12, 1793, governor of Berwick in 1795. On the death of his brother, Lord Viscount Howe, in 1799, he succeeded to his titles. In 1808 he was appointed governor at Plymouth. He died July 12, 1814. *Vide* British Army Lists, *in loco;* Siege of Boston (Frothingham), pp. 133–149 *et passim;* Burke's Peerage and Baronetage, *in loco;* Historical Record Forty-Sixth Foot; History of New York During the Revolutionary War (Jones), vol. 1, pp. 252, 716 *et passim;* vol. 2, pp. 86, 423 *et passim.*

[124] Richard Earl Howe was born in 1725, and succeeded to the titles of his elder brother, the friend of Schuyler, who was killed at Ticonderoga in 1758. He was a midshipman at the age of fourteen under Lord Anson, and was a lieutenant at twenty. He had risen to the rank of rear-admiral in 1770, and, in 1775, was made vice-admiral of the Blue. After his return from America he became first lord of the admiralty and commanded the British fleet successfully against the French in 1794. He died August 5, 1799. *Vide* Burke's Peerage and Baronetage, *in loco.*

great deal of service and rose from a private life, though a very good family, by mere merit to the rank he at present bears. In time of danger he possesses a coolness and steadiness, (the attendant on true courage) which few can attain; yet he was far from being the favorite of the army. Genl Burgoyne alone engrossed their warmest attachment. From haveing seen a great deal of polite life, he possesses a winning manner in his appearance and address, far different from the severity of Carlton, which caused him to be idolized by the army, his orders appearing more like recommending subordination than enforcing it. On every occasion he was the soldiers friend, well knowing the most sanguine expectations a general can have of success, must proceed from the spirit of the troops under his command. The manner he gained their esteem was by rewarding the meritorious when in his power, which seldom failed from the praise which they received, to cause a remissness in duty [to be] odious and unmanly, and a desire of emulation soldier like & honourable. But I shall often have occasion to mention him in the following pages.

10th. About 12 o clock our small fleet sailed up with a fair wind, which was a most pleasing sight to the army. Their decks were all cleared & ready for immediate action. Genl Carlton went in person (tho. many blamed his hazarding himself on an element so much out of his line), on board the *Maria*, and gave the command of the fleet to Pringle as commodore, by which he was of very little service on board, excepting proveing his courage, which no man in the army has the least doubt of. The wind blowing fresh, we expected shortly to hear of their engageing, on which our fate in a great measure depended.

11th. We were in hourly expectation of intelligence. Our Indians were on the banks on the lake, who, we eagerly hoped, would come down to inform us of any thing particular, and that day passed over in the greatest state of uncertainty.

12th. Was awoke very early in the morning by a confused noise about my tent, and on hearing the word Carlton named, imagined something had happened, so arose and made the greatest haste to the shore side, where a boat had just arrived with our wounded men from the fleet. The accounts were, that our fleet came pretty near them, when the wind shifted a little about, when none of our vessels could haul so much to the windward as the *Carlton*, who made all the sail possible for them and stood most of their fire for a long time, assisted by a few gun boats; that the *Royal Savage*[125] engaged her, and at last was obliged to strike to the *Carlton*, but,

---

[125] The *Royal Savage* was a schooner, and had been built under the supervision of General Arnold. She carried four six and eight four-pound guns, and was manned by fifty men. The account of her destruction, here given by Digby, is doubtless as it was given to him, but is incorrect. The *Royal Savage*, while beating up against the wind where there was insufficient room, was stranded on Valcour Island. She

against all the rules of war, after strikeing, they ran her on shore, blew her up and escaped in the wood. The greatest praise was given to lieut Decars for his spirited behaviour, as he did not retire till so much shattered in masts & rigging, as made it necessary to tow the vessel off by boats. Our gun boats also did great execution, but unfortunately, one of them blew up on the water. The sailors also informed us, that the enemy wanted to fly from us, but that our fleet had got them into a bay which they could not escape from, without fighting, and that our Floating battery was moored at the entrance of the bay, and three 24 pounders ready to open on them by day light. From these accounts, it was imagined that in all probability, a few hours would determine who should be masters of the Lake—though we made but little doubt of our being victorious; and all that day, waited with the greatest impatience—watching earnestly with our glasses for the appearance of a boat.

13th. Was passed over in the same state of suspense and uncertainty.

14th. We were very impatient for an express, and did not well know what to think, when about 3 o'clock a cannoe was perceived at a great distance makeing all the way possible for our camp. On her

---

had been much injured in the engagement, and as it was found impossible to get her afloat, she was abandoned, and her crew escaped. A party of British troops boarded her during the night, and to prevent the Americans from making any use of her again, set her on fire and so destroyed her.

nearer approach we perceived it was Sir Francis Clark,[126] the general's aid-de-camp, who waving the

[126] Sir Francis Carr Clerke was born in London, October 24, 1748, and entered the Third Foot Guards, January 3, 1770, as an ensign, and received a lieutenant's commission, July 26, 1775, which was equivalent to the rank of a captain in the army. He was made adjutant, February 3, 1776, and accompanied Burgoyne, with whom he was a favorite, to America as an aide-de-camp. When Burgoyne returned to England, after the campaign of '76, Clerke accompanied him, and also returned with him the next spring in the capacity of private secretary and aide-de-camp. In the battle of October 7, 1777, while riding to deliver an order which Burgoyne said would have changed the fortunes of the day had it been delivered, he was shot in the bowels and taken prisoner. He was taken to the tent of General Gates, where he remained, tenderly cared for, until his death. Wilkinson gives the following affecting particulars of the closing scenes of Clerke's life: "On one occasion, the wounded general inquired if the American surgeons were good for anything, as he did not like the direction of his wound, and wished to know whether it was fatal, or not. The physicians concealed their fears from him, but carefully watched him day and night. Seeing Dr. Townsend hesitate when he pressed him for an opinion, he exclaimed in his usual frank way, 'Doctor, why do you pause? Do you think I am afraid to die?' and upon being advised by that physician to adjust his private affairs, he thanked him, and quietly complied." Burgoyne said of him: "He had originally recommended himself to my attention by his talents and diligence; as service and intimacy opened his character more, he became endeared to me by every quality that can create esteem. I lost in him a useful assistant, an amiable companion, an attached friend; the State was deprived by his death of one of the fairest promises of an able general." He died on the 13th of October following his injury. *Vide* British Army Lists, *in loco;* Burke's Peerage and Baronetage, *in loco;* Memoirs of My Own Times, vol. 1, p. 269; A State of the Expedition, p. 125.

enemies colors, thirteen stripes,[127] declared the day was all our own. This happy intelligence was answered by the troops in three huzzas, and the joy expressed by the whole, gave evident signs of their satisfaction on so important a victory. He informed General Frazier that the enemies fleet had by some means escaped ours on the night of the 12th; but the following day ours came up, and after a smart action, burnt, took or destroyed all their vessels on

[127] A flag bearing thirteen stripes, alternate red and white, emblematical of union, suggested, perhaps, by the Roman fasces, was first displayed over the American camp at Cambridge on the 1st of January, 1776, and the next month Commodore Esek Hopkins sailed from the Delaware to operate against Lord Dunmore's fleet, which was then on the Virginia coast, bearing the striped flag with the addition of a rattlesnake stretched diagonally across it with the words "*Don't tread on me*" underneath. It was not until the 14th of June, 1777, that Congress "resolved that the flag of the United States be thirteen stripes, alternate red and white; that the Union be thirteen stars, white, in a blue field, representing a new constellation." When St. Leger appeared before Fort Schuyler, in the beginning of the following August, the fort was without a flag, and as it was necessary to have one, General Gansevoort caused one to be made, in accordance with the resolve of Congress, by cutting the white stripes from a shirt, and the red ones from the petticoat of a soldier's wife, using the blue cloak of Captain Abraham Swartwout to make a field upon which to display the new constellation. This flag, Mr. Wm. L. Stone informs us, is in the possession of a descendant of General Gansevoort, by whom it is cherished as a most precious relic. As Digby does not mention that the flag which Sir Francis Clerke had captured bore upon it the stars or the serpent, we must infer that it was like the one displayed at Cambridge at the beginning of the year.

the lake. That a general Waterbury[128] and a great many were made prisoners; and that it was general Carlton's orders we immediately strike our camp, embark in our boats without loss of time, and make the best of our way to Crown Point, where we should receive further orders. I shall here insert the fate of the enemies fleet on the 11th and 13th of October.

ACCOUNT OF THE ENEMIES FLEET ON LAKE CHAMPLAIN, COMMANDED BY BENEDICT ARNOLD.

	SHIPS NAME.	October.	Guns.	WEIGHT OF METAL. 129						
				Pounders. 24	Pounders. 18	Pounders. 12	Pounders. 9	Pounders. 6	Pounders. 4	Pounders. 3
Row galleys......	Congress — burnt............	13	16	2	2	2	2	6	--	2
	Washington — taken........	13	14	2	1	1	2	6	--	2
	Turnbull — escaped.........	10	10	--	1	1	2	6	--	--
Gondolas. .	Philadelphia — sunk	11	3	--	--	1	2	--	--	--
	New York — burnt..........	13	3	--	--	1	2	--	--	--
	Jersey — taken	12	3	--	--	1	2	--	--	--
	Providence — burnt..........	13	3	--	--	1	2	--	--	--
	Newhaven — burnt	13	3	--	--	--	3	--	--	--
	Spitfire — burnt............	13	3	--	--	1	2	--	--	--
	Boston — burnt	13	3	--	1	--	2	--	--	--
	Connecticut — burnt........	13	3	--	1	--	2	..	--	--
Schooners .	Royal Savage — blown up..	11	14	2	--	8	--	4	--	--
Cutters	Revenge — escaped.........	----	8	--	--	--	--	--	2	6
	Enterprise — escaped	----	10	--	--	--	--	--	10	--
	Lee cutter — taken..........	13	6	--	--	2	--	4	--	--

[128] David Waterbury, Jr., was born at Stamford, Connecticut, February 12, 1722. He was a man of great energy and had a predilection for military affairs, having, in 1747, nearly thirty years before this date, been an ensign in the

[129] The number of guns and weight of metal here given are much exaggerated. The following is the correct armament of the vessels, with the names of their commanders:

At Ticonderoga and had not joined the fleet,—one row galley 10 guns, and the schooner *Liberty*, 8

State militia, and subsequently having served through six campaigns against the French and Indians. Naturally he was one of the first to actively espouse the American cause, and we behold him in July, 1775, at the head of his regiment marching to occupy Crown Point and Ticonderoga. His uncompromising patriotism rendered him harsh and severe toward those who did not support the popular cause; indeed, the historian of Stamford says that "he seems to have shown them no mercy. One of the reasons given by citizens in this vicinity for going over to the enemy was the excessive rigor of Colonel Waterbury." This resentment, however, against traitors, as they were popularly but not reasonably called, was general. Lord Mahon says in reference to it, that "a ferocious saying came to be current in America that, though we are commanded to forgive our enemies, we are nowhere commanded to forgive our friends." General Carleton was elated at his capture, and immediately reported it to Germaine. He was soon exchanged and again in service. At the close of the war, he returned to the plough, and died on his farm at Stamford, June 29, 1801. *Vide* History of Stamford, Ct. (Huntington), pp. 417–23; History of England (Mahon), vol. 6, p. 127; Sparks' Life of Washington, vol. 7, p. 288; vol. 8, pp. 88, 92, *et passim*.

	Vessels' names.	Captains.	Number of guns.	Weight, 18 lb.	Weight, 12 lb.	Weight, 9 lb.	Weight, 8 lb.	Weight, 6 lb.	Weight, 4 lb.	Weight, 2 lb.
Row Galley	Congress	Arnold	8	--	2	--	2	4	--	--
"	Washington	Waterbury	8	1	1	2	--	--	4	--
"	Trumbull	Wigglesworth	8	1	1	2	--	4	--	--
Gondola	Philadelphia	Rice	3	--	1	--	--	2	--	--
"	New York	Reed	3	--	1	--	--	2	--	--
"	Jersey	Grimes	3	--	1	--	--	2	--	--
"	Providence	Simonds	3	--	1	--	--	2	--	--
"	New Haven	Mansfield	3	--	1	--	--	2	--	--
"	Spitfire	Ulmer	3	--	1	--	--	2	--	--
"	Boston	Sumner	3	--	1	--	--	2	--	--
"	Connecticut	Grant	3	--	1	--	--	2	--	--
Schooner	Royal Savage	Hawley	12	--	--	--	--	4	8	--
"	Revenge	Seaman	8	--	--	--	--	--	4	4

guns. One of the gondaloes, I have no confirmed account of, but believe she was burned 13th October

THOS PRINGLE

Sir Francis also informed that general Arnold who acted as commodore, after finding all was lost some how escaped on shore, after behaving with remarkable coolness and bravery during the engagement. In the following pages will be seen how great an acquisition his being taken would have been to us, as he is certainly a brave man, and much confidence reposed in him by their Congress. We embarked about 4 o'clock in the evening, and though we made the greatest expedition possible did not arrive at Crown Point until the 20th, where our fleet had been for some days. The lake in ruff weather is dangerous for battows, as there are great swells in many parts, but none that did our small fleet any damage; and we arrived there without any accident happening to us. We had good sport in shooting

	Vessels' names.	Captains.	Number of guns.	Weight, 18 lb.	Weight, 12 lb.	Weight, 9 lb.	Weight, 8 lb.	Weight, 6 lb.	Weight, 4 lb.	Weight, 2 lb.
Sloop	Enterprise	Dickenson	12	--	--	--	--	--	12	--
Row Galley	Lee	Davis	6	--	1	1	--	--	4	--
Schooner	Liberty	Premier	8	--	--	--	--	--	4	4
Total, 16 vessels.			94	--	--	--	--	--	--	--

Manned by 800 men.

It will be seen that the British fleet carried a much heavier weight of metal.

pidgeons, flocks of which flew over us thick enough to darken the air, also large eagles. There were herds of deer all along the shore side, which were seldom disturbed, the country being but little altered since its first state of nature, except now and then a wandering party of savages comeing there to hunt for their subsistance. At night we landed and lay warm enough in the woods, makeing large fires. When it rained, it was not so pleasant, but use reconciled all that soon to us, and we slept as sound under the canopy of the heavens as in the best feather bed. Crown Point is a remarkable fine plain, an uncommon sight to us after being so long buried in such boundless woods, where our camp formed a grand appearance. Some few families who had not joined the enemy lived there; but had suffered much, as their cattle were mostly drove away for their loyalty. They had a force at Crown Point under the command of a Major Heartly,[130] who thought proper to

---

[130] Thomas Hartley was a native of Reading, Pennsylvania, and was born September 7, 1748. He was bred to the law, and was practicing his profession at York when the war broke out with the mother country. He at once threw aside his Coke and Blackstone and hastened with other patriots to offer his services to his country. He received a commission as lieutenant-colonel of the Sixth Pennsylvania Regiment, January 9, 1776, and, after Colonel Irvine was taken prisoner, the command devolved upon him. He was an energetic officer, and showed great zeal in the prosecution of the plans which were assigned to him to carry out. In common with Waterbury and other commanders in the American army, he was hostile to those who espoused the royal cause, or who, while professing neutrality, were ready

retire to Ticonderoga on our fleet comeing so near his works, where they were thunder struck at hearing of the defeat of theirs, thinking it scarce possible. Our loss on the lake was about 60 men killed and wounded. Their general Waterbury, & the rest of the prisoners were sent back to them by general Carlton to Ticonderoga on their parole, and Capt Craig[131] 47th light Infantry, went as a flag of truce

---

to afford aid and comfort to the enemy, and he showed them no favor. In 1778, after the massacre of Wyoming, he led an expedition into the valley, and for his brave and efficient conduct in the prosecution of this enterprise, was highly commended by the government. Shortly after, he retired from military life, and was a member of the Council of Censors in 1783, and one of the convention delegates of Pennsylvania which ratified the Constitution of the United States, December 12, 1787. He was a member of Congress from 1789 until the day of his death, which took place at York, in his native State, December 21, 1800. *Vide* Revolutionary Record, p. 202; Sparks' Washington, vol. 4, p. 12; vol. 5, p. 422, *et passim;* Field Book of the Revolution (Lossing), vol. 1, p. 362, *et seq.;* Campaign for the Conquest of Canada, pp. 73, 100, 107, *et passim.*

[131] James H. Craig was born at Gibraltar in 1748, his father being judge of civil and military affairs there. When he was fifteen years of age, the Thirtieth Foot was in garrison at Gibraltar, and young Craig, being infected with the military fever, obtained through the influence of his father a commission as ensign, which bore date June 1, 1763. He was promoted, July 19, 1769, to a lieutenancy, and March 14, 1771, was commissioned a captain in the Forty-seventh Foot, which he accompanied to America in 1774. This regiment was stationed at Boston during the siege of that city, and formed part of Lord Percy's command on that memorable nineteenth of April, when the first battle for American independence took place. Captain Craig was at

with them. In return, they sent the general a letter of thanks, but would not permit even the prisoners to enter the fort, but sent them directly away, which was politic enough, as by their informing their country men how well they had been used, might

---

the battle of Bunker Hill in which he was wounded. He joined Carleton at Quebec in the spring of 1776, and accompanied him in the campaign of that year. He was also in the disastrous campaign of Burgoyne, was wounded at Hubbardton and Freeman's Farm, and conducted the negotiations for the surrender of the army. In these negotiations every thing was done to salve the wounded pride of Burgoyne and his aristocratic officers, and, among other things, the term *convention* was substituted for *capitulation* in the preparatory articles of surrender, at Captain Craig's solicitation. He went to England after the surrender with dispatches, where he received the appointment of major in the Eighty-second Foot, and returned to Halifax in 1778, and was engaged during the following year in operations in eastern Maine. He served through the war of the Revolution, was promoted to the rank of lieutenant-colonel of his regiment, December 31, 1781, and of colonel in the army, November 18, 1790. In 1794 he was made major-general, and the next year was appointed governor of the Cape of Good Hope, having conducted a successful expedition thither. He returned to England in 1797, and was raised to the peerage for his efficient services. In January, 1801, while in India, where he had been in service nearly four years, he received a commission of lieutenant-general, and the next year returned to England, where he was at once assigned to a command. At the close of a successful service in the Mediterranean, he received, in 1807, the appointment of governor-general of British North America. His hatred of every thing savoring of democracy caused him to act harshly toward every movement of a liberal character, and he soon found himself surrounded by enemies. For four years he held the reins of office, when, broken in health and disgusted with the people of the province, who it would seem were equally disgusted

induce some to turn on our side. Gen Gates[132] then commanded there; of whom I shall have occasion to speak more of hereafter. He was formerly in our service, but from his wife's connections, who is an American, he was induced to change into theirs. He is a man much confidence is reposed in by their Con-

---

with him on account of his tyrannical administration of affairs, he returned home in the summer of 1811, and died the January following. *Vide* British Army Lists, *in loco;* Memoirs of My Own Times, pp. 309–317; Journal of Occurrences During the Late American War, Dublin, 1809, p. 174; Gentleman's Magazine, vol. 48, p. 551.

[132] Horatio Gates was born in 1728, and it has been asserted that he was a natural son of Horace Walpole. Even as recent and generally accurate a writer as Fonblanque says, "he was related by marriage to the Earl of Thanet, and was a godson (scandal attributed a nearer relationship) of Horace Walpole," a statement precisely similar to that made with respect to the parentage of Burgoyne, which was attributed to Lord Bingley, and which Fonblanque labors to disprove. Strange to say, Fonblanque does not seem to have thought of examining the life of Walpole to ascertain what probability existed for this story. Horace Walpole was born October 5, 1717, and at the time of Gates' birth was less than eleven years of age, and this fact, hitherto unnoticed, should set this idle story at rest; but it will probably be repeated by careless writers till the end of time. Horace Walpole was his godfather, and had a brother Horatio, Baron of Wolterton, and what more probable than that the name of his august kinsman applied to the obscure infant of the housekeeper who was intimate with "my mother's woman," was an incipient display of that humor which subsequently made the genius of Walpole conspicuous? Walpole's journals have been published, and, fortunately, he has left an item relating to the matter. He says that Gates "was the son of a housekeeper of the second Duke of Leeds, who, marrying a young husband when very

gress, but as to what he deserves for the exchange, I shall leave the reader to judge. Their force then at Ticonderoga, about 14 miles, was said to be 20,000, and it was thought from the lateness of the season and many other reasons, but this, the one most material, that it would be but a vain attempt to

old, had this son by him. — My mother's woman was intimate with that housekeeper, and hence I was godfather to her son, though I believe not then ten years old myself." It would almost seem that Walpole had heard that the parentage of Gates had been ascribed to him, and therefore placed this statement on record to refute it. When twenty-six years of age, Gates, who had been bred to the profession of arms, and had served as a volunteer under Cornwallis while the latter was governor of Halifax, joined General Braddock at Fort Cumberland, and participated in the unfortunate campaign which ended so disastrously to the British arms. In this battle he was wounded, but more fortunate than many of his brother soldiers, escaped with his life. He was subsequently stationed in western New York with his company, and while there was commissioned a brigade major. He was then selected by General Monckton as aide-de-camp, and accompanied that officer to the West Indies, where he gained attention by his gallantry in the capture of Martinico. He was bearer of dispatches to London announcing the victory, and was rewarded by being made a major in the Royal Americans. Although his advancement had been unusually rapid, he was disappointed; and having married a lady of high connections, he sold his commission and endeavored, through the influence of his friends and the family relations of his wife, to obtain a lucrative appointment under the government. Failing in this, he emigrated to America and settled on an estate which he purchased in Berkeley county, Virginia. He was a friend of Washington, and was dining at Mount Vernon when the news of the battle of Lexington was received. He was at once aroused to take part in the popular cause, and Washington procured his appointment as

besiege it that year, we having but a small part of the army on that side of the lake ; viz, the first Brigade and our Advanced corps. The remainder of the army nor having battows ready to remove from St Johns, and the Isle-aux-Noix, from whence it was thought by the advice of the engineers who were

---

adjutant-general with the rank of a brigadier. He joined the camp at Cambridge in July, and busied himself in organizing the raw recruits, in which service he was very efficient. He was made a major-general in May, 1776, and in the June following, was appointed to the command in Canada. Naturally of a jealous disposition, he was disturbed at the ever-growing popularity of Washington and instead of assisting, as in duty bound, his old companion-in-arms in his arduous campaign during the winter of '76 and '77, he busied himself in efforts to supplant him. Washington was, however, too magnanimous to allow the treachery of Gates to disturb him, and he endeavored to secure his really valuable services in reorganizing the army at his old post, as adjutant-general. A conflict of authority now arose between him and Schuyler, a pure and reasonably disinterested patriot, which was settled by Congress, which decided in favor of Schuyler. Gates at once proceeded to Philadelphia to lay his grievances before Congress, but made so poor a display of himself as to excite the opposition of that body, and he retired with indignation. The failure of St. Clair to maintain his position at Ticonderoga, which was in Schuyler's department, gave an opportunity for the enemies of Schuyler and the friends of Gates to get the former removed, and he was superseded by Gates. When he assumed the command, every thing was in readiness, as far as it possibly could be, to meet the onset of the advancing army of Burgoyne, Schuyler having bent all his energies toward rendering the advance of the enemy difficult and the American army efficient, so that he found nearly every thing shaped to his hand. Many writers have criticised the action of Gates in this campaign, one of whom we will quote: Says Lossing: "While

consulted respecting works, &c., that the enemy must return to winter in Canada, they not being then able to throw up lines for above 1300 men, and even then, we should have no place to cover our troops from the

---

Arnold was wielding the fierce sickle of war without, and reaping golden sheaves for Gates' garner, the latter was within his camp, more intent upon discussing the merits of the Revolution with Sir Francis Clarke, Burgoyne's aide-de-camp, who had been wounded and taken prisoner, and was lying upon the commander's bed at his quarters, than upon winning a battle all important to the ultimate triumph of those principles for which he professed so warm an attachment. When one of Gates' aids came up from the field of battle for orders, he found the general very angry because Sir Francis would not allow the force of his arguments. He left the room, and, calling his aid after him, asked, as they went out: 'Did you ever hear so impudent a son of a b—h?' Poor Sir Francis died that night upon Gates' bed." That, in spite of his faults, which have perhaps been exaggerated, and for which he subsequently suffered, Gates possessed noble qualities, is evidenced by his domestic correspondence, the emancipation of his slaves and generous provision for their support. Not long before his death, near the end of a disappointed life, he wrote, expressing these noble sentiments: "I am very weak and have evident signs of approaching dissolution. But I have lived long enough since I have lived to see a mighty people animated with a spirit to be free and governed by transcendent abilities and power." He died in New York, April 10, 1806, at the age of 78. *Vide* Political and Military Episodes, p. 283; British Army Lists, *in loco;* Last Journals of Horace Walpole, London, 1859, vol. 2, p. 200; George III (Horace Walpole), London, 1847, vol. 1, p. 401; Irving's Life of Washington, vol. 1, p. 422, *et seq.;* vol. 3, p. 66; Life of Washington (Sparks), vol. 2, p. 469; vol. 3, pp. 6, 7, 483, 481, *et passim;* Curwen's Journals and Letters, N. Y., 1842, p. 475, *et seq.;* Field Book of the Revolution, vol. 1, p. 63; Memoirs of My Own Times, vol. 1, p. 269.

very severe cold shortly expected to set in.[133] The cruelty exercised by Major Heartly over the poor inhabitants was great; burning many of their habitations and small effects, and driveing away their cattle, many of which we found in the woods, which, by the general's order, were either returned to the owners, or an adequate price paid them for such cattle as were wanted for the use of the troops, and it gave me the sincerest pleasure to think our troops could relieve the miseries of the unfortunate as well as conquer the enemies of our country. On general Burgoyne's first hearing of the compleat victory gained by our fleet over the enemy, he gave out the following orders to the army, and which I should have inserted sooner. In it, he pays the greatest compliment to General Carlton.—

[133] The Americans were waiting at Ticonderoga with anxious impatience for Carleton to attack them, and were in excellent condition to receive him. Arnold held an important command, and was active in strengthening his position. It was supposed that an attack would be made upon the old French lines, and every preparation was made to meet it there. Every precaution was taken by the Americans to prevent a surprise, and every effort resorted to in order to obstruct the approaches to their works. The weather continued bad, but supplies of munitions of war and of men continued to arrive. Gates wrote to Schuyler on the 24th: "Carleton keeps very close to Crown Point, his navy at anchor on his flanks. I have scouts constantly down on both sides of the lake. I apprehend by this time his force is all collected, and expect this stillness will be succeeded by a grand attack. The army here are in good spirits and think only of victory." Had Carleton followed the urgent advice of Burgoyne and Phillips, there is a fair probability that he would have met with defeat.

GENERAL ORDERS.

17th Octr Riviere Sable, Lieut. Gen. Burgoyne, haveing received authentic intelligence of the late victory, obtained by the commander in chief in person, takes the first moment to communicate to the army, that of the 16 vessels of which the rebel fleet consisted before the action, three only escaped, all the others either taken or destroyed. The importance of the conquest is not greater to the national cause, than is the glory achieved to his majesty's arms, conspicuous by the general behaviour of the officers and men. It is a part of magnanimity to spare public demonstration of triumph on the present occasion; but it is not doubted that this army will be affected with every sentiment the brave are accustomed to feel from present great & glorious examples.

24th. Lieut Gen Burgoyne sailed in the *Washington* prize for St Johns, from where he was to go by land for Quebec where a frigate was ready to sail with him to England, as it was then determined the army was to return to winter in Canada, & make their appearance early the following season before Ticonderoga, when every thing necessary for the reduction of that fort would be in greater readiness, and the season more favourable for our operations than so late in the year, during which time our fleet would be masters of the Lake, and the severity of the winter too great for them to build any vessels that could obstruct our movements early in the spring; even at that time the cold was very severe and our tents but a small covering against it.

25th. Our Indians, who with Captn Frazier were advanced nearer their lines, took a prisoner and before they brought him to us painted the poor devil in a most curious manner, which almost frighted him out of his wits. It often surprised us their not attacking us at Crown Point, their numbers being so greatly superior to ours.

29th. Gen Carlton and General Phillips,[134] who command the Artillery, went up towards their lines

---

[134] William Phillips entered the Royal Military Academy at Woolwich, August 1, 1746, as a cadet; was made lieutenant-fireworker in the Artillery, January 2, 1747; quartermaster of the First Battalion, April 1, 1750; second lieutenant, March 1, 1755, and first lieutenant, April 1, 1756. As captain in the Royal Artillery, to which he was commissioned May 12, 1756, he distinguished himself in Germany. At the battle of Minden, in 1759, he commanded three companies of the Royal Artillery, and was particularly thanked by Prince Ferdinand, who testified his appreciation of his distinguished services by a present of a thousand crowns. At Warbourg the next year he gained attention by his skill and efficiency in handling his artillery, and August 15th, was promoted to the rank of lieutenant-colonel in the army. In 1768 he received the appointment of lieutenant-governor of Windsor Castle, and was commissioned a colonel in the army, May 25, 1772. He was elected in the autumn of 1774 to represent Boroughbridge in Parliament, and when the war between England and her trans-Atlantic colonies broke out, he was commissioned, January 1, 1776, a major-general for service in America. He had seen long and arduous service, in which he had always shown great skill and bravery. He it was who planted his batteries upon Sugar Loaf Hill, which forced the evacuation of Ticonderoga without a battle, and sent St. Clair, discomfited and disgraced, on his flight south

to reconnoitre their strength, situation &c. and which by them were thought of great extent & force. By deserters we heard they were then receiving fresh supplies of cannon and other stores. During the months of October and November, there are frequent squalls of wind on the Lake, which come momentary

---

with his shattered army. On April 25, 1777, he had been appointed major in the artillery, and on August 29th, he was promoted to the rank of major-general in the army. He was fully trusted by Burgoyne, and assumed command of the captive troops after the latter's return to England. He was proud and passionate; and, during his captivity at Cambridge, was confined by General Heath to the limits of his house and grounds and the road leading to the quarters of his troops, for using language which reflected upon the honor and dignity of Congress. When in Virginia with the captive army, he made the acquaintance of Jefferson, and was hospitably entertained by him and Mrs. Jefferson at their mansion. Jefferson afterward spoke of him as "the proudest man of the proudest nation on earth." He was exchanged on the 25th of October, 1780, and the following spring set out upon an expedition into Virginia. He was accompanied by Benedict Arnold, who had, since his last battle against Phillips, at Saratoga, joined the British side. On this expedition Phillips contracted a fever and died at Petersburg, May 13th. While he lay upon his death-bed, Lafayette appeared upon the heights opposite Petersburg and began a cannonade of the British position, one of his cannon balls going through the dying general's chamber and killing a female negro attendant. *Vide* Travels Through the Interior Parts of America, vol. 2, p. 506, British Army Lists, *in loco;* History of the Royal Artillery (Duncan), London, 1872, vol. 1, pp. 207–217; A State of the Expedition, Appendices XLVIII, LIV; Memoirs of General Heath, pp. 166, 169, *et passim;* Simcoe's Journal, London, 1787, pp. 129–146; Life of Jefferson (Randolph), pp. 50, 53; Historical Magazine, vol. 9, p. 247.

off the land and do great damage particularly to small craft. A few days before, the *Carlton* being under way and cruising on the Lake, one of these sudden squalls was very near laying her on her beam ends.

30. Our floating battery sailed for St Johns with stores &c, which opportunity we took to forward letters to Montreal post, in order to their being sent to our friends in Great Britain, as few vessels ever sail from Quebec after the 15th November on account of the frost, which begins to set in with great violence about that time, after which Canada is as much shut out from all communication with the rest of the world as possible, particularly then, as the country from Ticonderoga was in possession of the enemy.

November 2nd. We embarked in our battows and long boats for Canada, and proceeded about 17 miles, where our small fleet were obliged to put into a creek, the wind blowing very fresh, though fair for us, but causing a deep swell which was not so safe for the battows; as to the long boats there was but little danger. Our soldiers called this place Destruction Bay, and not unaptly, as there we saw the great execution the enemy suffered from the fire of our fleet in the engagement on the 11th and 13th October. Some of their dead were then floating on the brink of the water, just as the surf threw them; these were ordered to be directly buried. During the night it blew fresh and was attended with a fall of snow which was the first we had experienced.

The weather being fair we got under way, and with both sails and oars got a good distance before night.

6th. After a variety of weather, we made Point-au-faire. We had a strong gale of wind crossing over Cumberland Bay, where we could not keep the shore without going six times the distance at least, and this short cut, if I can call it so, was near endangering many of our battows. Near that, we saw the wreck of the *Royal Savage*, and had the rest of their fleet behaved as well as she did, we should not have been so easyly masters of the Lake, We found one Artillery man of ours who fell the 13th; him we buried. At night we made large fires as before, and lay round them, keeping our feet always next the fire, as when they are warm the body is seldom cold.

9th. Embarked for St Johns after remaining at Point-au-faire from the 6th, on account of the delay in getting over provisions ammunition &c. &c., all which were sent down to St Johns before our moveing from that post. We also brought with us the families who resided before at Crown Point, as it would have been cruel to have left them to the mercy of the enemy, who no doubt would persecute them, for their attachment to us. We had scarce pushed off the shore, about break of day, when the greatest fog arose I ever beheld, and which prevented our seeing above 3 or 4 yards from our boat's bow, in consequence of which we separated, some steering one way and some the other. Brig Gen Frazier caused drums to beat in his boat, by which he collected many others, but in place of going to St Johns he went directly the opposite course back to the Isle of mott, where he thought proper to land and wait till next day, which was clear. Our boat, by great good fortune, made St Johns before night, though we saild round a small island twice, thinking it the main land. At night we found a hearty reception from our Regiment, who garrisoned that fort and had not crossed the Lake.

10th. The remainder of our Corps came down, the day being clear. Our ships were all laid up at this place for the winter, masts and rigging taken from them, and the ice broke round every morning and evening to prevent their keels from suffering by the severe frosts then shortly expected.

13th. We marched for Vershere,[135] a neat village on the banks of the river St Lawrence, and about six leagues below Montreal.

---

[135] Vercheres is a small village on the right bank of the St. Lawrence, twenty-three miles below Montreal, and is still a small village, its population not greatly exceeding one thousand persons. It derives its name curiously from a heroine, Madame de Verchere, who in the year 1690, being left alone in the little palisaded block-house here, while the few people who composed the hamlet were at work in a distant clearing, perceived a party of Indians approaching to attack the place. She instantly seized a gun and fired upon them; and although several attempts were made to scale the palisade, she kept them at bay until help arrived. At another time a larger body of savages attacked and took prisoners all the men who were laboring in the fields. Madame Verchere with one soldier, her daughter and other women, were in the block-house, and seeing their husbands

16th. Our battallion of Grenadiers arrived at Verchere our winter quarters, after a pleasant and agreeable march, and our men were billeted through the parish, 2 or 3 in each house. The army were quartered in like manner through the province, where there were prepared good stoves and plenty of fuel to enable us to bear comfortably the severity of the approaching season, as during that time every thing is froze. All kinds of provisions are laid up in that frozen state, during the winter, and when wanted to be used, are gently thawed in cold water for some time and then cooked, when they eat perhaps after being months killed, as well as if just before slaughtered; and, were a thaw to take place during the winter months, there would be every prospect of a famine in the province, as at the setting in of the frost, such eatables as are to serve the inhabitants for near half the year are all slaughtered; cows,

---

taken prisoners, many of the women made loud lamentations. To prevent their cries from reaching the Indians, and encouraging them in their designs upon the fort, she shut them up, and hastily assuming the garb of a soldier, trained a cannon upon the foe. She resorted to the stratagem of firing first from one embrasure and then from another, and prevented the Indians, who supposed the fort held a considerable number of defenders, from taking it until a force arrived from the fort at Chambly where the cannon had been heard, and not only raised the siege, but was fortunate enough to rescue the prisoners who were in the hands of the savages. Madame Verchere subsequently returned to Normandy, where, at her death, a tombstone was reared over her, upon which was placed an inscription commemorating these acts of bravery.

beeves pigs and all sorts of fowls [are] laid up in this manner, nay, I have seen cream hawked through the streets of Quebec and sold by weight, carried in a basket. The great river St Lawrence in one night's frost will have ice thick enough to bear any carriage. Then the Carrioling,[136] which is the principal amusement of the Canadians, commences. That carriage from the great velocity it moves on the snow & ice, from its easy and pleasant motion seems to engross all their attention during the winter months. It is drawn by one or two horses, which in Canada are excellent for the draught, tho in general small, and is rather a help, so very easy is the draught to the horses, to keep them steady on the ice. The persons seated in the Caryole, generally two, are dressed entirely in furs. The ladies' [furs] in general and of the higher rank are elegant, so famous in that part of the world to protect them from the severe cold; but, yet it is pleasant, the sky being quite serene and not a cloud to be seen in the hemisphere. Thus equipt you parade over the ice & snow amidst perhaps a hundred other caryoles, painted in the most gaudy

[136] This is a word of purely Canadian coinage, and has passed unnoticed by lexicographers. "*Carriole*" is a French word for a small, light carriage, and, strangely enough, has been metamorphosed into carryall and applied to a cumbersome vehicle formerly much in vogue in New England, but unknown in Europe. Hadden gives the word as "*cabrioling*," a word of very different etymology, from *caper*, a goat, referring especially to the leaping motion of that animal, and applied also to a carriage (cabriolet and cab), which originally was a small one-horse carriage (cabriolet and cab), to which the horse imparted a jerking motion.

colours, which from the great contrast of the snow has a beautiful effect. The ice is much smoother and better for this amusement before a snow storm, which is there frequent; but yet the idea of the water being deep enough under you to float a ship of the line, and the ice so very transparent as fish to be seen under it, has rather an alarming appearance to a stranger, though very seldom accidents happen — as by an order from the governor the roads are marked out on the river, keeping clear of all springs, many of which are to be found on the St Lawrence — except at the breaking up of the ice — the thaw generally coming on about the latter end of March — when Caryoles are sometimes lost; for example one officer of our regiment, Captain Scott[137]

[137] Alexander Scott belonged to a noted Scotch family known as the Scotts of Logie, and was commissioned an ensign in the Thirty-seventh Foot, October 3, 1757. He was advanced to the rank of lieutenant, May 17, 1759, and served with his regiment through the French war, when, in 1763, his regiment, the Seventy-fifth Foot, which was composed of the Second Battalion of the Thirty-seventh Foot — that battalion having been detached and so numbered in 1759 — was disbanded. From that time until February 11, 1767, he was on half pay, but on the date named was made a lieutenant in the Fifty-third Foot while it was stationed at Gibraltar. The next year he accompanied his regiment to Ireland, and, when it was ordered to America in the spring of '76, he accompanied it, and served through the campaign of that year, being assistant commissary of Powell's Brigade. In a note to Hadden's Journal and Orderly Books, p. 206, he is stated to have served through the Burgoyne campaign, and to have died in 1778; but this statement of Digby corrects the error. *Vide* Burke's Landed Gentry and British Army Lists, *in loco*.

and one of 47th regiment, Cap Lestrange,[138] both unfortunately lost their lives in this manner. The thaw is attended with a tremendous noise, the ice rushing down from the great Lakes in large bodies crushing all before them many leagues after clearing the gulph, and rendering the approach of ships to that coast at this time of the year very dangerous.

All the great Lakes and Rivers we passed during the summer in boats and battows were at this season of the year fine plains for caryoling.—The cold is so very intense, that we have had port wine froze in the bottles, though in a room with a stove. On going out in the air, you must be very well raped up with furs or the most tender parts will be frost bitten, which the only remedy for is being well rubbed with snow, else the part will, perhaps, mortify or drop off. Some few of our men have suffered in this manner through their own carelessness, as they

---

[138] Richard L'Estrange entered the Forty-seventh Foot as an ensign, June 13, 1765. He was promoted, November 6, 1769, to the rank of captain-lieutenant, and to that of captain, May 25, 1772. At the date of his latter promotion, the Forty-seventh was stationed at Ireland, from whence it sailed for America in 1773. The Forty-seventh, which had before seen service in America, having distinguished itself under Wolfe at the fall of Quebec, was one of the regiments ordered to Boston at the beginning of troubles there, and in the battles of Lexington and Bunker Hill, Captain L'Estrange participated. After the evacuation of Boston, he sailed with his regiment to Halifax, and soon after joined General Carleton's command and participated in the campaign of '76, which was his last. *Vide* Historical Record of the Forty-seventh Foot and British Army Lists, *in loco.*

were all provided with caps, gloves, blankets coats, &c. &c.

A poor fellow of our company died during the winter, and we found it a most difficult affair to bury him. After near a days labor with crows, pick-axes &c, we had a grave dug for him, the ground being froze above six feet deep. This was matter of surprise to the Canadians, who place their dead at this season in a small habitation built beside their places of worship, where they remain froze till the warm weather allows them burial.—At this time the wolves and bears come from the woods to pick up food, when the former are dangerous; they are taken in traps when they howl most dreadfully. We killed a fine bear and his flesh proved not very bad; at least it was a variety. It had a young cub which we tamed and in a little time was very tractable. All the hares turn at this season as white as snow, as indeed do many other beasts in more nothern countrys. Nothing but a melancholy white strikes the eye on every side, and [there is nothing] which takes the place [better] of that beautiful variety of colours, which is the greatest ornament of the country, than [the] trees, which appear planted in the snow and which present to our sight only hoary heads and branches loaded with icicles. During the winter there were balls, assemblys &c at Quebec and Montreal; the former is the seat of the Governor, who lives in a great degree of elegance, and as absolute in his government as possible. Gen Carlton, notwithstanding his severity, was much liked by the Canadians, perhaps fear might have something to say in that case.[139] General Phillips commanded at Montreal, and general Riedzel, of the foreign troops, at Trois Riviere. The persons of the Canadians ——, but I am exceeding the bounds, I at first prescribed in my preface, by a digression no doubt tedious & tiresome to the reader.—

Thus situated we passed the Winter in as agreeable a manner as was in our power, with an expectation of opening the campaign early the ensueing season.

---

[139] Reference has been made—*ante*, note 68—to the French historian, Garneau's statement, that General Carleton, on his return to Canada, punished most barbarously with fire and sword those Canadians who had exhibited sympathy with their brother colonists from the south, who had invaded their country. It is strange that neither Hadden, Pausch nor Digby alluded to this, a matter which ought naturally to have engaged their attention. The nearest approach to such an allusion is this of Digby, and is not sufficient to base an opinion upon. From the absence in these journals of any statement bearing out the assertion of Garneau, we may infer that it is exaggerated.

END OF THE FIRST CAMPAIGN.

CAMPAIGN OF 1777.

BY AN OFFICER IN THE NORTHERN ARMY,

UNDER THE COMMAND OF HIS EXCELLENCY

LIEUT.-GEN. JOHN BURGOYNE.

TO THEIR CAPTURE AT

SARATOGA.

SECOND CAMPAIGN,

1777.

MAY 6, 1777. Lieut. General Burgoyne made Quebec in the *Apollo* frigate, with orders from Government, to take the command of the army, which, though it pleased the troops in general, yet caused some surprise at General Carlton's being set aside; and which could be accounted for only in the following manner; first his not being able as Governor to leave the province, as were he to effect a junction with General Howe, who was appointed Commander in chief of all America, and which was thought very probable, General Carlton, as the oldest officer, must have taken the command, from whence it was judged better not to let them clash; some gave another reason, which, I think, must appear an unjust one, namely, his not attempting to reduce Ticonderoga the preceding season; and I am positive every officer in the army, if called upon, would acquit him of acting imprudently in retireing from that place to winter in Canada, the season being so very severe and far advanced.[140] The troops were assembled at St Johns ready to cross over Lake Champlain. The 31st, 29th and 34th regiments were left to garrison Canada. The troops were all in the greatest health and much improved since their sailing from Great Britain; as many were then recruits, they were also better inured to the climate than the preceding season, and General Burgoyne seemed extremely pleased, as indeed he must have been, with the good appearance of the army on taking the field; and I make no doubt, but the expectations of the people at home were sanguine respecting his opperations necessary for the junction with the Southern army, under the command of General Howe. On his takeing the command, he gave out the following manifesto or proclamation, intending it for the benefit of the Americans, where his army was intended to act, and as he afterwards says in the House of Commons, rather to hold out terrors, than put them into execution. Many copies were soon dispersed through the Provinces of the enemy. How it was attended to will be seen in the following pages.

---

[140] The subject of placing Burgoyne in command of the campaign about to be inaugurated, was widely discussed at home as well as in the army, and Burgoyne was openly accused by his adversaries of having supplanted a brother officer by the use of means not honorable to a soldier. This charge he met and refuted in Parliament. On the other hand, many saw in the action of the government a disapproval of Carleton's management of the previous campaign.

BY JOHN BURGOYNE, E[SQ]

Lieutenant General of his Majesties Armies in America, Col° of the Queen's regiment of Light Dragoons, Governor of Fort William in North Britain, One of the representatives of the Commons of Great Britain in Parliament and Commanding an army and fleet employed in an expedition from Canada &c. &c. &c.

The forces intrusted to my command are designed to act in concert and upon a common principle with the numerous armies and fleets which already display in every quarter of America the Power, the Justice (and when properly sought) the Mercy of the King. The cause, in which the British arms are exerted, applies to the most affecting interests of the human heart, and the military servants of the crown, at first called forth for the sole purpose of Restoring the rights of the Constitution, now Combine with love of their Country, and duty to their Sovereign, the other extensive incitements which spring from a true sense of the general privileges of mankind. To the eyes and ears of the temperate part of the public, and to the breasts of the suffering thousands in the Provinces, be the melancholy appeal, whether the present unnatural Rebellion has not been made a foundation for the completest system of tyranny that ever God, in his displeasure suffered for a time to be exercised over a froward and stubborn generation. Arbitrary Imprisonment, confiscation of property, Persecution and torture unprecedented in the Inquisition of the Romish Church are amongst the palpable enormities that verefy the affirmative. These are inflicted by Assemblys and Committees, who dare to profess themselves friends to Liberty, upon the most quiet subjects, without distinction of age or sex, for the sole crime, often for the sole suspicion, of having adhered in principle to the Government under which they were born, and, to which, by every tie Divine & Human, they owe allegiance. To consummate these shocking proceedings, the profanation of religion is added to the most profligate prostitution of common reason; the consciences of men are set at naught, and multitudes are compelled, not only to bear arms, but also to swear subjection to an usurpation they abhor. Animated by these considerations, at the head of troops in full power of health, discipline and valour, determined to strike when necessary, and anxious to spare when possible. I by these presents, invite and exhort all persons, in all places where the progress of this army may point, (and by the blessing of God I will extend it far) to mentain such a conduct as may justify in protecting their lands, Habitations and Families. The intention of this address, is to hold forth security, not depredation to the country. To those whom spirit and principle may induce to partake [in] the glorious task of redeeming their countrymen from dungeons, and reestablishing the blessings of Legal Government, I offer encouragement and employment, and upon the first intelligence of their associating, I will find means to assist their undertakings. The Domestic, the industrious, the infirm and even the timid inhabitants I am desirous to protect, provided they remain quietly in their houses; that they do not suffer their cattle to be removed, nor their corn or forage to be secreted or destroyed; that they do not break up their bridges or roads, nor by any other acts, directly or indirectly, endeavor to obstruct the opperations of the Kings troops, or supply or subsist those of the enemy, every species of provision brought to my camp will be paid for at an equitable rate and in solid coin. The consciousness of Christianity, my Royal Master's clemency, and the honour of soldiership, I have dwelt upon in this invitation, and wished for more persuasive terms to give it impression; and let not people be led to disregard it by considering their distance from the immediate situation of my camp. I have but to give stretch to the Indian forces under my direction, (and they amount to thousands) to overtake the hardened enemies of Great Britain and America. I consider them the same where ever they may lurk. If notwithstanding these endeavours, and sincere inclinations to effect them, the phrensy of hostility should remain, I trust I shall stand acquitted in the eyes of God and men in denouncing and executing the vengeance of the State against the wilful outcasts. The messengers of Justice and wrath await them in the field, and Devastation, famine and every concomitant horror that a reluctant but indispensible prosecution of military duty must occasion, will bar the way to their return.[141]

GENERAL ORDERS.

Disposition of the army under the Command of Lieu^t^ Genl Burgoyne.

---

[141] Many humorous replies were made to this high-sounding proclamation of Burgoyne, one of which Digby himself gives us. Another, ascribed to William Livingston, Governor of New Jersey, was especially witty, and purported to be an agreement for exchange of prisoners, supposing the commander-in-chief himself fell into the hands of the Americans. It was arranged in articles, in which his various titles were appropriately numbered, and a value set upon each for purposes of exchange. Thus it was proposed to give, as follows:

"1. For John Burgoyne *Esquire*, some worthy justice of the peace.
"2. For J. B. lieut. gen. of his maj's armies in Am. 2 major generals.
"3. For J. B. Col. queen's reg. lt. dragoons, at least 3 Continental colonels.
"4. For J. B. gov. of fort Wm. in N. Britain, 1 Gov. because his multititulary excellency is gov. of a fort & 2 as that f. is in *North Britain*.
"5. For J. B. one of the representatives of Great Britain, the first member of Congress who may fall into the enemy's hands.
"6. For J. B. com. of a fleet employed on an expedition to Canada, the admiral of our navy.
"7. For J. B. com. of an army employed in an expedition from Canada, 1 commander in chief in any of our departments.
"8. For J. B. &c. &c. &c. which he humorously discusses, 3 privates."

Washington issued a counter-proclamation, which was in strong contrast to Burgoyne's, being characterized by simple, but lofty and dignified sentiments. It closed with these noble words: "*Harassed as we are by unrelenting persecution, obliged by every tie to repel violence by force, urged by self-preservation to exert the strength which Providence has given us to defend our natural rights against the aggressor, we appeal to the hearts of all mankind for the justice of our cause; its event we leave to Him, who speaks the fate of nations, in humble confidence that as his omniscient eye taketh note even of the sparrow that falleth to the ground, so he will not withdraw his countenance from a people who humbly array themselves under his banner in defense of the noblest principles with which he has adorned humanity.*"

Brigadier General Frazier will be joined by the Canadian companies of Moning and Boucherville,[142] Captn Frazier's detachment and a body of Savages. The German Grenadiers, Chassieures, Light Infantry under the command of Lieut Colo Bremen[143] form a corps of Reserve, and will never encamp in the line. The regiment of Riedesel's Dragoons is also out of the Line, and for the present, will be employed to cover head quarters. The provincial corps of Peters[144]

[142] Réné Antoine de Boucherville was born at Cataracouy, the Indian name of a settlement which occupied the site of the present busy town of Kingston, on February 12, 1735. He was an active partisan in the war, and subsequently attained prominence in political affairs, becoming a member of the Canadian Legislative Council, and occupying other official positions. He died at Boucherville, Canada, September 2, 1812. Colonel Rogers questions the identity of the officer mentioned in this journal with the Seigneur Réné Antoine, above noted. His reasons may be found in Appendix number twelve to Hadden's Journal and Orderly Books.

[143] Heinrich Christoph Breymann was lieutenant-colonel of the grenadiers loaned by the Duke of Brunswick to George the Third. He was a brave and efficient officer; but was severely criticised for tardiness in marching to the support of Baum, at Bennington. A report was current in Burgoyne's army, says Hadden, "that an old picque between *Brymen & Baume* might occasion his tardiness, as he was heard to say, 'we will let them get warm before we reach

[144] John Peters was a Connecticut yankee, and was born at Hebron in 1740. He was of sound rebel stock. His father, John, was a staunch patriot, and his cousin, John S., was governor of Connecticut. The historian of Connecticut, the Rev. Samuel, was his uncle. He was a graduate of Yale College in the class of 1759, and studied the profession of

and Jessop[145] are also out of the line. The recruits of the 33rd regiment, and the other regiments under

them' when he heard the firing." Be this as it may, he fought well after reaching the scene of action, was himself wounded, and his command suffered severe loss. He was subsequently killed in the battle of Bemus' Heights, October 7, 1777. *Vide* Hadden's Journal and Orderly Books, pp. 36, 136.

the law, removing in 1766 to Vermont, where he became a prosperous citizen, holding important civil offices until the opening of the war. He was a member of the provincial congress, but was hostile to independence, and allied himself to the Tories in the war, and accompanied General Carleton on the campaign of '76 as a volunteer. He went on the raid to Bennington with Baum, as lieutenant-colonel of the Queen's Loyal Rangers, expecting to add to his command from the disaffected after the expected defeat of his fellow-countrymen, but in the battle lost a large portion of his men. He fought with Burgoyne through the campaign of '77, and on the eve of that general's surrender of his army he escaped to Canada. Here he seems to have been neglected, and the promises made to him broken. His property was, of course, confiscated, and he was unable on account of the act of attainder, to return to his old home. Broken in health, and unable even to get pay for his services, he finally went to England to urge his claims upon the government, leaving his family, consisting of a wife and eight children, at Cape Breton, but a deaf ear was turned toward him, and for three years he hung about the back doors of royalty begging in vain, when death came to his relief in 1788. *Vide* History of New York During the Revolutionary War (Jones), vol. 1, pp. 686–692; History of Vermont (Hall), p. 769; Loyalists of the American Revolution (Sabine), Boston, 1864, vol. 2, p. 183.

[145] Ebenezer and Edward Jessup were brothers, born in the Province of Connecticut, who, several years before the commencement of the Revolution, removed to northern New York where they had acquired extensive possessions, and erected houses and mills. They were both justices of

the command of Lieu^t Nutt [146] are, for the present, to serve on board the Fleet.

---

the peace for the Province of New York, and engaged in business enterprises of importance, but when the war began, thought best to cast in their lot with the British invaders of their country. Edward Jessup had already had military experience, having been a captain of Provincials in 1759. Both brothers, it would seem, were considered competent to command, hence we find them both prominent among the commanders of Provincial loyalists. Burgoyne, however, did not regard these soldiers very favorably, as they did not stand by him with that constancy which he demanded of them, but we must remember that he had been bred in the regular service, and consequently would, of necessity, be prone to regard Provincial irregulars unfavorably. The brothers Jessup never returned to the United States and their property was confiscated. A Jessup genealogy by Prof. Henry G. Jessup is in press, to which the reader is referred for further particulars. Also, *vide* Hadden's Journal and Orderly Books, pp. 67–74, 112 *et passim.* I am indebted for several particulars in this note to Mr. Douglass Brymner, Canadian archivist.

[146] George Anson Nutt became an ensign in the Thirty-third Foot, August 28, 1771, and a lieutenant, October 26, 1775. He was in command of a body of about one hundred and fifty men to recruit the Thirty-third — the regiment of Lord Cornwallis, which had accompanied Sir Peter Parker's unsuccessful expedition against Charleston, South Carolina, and which was to have joined Carleton at Quebec, had not a change of plan taken place. He was attached with his command to the artillery in the campaign of '77, and suffered captivity with the surrendered army until September 3, 1781, when he was exchanged. On October 1, 1780, during his captivity, he was promoted to the rank of captain-lieutenant. In 1783 he went on half pay, but returned to active service in 1787, and became, on May 30, a captain in the Sixty-fifth Foot. Two years later his name disappears from the rolls. *Vide* British Army Lists, *in loco;* Hadden's Journal and Orderly Book, pp. lx, lxx; Burgoyne's Orderly Book, p. 178.

The line upon the next movement will encamp in order of Battle as follows, and will continue the same till Countermanded.

ORDER OF BATTLE.	RIGHT WING.	First Brigade British.	Brigdr Genl	47th Regiment.
				53rd Regiment.
			Powell [147]	9th Regiment.
		Second Brigade British.	Brigr General	21st Regiment.
				62nd Regiment.
			Hamilton [148]	20th Regiment.

[147] Henry Watson Powell became a lieutenant in the Forty-sixth Foot, March 10, 1753, and a captain, September 2, 1756, in the Eleventh, which afterward became the Sixty-fourth Foot. In this regiment he served against the French West Indies in 1759, and in 1768 accompanied his regiment to America. June 2, 1770, he was promoted to a majority in the Thirty-eighth, and July 23, 1771, to a lieutenant-colonelcy in the Fifty-third Foot. After his arrival in America in the spring of '76, General Carleton assigned him to the command of the Second Brigade with the rank of brigadier-general. Upon the evacuation by the Americans of Ticon-

[148] James Inglis Hamilton. Owing to the fact that there were several of this name in the army at the same period, it is difficult to identify the subject of this note during the early part of his career. Dr. O'Callaghan supposes him to have been commissioned captain in the army, February 28, 1755, and of the Thirty-fourth Foot, August 25, 1756. In 1758 this regiment formed part of the expedition against St. Malo, and in 1760 against Belle Isle. On October 17, 1761, he was appointed major in command of the One Hundred and Thirteenth Royal Highland Volunteers, which regiment being disbanded, he retired on half pay on May 25, 1772,

ORDER OF BATTLE.	LEFT WING.	Second Brigade Germans.	Brigr General................ Gall 149....................	Regiment of Frederick and Hannaw.
		First Brigade Germans.	Brigr General................ Speict 150..................	Regiment of Rhetz Speict Reidzel.

---

deroga, July 6, 1777, General Powell was left in command of the captured fortress. After the battle of Bennington, an attempt was made to sever Burgoyne's communication with Canada, and an attack was made upon Ticonderoga, which he repelled, though with such a considerable loss of men — a large number being taken prisoners — as to give to success

---

when he was appointed lieutenant-colonel in the army. On March 11, 1774, he was made lieutenant-colonel of the Twenty-first Foot. He served under Carleton in the campaign of '76, and was appointed brigadier-general November 5th of that year. He participated in the disastrous campaign of Burgoyne, acquitting himself "with great honor,

---

[149] W. R. Von Gall was colonel of the Hesse Hanau regiment, but at this time was in command of the Hessian regiments of Prince Frederick and Hesse Hanau, which had been formed into a brigade by General Carleton, and he therefore held the rank of brigadier-general during the campaign. Colonel Von Gall was in the various battles of the campaign of '77, and shared the hardships attendant upon it, and seems to have been a good and faithful officer. He was

---

[150] Johann Friederich Specht, colonel of the regiment of that name, did not arrive in Canada until the autumn of 1776; hence he did not take part in the campaign of that year. He, however, participated in the campaign of Burgoyne, and commanded the first German brigade. He was

If it should become necessary to form two lines, the second line is to be formed by the Second Brigade of British doubling upon the first, and the Second Brigade of Germans, doubling in the same manner upon their first. The Brigadiers are always to encamp with their Brigades.

Lieut Gen[1] Burgoyne takes the occasion of the Army's assembling to express publickly the high

---

the hue of defeat. After Burgoyne's surrender, he abandoned Ticonderoga and returned to Canada, where he held command for several years. He was made a colonel in the army, February 19, 1779, and in 1780 purchased an estate in the suburbs of Quebec. He was made a major-general, November 20, 1782; colonel of the Sixty-ninth Foot, April 16, 1792, and of the Fifteenth Foot, June 20, 1794; lieutenant-general,

---

activity and good conduct," according to Burgoyne. He was among the convention prisoners, and was exchanged September 3, 1781. He subsequently became colonel in the army, September 3, 1781; major-general, September 28, 1787; colonel of the Fifteenth Foot, August 22, 1792, and of the Twenty-first Foot, June 20, 1794; lieutenant-general, Janu-

---

among the captured officers and shared the captivity of his men. He was unjustly accused of appropriating money to his own use, a charge which grew out of an arrangement which he made, while in winter quarters, with some of the inhabitants, to board his men in exchange for their army rations. These rations he cut down in quantity, in order to accumulate a reserve fund for them, and although it appeared that he was not doing this for private gain, his tyrannical prince, when he returned, after his captivity in 1781, angrily turned him out of his service. There was another reason, however, quite as potent with the prince. As long as his officers remained out of the country, either in the service of

---

among the captured troops, and after his exchange in October, 1780, returned to Canada and remained there until peace was declared, when he returned home, in October, 1783. He

opinion he entertains of the Troops, which his Majesty has been graciously pleased to intrust to his command.

They could not have been selected more to his satisfaction, and the lieu[t] Gen[l] trusts it will be received as one mark of his attention to their glory and welfare, that with the promise of every encouragement the service will allow, he declares a determination and he calls upon every officer to assist him to mentain a steady, uniform system of subordination and obeydience.

May 3, 1796, and general, January 1, 1801. He died at Lyme, England, July 14, 1814. *Vide* British Army Lists, *in loco;* Burgoyne's Orderly Book, p. 10; Hadden's Journal and Orderly Books, pp. 45, 117, *et passim;* Journal of Occurrences During the Late American War, p. 173; Gentleman's Magazine, vol. 84, part 2, p. 190.

---

ary 26, 1797, and general, April 29, 1802. He died July 27, 1803. *Vide* British Army Lists, *in loco;* Burgoyne's Orderly Book, pp. 22, *et seq.*, 190, *et passim;* A State of the Expedition, Appendix 49; Hadden's Journal and Orderly Books, pp. 45, 176, *et passim.*

---

the British king, or in captivity, the result of that service, the prince received a considerable income from the treasury of Great Britain. Specht and others remained in Canada in the service of George the Third, until the peace, and Von Gall it appears did not have permission to return; hence he was made an example of, and the principal reason given was his return without permission. Certainly no other officer attempted to return after this salutary example. *Vide* Memoirs of General Riedesel, vol. 1, pp. 39, 100; vol. 2, pp. 101–105, 216–218.

---

died at Brunswick, June 24, 1787. *Vide* Memoirs of General Riedesel, vol. 1, pp. 26, 62, 66; vol. 2, pp. 47, 73, 100, *et passim;* Journal of Madame Riedesel, p. 160.

After which the standing regulations of the army respecting Dutys in camp &c are inserted, with orders for officer's strictly to observe on their several guards and out posts, which from their length I am obliged to omit inserting here.—

General Orders, June 29.

The army embarks tomorrow to oppose the enemy. We are to Contend for the King and the Constitution of Great Britain; to vindicate law and relieve the oppressed; a cause in which his majesties Troops, and those of the Princes, his allies, will feel equal excitement. The services required of this particular expedition are critical and conspicuous. During our progress occasions may occur in which no difficulty, nor labour, nor life are to be regarded.—

We crossed the Lake pretty much in the same manner before related, excepting that the season was a more pleasant one, and our being a longer time on the passage, owing to the great tediousness of bringing over Artillery and other stores, so requisite for such an expedition. We remained near a week at Bouquet river,[151] 30 miles North of Crown Point, where we were joined by a nation of Indians, and who, from General Burgoyne, received the most positive orders not to scalp, except the dead.

---

[151] The river Bouquet derives its name from Colonel Bouquet, who commanded an expedition against the Indians while Canada was under the French. It was at the place here mentioned that he negotiated a treaty of peace with the savages.

30. The Advanced Corps made their appearance before Ticonderoga. We encamped at Three Mile Point. The line, with the general, were at Putnam's Creek, about six miles in our rear, but expected shortly up. We had a full view from our post of their works lines &c and their flag of Liberty displayed on the summit of the Fort. Our gun boats were anchored across the river out of the range of their cannon, and our two frigates, the largest called the *Royal George* carrying 32 Guns, and built at St Johns during the winter, with the *Inflexible* at a small distance from the Gun boats, with a large boom ahead to prevent fire ships coming down from the Fort. Our Indians had many small skirmishes with parties of theirs, and always came off victorious, and what prisoners were taken, all seemed to agree that they intended to make a vigorous defence. With our glasses we could distinguish every thing they were about in the Fort, appearing very busy about their works, and viewing with their glasses our situation force &c. It was entertaining enough, being a scene of life I had not been accustomed to before, and its novelty made it amusing.

State of the Army rank and file fit for Duty.

British	3,252
Germans	3,007
Canadians	145
Indians	500
Total	6,904

I have not included sick officers, servants, Battmen[152] &c.

The Country round the Fort is covered with thick wood through [which] roads were to be made for our carrying on regular approaches.

July 1. About 12 o clock a small boat of theirs rowed down from the fort within reach of the cannon from our gun boats; she lay on her oars, when we saw her intent was to reconnoitre our post, at first it was proposed to fire on her, but the smallness of the object made it not worth perhaps expending a few shots on, and she returned quietly back to the Fort.

2d. A detachment of about 500 men from our corps were ordered, under the command of Brigr Genl Frazier, to take possession of an eminence, said to command the Fort. We moved at one o clock, and about three had a skirmish with a large party of the enemy, and drove them under cover of their cannon. We lost some Indians and poor Richd Houghton,[153] a

---

152 Batmen. *Bât* is a French word, signifying pack-saddle. The government formerly allowed to every company of a regiment in foreign service a batman, whose duty it was to take charge of the cooking utensils, etc., of the company. The term came to be applied to men in charge of baggage, and, finally, though inappropriately, to men in charge of officers' horses. The pack-horses were also called bat-horses, and money paid for service bat-money.

153 Richard Houghton was wounded on the night of July 2d while engaged in trying to save some savages from being captured or destroyed. They had been having a pow-wow, and had become drunk as usual, and probably in a spirit of bravado approached the American lines. Houghton, while

lieu[t] of our regiment [was] severely wounded. During that night they were constantly fireing on us from under cover of their guns, where they well knew we could not follow them. Our out sentries and theirs were very near each other, and sleep was a stranger to us. We had but two 6 pounders with us, the road not being cut for a large gun. We fired two evening guns to make them believe there were two Brigades on the ground, and also caused our drums to beat to alarm them in the Fort.

3[d]. At day break, the remainder of our corps joined us with the First Brigade of British, and soon after, they opened a nine pound battery on us, and by the direction of their shot, they must have seen our 6 pounders, as they killed a man and horse harnessed, in the carriage of the gun, on which we were obliged to move them under cover of a small hill. During the day they killed a few of our men, and some balls

---

endeavoring to get the worse than useless creatures back within the British lines, was fired upon by the Americans and wounded. One of the savages was killed and another wounded. Lieutenant Houghton obtained his first commission in the Fifty-third Foot as an ensign, August 30, 1768, and was promoted to a lieutenancy, April 30, 1771. Being wounded in the battle of the 7th of October, and carried to the rear, he was not among the convention prisoners, and undoubtedly remained with the Fifty-third in Canada until its return to England in the summer of 1789. He was commissioned as captain and captain-lieutenant, December 27, 1785, and his name so appears in the army lists of 1793, after which date it is dropped. *Vide* British Army Lists, *in loco;* Journal of Occurrences During the Late American War, pp. 174, 176; Hadden's Journal and Orderly Books, p. 83; Historical Record of the Fifty-third Foot, p. 4.

went through our tents, their ground commanding ours.

4th. Before day light, we shifted our camp farther back a small way from the range of their shot, until our 12 pounders could come up to play on them in return ; by their not throwing shells, we supposed they had none, which from our camp being on a rocky eminence would have raked us much ; as to their balls we did not much mind them being at too great a distance to suffer from any point blank shot from their cannon. About noon we took possession of Sugar loaf hill[154] on which a battery was imme-

[154] Sugarloaf Hill, or Mount Defiance, was an elevation difficult of ascent, which commanded the extensive works at Ticonderoga. The command of Ticonderoga and the defenses in the vicinity had been assigned to Gates by Schuyler, who was in command of the department; but the jealousy of Gates caused him to decline it, and this occasioned some delay in getting the defenses into a condition to meet an assault. Schuyler was bending all his energies toward strengthening the works in his department, and as soon as the decision of Gates was known, he dispatched General Arthur St. Clair to Ticonderoga, which he reached on the twelfth of June. With a strange want of foresight, he took no steps to fortify the important hill which commanded his works, but devoted himself to strengthening them. Burgoyne thus speaks of this neglect of St. Clair: "The manner of taking up the ground at Ticonderoga, convinces me that they have no men of military science. Without possessing Sugar Hill, from which I was proceeding to attack them, Ticonderoga is only what I once heard Montcalm had expressed it to be: '*Une porte pour un honnête homme de se deshonorer.*' They seem to have expended great treasure and the unwearied labor of more than a year to fortify, upon the supposition that we should only attack them upon the point where they were best prepared to resist." *Vide* Letter to Earl Hervey, 11th July, Fonblanque, p. 247.

diately ordered to be raised. It was a post of great consequence, as it commanded a great part of the works of Ticonderoga, all their vessels, and likewise afforded us the means of cutting off their communication with Fort Independent, a place also of great strength and the works very extensive. But here the commanding officer was reckoned guilty of a great oversight in lighting fires on that post, tho I am informed, it was done by the Indians, the smoak of which was soon perceived by the enemy in the Fort; as he should have remained undiscovered till night, when he was to have got two 12 pounders up tho their getting there was almost a perpendicular ascent, and drawn up by most of the cattle belonging to the Army. They no sooner perceived us in possession of a post, which they thought quite impossible to bring cannon up to, than all their pretended boastings of holding out to the last, and choosing rather to die in their works than give them up, failed them, and on the night of the 5th [day] they set fire to several parts of the garrison, kept a constant fire of great guns the whole night, and under the protection of that fire, and clouds of smoke they evacuated the garrison, leaving all their cannon, amunition and a great quantity of stores. They embarked what baggage they could during the night in their battows, and sent them up to Skeensborough under the protection of five schooners, which Captain Carter[155] of the Artillery

[155] John Carter became a cadet at Woolwich, February 18, 1752; lieutenant-fireworker in the artillery, March 1, 1755;

with our gun boats followed and destroyed with all their baggage and provisions. As I happened to be one of the Lieutenants of the Grenadiers piquet that night, when we perceived the great fires in the Fort, the general was immediately made acquainted with it and our suspicion of their abandoning the place, who with many other good officers imagined it was all a feint in them to induce us to make an attack, and seemingly with a great reason of probability, tho to me, who could be but a very poor judge, it seemed quite the contrary, as I never before saw such great fires. About 12 o clock we were very near committing a most dreadful mistake. At that hour of the night, as I was going my rounds to observe if all the sentrys were alert on their different posts, one sentry challenged a party of men passing under his post, which was situated on the summit of a ravine or gully, and also heard carriages dragging in the same place, who answered friends, but on his demanding the countersign, they did not give it, and by their hesitating appeared at a loss; when the fellow would have instantly fired upon them according to

second lieutenant, April 1, 1756; first lieutenant, April 2, 1757; captain-lieutenant, January 1, 1759, and captain, December 7, 1763. He participated in the campaign of 1776. At this time he was in command of a park of artillery. He was created a major in the army, August 29, 1777, and was among the captured officers, but died a prisoner, on March 17, 1779. *Vide* Kane's Artillery List; British Army Lists, *in loco;* History American War (Stedman), vol. 1, p. 324; History Royal Artillery (Duncan), vol. 1, pp. 176, 244; Hadden's Journal and Orderly Books, pp. 91, 250, 317, *et passim.*

his orders, had not I come up at the time, on which I caused him to challenge them again; they not answering, I called to the piquet to turn out and stand to their arms, still lothe to fire. Just at the time, Captain Walker[156] came up in great haste and told me it was a party of his Artillery with two 12 pounders going to take post on Sugar loaf hill, and his orders to them was to cause it to be kept as secret as possible, which by their too strictly attending to, in not answering our challenge, which

[156] Ellis Walker was made a cadet at Woolwich, March 1, 1755, and became a lieutenant-fireworker in the Royal Artillery October 29th of the same year. He advanced rapidly in his profession, being commissioned as second lieutenant, April 2, 1757; first lieutenant, January 1, 1759, and captain-lieutenant, August 5, 1761. In this year, war again broke out between England and France, and Captain-Lieutenant Walker sailed on the expedition under Major-General Hodgson against Belle-Isle, in the Bay of Biscay, which, after several attacks and the loss of many men, was captured on the seventh of June, two months after the appearance of the fleet before Port Andre. Walker became a captain, January 1, 1771, and was in the campaign of 1776. In the campaign of 1777 he had charge of the artillery of General Fraser's brigade. He returned to England after the war, and appears on the army list as late as 1820, sixty-five years from the date of his first commission, being then a general, having received the following commissions, viz.: Of major in the army, June 7, 1782; lieutenant-colonel in the artillery, December 1, 1782; colonel in the army, October 12th, and in the artillery, November 1, 1793; major-general, February 26, 1795; colonel commanding, September 25, 1796; lieutenant-general, April 29, 1802, and general, January 1, 1812. *Vide* British Army Lists, *in loco;* Kane's Artillery List; History Royal Artillery (Duncan), vol. 1, pp. 224, 229; Hadden's Journal and Orderly Books, pp. 154, 159, 250–254, *et passim.*

could never be the intention of their orders, was near involving us all in a scene of the greatest confusion, which must have arose from our piquet firing on them. I own I was somewhat alarmed, still thinking the great fires in their lines a feint, and their coming to attack us with more security, imagineing we gave into that feint.

6th. At the first dawn of light, 3 deserters came in and informed that the enemy were retreating the other side of mount Independent. The general was, without loss of time, made acquainted with it, and the picquets of the army were ordered to march and take possession of the garrison and hoist the King's colors, which was immediately done, and the Grenadiers and Light Infantry were moved under the command [of] Brigadier General Frazier, if possible to come up with them with the greatest expedition. From the Fort, we were obliged to cross over a boom of boats between that place and Mount Independent,[157] which they, in their hurry, attempted to burn without effect, as the water quenched it, though in some places we could go but one abreast, and had they placed one gun, so as the grape shot [could]

[157] Mount Independence. It had received this name on the eighteenth of the previous July. On the morning of that day, just after the beating of the reveille, a courier reached the camp of the Americans, who were posted on this hill, with a copy of the Declaration of Independence, which caused great enthusiasm in the camp. A *feu-de-joie* of thirteen guns, in honor of the thirteen Confederated States, was fired, and the hill was named Mount Independence to commemorate the event.

take the range of the bridge — and which surprised us they did not, as two men could have fired it, and then made off — they would, in all probability, have destroyed all or most of us on the Boom. We continued the pursuit the whole day without any sort of provisions, and, indeed, I may say, we had very little or none, excepting one cow we happened to kill in the woods, which, without bread, was next to nothing among so many for two days after, a few hours rest at night in the woods was absolutely necessary

7th. After marching 4 or 5 miles we came up with above 2000 of the enemy strongly posted on the top of a high hill, with breast works before them, and great trees cut across to prevent our approach; but notwithstanding all these difficulties, they had no effect on the ardor always shewn by British Troops, who with the greatest steadiness and resolution, mounted the hill amidst showers of balls mixed with buck shot, which they plentifully bestowed amongst us. This being the first serious engagement I had ever been in, I must own, when we received orders to prime and load, which we had barely time to do before we received a heavy fire, the idea of perhaps a few moments conveying me before the presence of my Creator had its force; but a moment's thought partly reconciled it; and let not the reader imagine from that thought, that it was the cause of my deviating at the time from my duty as a soldier, as I have always made it a rule that a proper resignation to the will of the Divine Being is the certain foundation for true bravery; but to return, we no sooner gained the ascent, than there was such a fire sent amongst them as not easily conceived; they for some hours maintained their ground, and once endeavoured to surround us, but were soon made sensible of their inferiority, (altho we had not more than 850 men engaged, owing to our leaving the camp in so great a hurry, half of our companies being on guard and other duties), and were drove from their strong hold with great slaughter. They continued retreating from one post to another, the country affording them many. After killing and taking prisoners most of their principal officers, they were totally routed and defeated with great loss. The numbers they had killed cannot easily be ascertained, as a great many fell in the pursuit which continued some distance from the field of action. They had two Colonels killed, one taken prisoner, with many other officers killed and taken prisoners. The action lasted near three hours, before they attempted retreating, with great obstinacy. We had near two hundred killed and wounded. Major Grant,[158] 24th Regiment who

[158] Robert Grant was killed early on the morning of the seventh. Being on the advance-guard, he surprised a party of Americans while cooking their breakfasts and drove in their pickets. He had climbed upon a stump to get a view of the situation, when he was picked off by a sharpshooter. Anburey speaks of him as "a very gallant and brave officer." He had served on this same ground twenty years before with the Americans against the French, as a lieutenant. He received his captain's commission in 1762, and, two years later, was assigned to the command of a company in the

had the advanced guard was the first who fell. We had two other majors wounded, which were all we had with us. Lord Balcarres, Major to the Light Infantry, and Major Ackland of our Battallion, with 15 or 16 other officers killed & wounded, the fire being very heavy for the time. On Col^{l} Frances [159]

Fortieth Foot. His commission to a majority in the Twenty-fourth Foot he had enjoyed but two years, it having been dated March 5, 1775. *Vide* British Army Lists, *in loco;* Travels in the Interior Parts of America, vol. 1, p. 327; Naval and Military Memoirs (Beatson), vol. 6, p. 69.

[159] Ebenezer Francis was the son of Ebenezer Francis and Rachel Whitmore, and was born in Medford, December 22, 1743. After receiving a careful education, he moved to Beverly, where, in 1766, he was married to Judith Wood. He was commissioned by Congress as captain, July 1, 1775, and was the next year promoted to a colonelcy. By authority of Congress in January, 1777, he organized a regiment — the Eleventh Massachusetts — with which he marched to oppose the advance of Burgoyne. Anburey says that, "At the commencement of the action, the enemy were everywhere thrown into the greatest confusion, but being rallied by that brave officer, Colonel Francis, whose death, though an enemy, will ever be regretted by those who can feel for the loss of a gallant and brave man, the fight was renewed with the greatest degree of fierceness and obstinacy." So interesting is Anburey's relation of two incidents connected with Colonel Francis' death, that it may be pardonable to repeat them here, though they have been often before repeated. He says: "After the action was over and all firing had ceased for near two hours, upon the summit of the mountain I have already described, which had no ground anywhere that could command it, a number of officers were collected to read the papers taken out of the pocket-book of Colonel Francis, when Captain Shrimpton of the Sixty-second regiment, who had the papers in his hand, jumped up and fell, exclaiming 'he was severely wounded.' We all

falling, who was there second in command, they did not long stand. I saw him after he fell, and his appearance caused me to remark his figure, which was fine & even at that time made me regard him with attention. Our men got more plunder than they could carry, and great quantities of paper money which was not in the least regarded then, tho had we kept it, it would have been of service, as affairs turned out. I made prize of a pretty good mare. In general Burgoyne's letter to Government, he makes particular mention of the Grenadiers, who with the rest of the troops behaved with the greatest bravery. A party of Germans came up

---

heard the ball whiz by us, and turning to the place whence the report came, saw the smoke. As there was every reason to imagine the piece was fired from some tree, a party of men were instantly detached, but could find no person, the fellow, no doubt, as soon as he had fired, had slipped down and made his escape." The sequel is curious. After the surrender, while Anburey and some brother officers were prisoners at Cambridge, he says: "A few days since, walking out with some officers, we stopped at a house to purchase vegetables. Whilst the other officers were bargaining with the woman of the house, I observed an elderly woman sitting by the fire, who was continually eyeing us, and every now and then shedding a tear. Just as we were quitting the house she got up, and bursting into tears, said: 'Gentlemen, will you let a poor distracted woman speak a word to you before you go?' We, as you must naturally imagine, were all astonished, and upon inquiring what she wanted, with the most poignant grief and sobbing as if her heart was on the point of breaking, asked if any of us knew her son, who was killed at the battle of Huberton, a Colonel Francis. Several of us informed her, that we had seen him after he was dead. She then inquired about his pocket-book, and if

time enough also to share in the glory of the day, and the regular fire they gave at a critical time was of material service to us. After the engagement, we made sort of huts covered with the bark of trees for our wounded, who were in a very bad situation, as we had nothing to assist them till the return of an express which was sent to Ticonderoga for surgeons &c. &c. But here the reader will forgive my leaving that place, (& recollect the hurry we were ordered from it) without giving a description of that important fortress. Ticonderoga lies on the western shore, and only a few miles to the northward from the commencement of that narrow inlet

---

any of his papers were safe, as some related to his estates, and if any of the soldiers had got his watch; if she could but obtain that in remembrance of her dear, dear son, she should be happy. Captain Ferguson, of our regiment, who was of the party, told her, as to the colonel's papers and pocket-book he was fearful that they were either lost or destroyed, but pulling a watch from his fob, said 'There, good woman, if that can make you happy, take it and God bless you!' We were all much surprised, as unacquainted, as he had made a purchase of it from a drum boy. On seeing it, it is impossible to describe the joy and grief that was depicted in her countenance; I never in all my life beheld such a strength of passion. She kissed it, looked unutterable gratitude at Captain Ferguson, then kissed it again; her feelings were inexpressible. She knew not how to express or show them. She would repay his kindness by kindness, but could only sob her thanks. Our feelings were lifted up to an inexpressible height. We promised to search after the papers, and I believe, at that moment, could have hazarded life itself to procure them." *Vide* History of Medford (Brooks), Boston, 1855, pp. 194–196, 513; Travels in the Interior Parts of America, vol. 1, pp. 331, *et seq.*, 336; vol. 2, pp. 208–210.

by which the water from Lake George[160] is conveyed to Lake Champlain. Crown Point lies about a dozen miles farther north at the extremity of that inlet. The first of these places is situated on an angle of land, which is surrounded on three sides by water and that covered by rocks. A great part of the fourth side was covered by a deep morass; where that fails, the old French lines still continued as a defence on the north west quarter. The Americans strengthened these lines with additional works and a block house. They had other posts and works with block houses on the left towards Lake George. To the right of the French lines they had also two new block houses with other works. On the eastern shore of the inlet, and opposite to Ticonderoga, they had taken still more pains in fortifying a high circular hill, to which they gave the name of Mount Independent; on the summit of this, which is table land, they had erected a star fort inclosing a large square of barracks well fortified and supplied with artillery. The foot of the

[160] Champlain was the first European who penetrated the gloom of this wild region, and to the great lake he gave his own name. Four decades later, that self-sacrificing and heroic man, the Pere Jogues, with a wild band of savages, traversed painfully the dangerous trail into the Iroquois country, and on the eve of one of the many festival days of his church — that of *Corpus Christi* — he came to the bank of this romantic lake, and with religious fervor bestowed upon it the name of *St. Sacrament*. This name it retained for more than a century, when, in 1755, General Johnson changed its name to Lake George, in honor of the British king, and in evidence of his dominion over this region.

mountain, which on the west side projected into the water, was strongly intrenched to its edge, and the intrenchment well lined with heavy artillery. A battery about half way up the mount, sustained and covered these lower works.

The enemy, with their usual industry, had joined those two posts by a bridge of communication thrown over the inlet. This was like many other of their performances, a great and most laborious work. The bridge was supported on 12 sunken piers of very large timber planted at nearly equal distances; the spaces between these were filled with separate floats, each about 50 feet long & 12 feet wide, strongly fastened together with chains and rivets, and as effectually attached to the sunken pillars on the Lake Champlain side of the bridge. It was defended by a boom composed of very large pieces of timber fastened together by riveted bolts, and double chains made of iron an inch and an half square. Thus not only a communication was maintained between these two posts, but all access by water from the northern side was totally cut off. But to return, soon after the action, about 200 prisoners with a Col^l Hale[161] came in to us, and

[161] Nathan Hale was born in Hampstead, New Hampshire, September 23, 1743. His father, Moses Hale, removed to Rindge, a border settlement of his native State, when he was about seventeen years of age, and died two years later. Nathan, who had become a farmer and merchant, was married on January 28, 1766, to Abigail Grout of Lunenburg, Mass. From this date he appears as an active and influential

them we obliged to fell trees in order to make a breast work for our protection, not knowing but the enemy might be reinforced and come again to the attack. We were very badly off for provisions, and nothing but water to drink, and tho it rained very hard after the engagement (for the day before and while the action lasted, it was I may say burning hot weather), we had no covering to shelter us, our poor huts being a wretched security against the heavy rain [which] poured on us.

8th. About 11 o'clock the Germans under the command of General Reidzel marched from us towards

---

citizen of the town, and when, in 1774, a company of minute-men was formed in Rindge, he became its commander, and was commissioned by the Provincial Congress a captain of militia, June 2, 1774. "The people were nervously waiting for the clouds to break, or, if needs be, for hostilities to commence," when the news of the fight at Lexington reached them, and Hale, at the head of his command of fifty men, marched at once to Cambridge and tendered his services to Washington, which were accepted. He participated in the battle of Bunker Hill, and was commissioned as follows: June 6, 1775, major of Colonel Reed's regiment, the Third New Hampshire Foot; January 1, 1776, major of the Second New Hampshire Foot; November 8th, lieutenant-colonel of the second battalion of New Hampshire troops, and, April 2, 1777, colonel of the same. Hale was held a prisoner by the British, and died in captivity, September 23, 1780. Much discussion has been held over his conduct in surrendering, and different opinions still exist regarding it. These have been ably presented by Colonel Rogers, who, as usual, has not left much for those coming after him to say on the subject. *Vide* History of Rindge (Stearns), Boston, 1875, pp. 85–177, 541, *et passim;* Hadden's Journal and Orderly Books, Appendix 15.

Skeensborough,[162] (where it was supposed the main body of our army had by that time arrived) to our very great amazement, and which I believe arose from some little jealousy between the two Generals.[163] By this movement, we were left with about 600 fighting men, all our wounded to take care of, and a number of prisoners, in the midst of thick woods, and but little knowledge of the country around, also at too great

---

[162] Skenesborough was named for Captain Phillip Skene, a British officer, who was under General Abercrombie in the war with the French, in 1758. Becoming in that war familiar with the region of country about Lake Champlain, he obtained extensive grants of land in the vicinity, sold out his commission in the army, and began a settlement to which his own name became attached. He commonly went by the title of Colonel Skene. The following incident related by Palmer, is worthy repeating: "The history of the surprise of Skenesborough is embellished by an account of a singular discovery made there by the patriots. It is said that some of Herrick's men, while searching Skene's house, found the dead body of a female deposited in the cellar, where it had been preserved for many years. This was the body of Mrs. Skene, the deceased wife of the elder Skene, who was then in Europe, and who was then in receipt of an annuity which had been devised to his wife '*while she remained above ground.*'" *Vide* British Army Lists, *in loco;* Survey of Washington County, New York (Fitch); History of Lake Champlain (Palmer), p. 104.

[163] Digby is mistaken in this surmise. There was, as we well know, considerable jealousy between the German and English portions of the army; but in this instance, the advance of Riedesel was part of a plan which resulted in success to the British arms. Had not Riedesel marched to the support of the troops under Fraser, who had preceded him, it is probable that the Americans would have been the victors in the conflict which followed. *Vide* Memoirs of Major-General Riedesel, vol. 1, pp. 114–117.

a distance from our Army to expect any reinforcements; and by our scouts a certainty of the enemys main body, commanded by general St. Clair,[164] not above six miles from us at Castletown; tho we afterwards found that he, since his retreat from Ticonderoga with the army under his command, was compleatly dispirited and thought of nothing but getting farther from us. In this situation General Frazier

[164] Arthur St. Clair was born in Edinburgh, Scotland, in 1734, and accompanied Admiral Boscawen to America in 1759. He was a lieutenant under Wolfe, and was with that brave man when he fell on the Heights of Abraham. After the peace, he was for a short time in command of Fort Ligonier, in Pennsylvania; but, becoming enamored of a farmer's life, he left the army and assumed the duties of a civilian. The war of the Revolution found him surrounded by a rising family and with every thing about him to make life happy; but he felt that duty called him from the happiness of home-life, and he at once cast in his lot with the patriots. He was appointed a colonel in the Continental army, in January, 1776, and ordered to raise a regiment. Within six weeks he had gathered and equipped his regiment, and was on the march to Canada. He was appointed a major-general, in February, 1777, and on the fifth of June, was ordered to the command, which Gates had declined, of Ticonderoga. He arrived there on the twelfth and assumed command. He has perhaps been censured unjustly for his surrender of that post, but he certainly showed great want of foresight and knowledge in neglecting to fortify Mount Defiance, which commanded his works, and for not destroying his stores before retreating. Palmer says: "When Burgoyne placed his batteries upon the summit of Mount Defiance, he effectually destroyed all hopes of resistance on the part of the Americans. Their only alternative was to surrender or evacuate the works. By adopting the latter course, St. Clair saved the greater portion of his garrison and preserved the nucleus of an army, which ultimately baffled

was obliged to detach a capt's command with the prisoners to Ticonderoga that night, which weakened us a good deal, during which, it rained very hard, and about day break.

9th, we received orders to march towards Skeensborough. We were obliged to leave all our wounded behind us with a sub alternguard,[165] who received orders, if attacked to surrender and rely on the mercy

---

Burgoyne and compelled him to capitulate. At the moment, however, all classes of people were astonished at the unexpected result. 'It is an event of chagrin and surprise,' says Washington, 'not apprehended, nor within the compass of my reasoning.' The Council of Safety of New York signalized it as a measure 'highly reprehensible' and 'probably criminal.'" People asserted that Schuyler and St. Clair were bribed by Burgoyne, who fired *silver bullets* against the fort, which Schuyler and St. Clair gathered and divided. Even Thatcher, in his Military Journal, gravely denies the report. St. Clair suffered much from the severe criticisms passed upon his conduct, from which, indeed, he never recovered, although he remained in the service. In 1781 he was in command of the troops at Philadelphia for the protection of Congress, and, in 1781, was at the siege of Yorktown, and, after the surrender of Cornwallis, joined General Greene in the south. He was a member of Congress in 1786, and president of the House of Representatives in 1787. He was governor of the North-western Territory from 1788 until 1802. He died at Laurel Hill, Pennsylvania, August 31, 1818. *Vide* British Army Lists, *in loco;* History of Lake Champlain, p. 146; The Writings of George Washington (Sparks), vol. 4, p. 493.

[165] It was Sergeant Lamb who was left in charge of the wounded, and his account of his experiences is very interesting. He says: "It was a distressing sight to see the wounded men bleeding on the ground; and what made it more so, the rain came pouring down like a deluge upon us.

of the enemy. This was a severe order, but it could not be helped in our situation. We had about 30 miles to march and for the first six, we every minute expected to be attacked, and which I must say we were not so well provided for, as on the seventh, part of our ammunition being expended, and our force much reduced; this genl Frazier prudently foresaw, and though he wished to avoid it, yet by his orders, we marched in such a form as to sustain an action with as little loss as possible. By the knowledge of our Indians, we struck into a path that led us to Skeensborough, after a most fatigueing march thro rivers, swamps and a desolate wilderness. The enemy had evacuated that place some days before, not think-

---

And still, to add to the distress of the sufferers, there was nothing to dress their wounds, as the small medicine-box, which was filled with salve, was left behind with Surgeon Shelly and Captain Montgomery at the time of our movement up the hill. The poor fellows earnestly entreated me to tie up their wounds. Immediately I took off my shirt, tore it up, and, with the help of a soldier's wife (the only woman that was with us, and who kept closely by her husband's side during the engagement), made some bandages, stopped the bleeding of their wounds, and conveyed them in blankets to a small hut about two miles in our rear. Our regiment now marched back to Skeensborough, leaving me behind to attend the wounded, with a small guard for our protection. I was directed, that in case I should be either surrounded or overpowered by the Americans, to deliver a letter, which General Burgoyne gave me, to their commanding officer. Here I remained seven days with wounded men, expecting every moment to be taken prisoner." *Vide* Journal of Occurrences During the Late American War, p. 143, *et seq.*

ing it tenable, and retired to Fort Anne,[166] where they were pursued on the 8th by the 9th regiment, and defeated with great loss, though vastly superior in numbers, the 9th not having above 200 men engaged, which was, I think, risking a great deal to send so small a body, when the 47th and 53d regiments were then at Skeensborough, and might as well have supported them. Hereafter will be seen the consequences of detaching such small numbers from the main body of the army, as it has always been the wish of the Americans to avoid a general engagement, except they have a great superiority, and to surround small parties of ours, and get them into a wood, where the discipline of our Troops is not of such force. We had but one officer killed, and Captn Mt Gomery[167] wounded and taken prisoner, with the

---

[166] Fort Anne, named thus in honor of the queen, was built in 1709 by the expedition under Colonel Nicholson, which was organized against the French in that year. It was built of timber and surrounded by a palisade, and was intended only to protect the garrison against the fire of musketry.

[167] William Stone Montgomery was the only son of Sir William Montgomery of Dublin, and was born August 4, 1754. He entered the British military service at the age of seventeen, his first commission as cornet in the Ninth Dragoons being dated December 16, 1771. On March 20, 1775, he exchanged into the Forth-fourth Foot, at which date he received a lieutenant's commission, and January 9, 1776, was commissioned a captain in the Ninth Foot. He was wounded at Fort Ann on the ninth of July, and was taken prisoner. The report of General Burgoyne in the History of the Ninth Foot contains the following reference to Captain Montgomery: "An officer of great merit, was

surgeon. At Skeensborough, the whole army rendezvoused, where Divine service was performed, returning God thanks for our late successes, after which a feu-de-joi was fired, beginning from the ships and great guns, and answered by the small arms of the army. Captⁿ Gardner[168] went from that to England express

---

wounded early in the action, and was in the act of being dressed by the surgeon, when the regiment changed ground; being unable to help himself, he and the surgeon were taken prisoners." Lamb also speaks of the event as follows: "Captain Montgomery, son to Sir W. Montgomery, bart. of Dublin, was wounded in the leg and taken prisoner, with the surgeon who was dressing his wound, just before we retired up the hill. I very narrowly escaped myself, from being taken prisoner at that time, as I was just in the act of assisting the surgeon in dressing the captain's wound, when the enemy came pouring down upon us like a mighty torrent, in consequence whereof, I was the last man that ascended the hill." Although Captain Montgomery was wounded in the leg, and from Lamb's account it would appear not seriously, for some cause of which we are ignorant, he did not recover, as he is reported in Betham's Baronetage to have died in America at the age of nineteen years. This is an error as he was twenty-three years of age. *Vide* British Army Lists, *in loco;* Historical Record of the Ninth Foot; Journal of Occurrences During the Late American War, pp. 142, *et seq.;* Betham's Baronetage, vol. 5, p. 474; British Family Antiquity, vol. 7, p. 194.

[168] Henry Farington Gardner entered the army and was commissioned a cornet of the Sixteenth Light Dragoons — Burgoyne's regiment — on May 22, 1761. The next year he served with Burgoyne in his brilliant campaign in Portugal. On June 8, 1768, he was made a lieutenant, and on the 20th of July succeeding, adjutant of his regiment. He became captain, November 6, 1772, and accompanied Burgoyne to America as aide-de-camp. He reached Quebec on the twenty-second, five days after leaving Burgoyne's camp, and found

with the account of our successes since the takeing of the field. I shall here insert the General orders to the Army.

HEAD QUARTERS OF THE KING'S ARMY
AT SKEENSBOROUGH, 10th *July*, 1777.

On the 6th July, the enemy were dislodged from Ticonderoga by the mere countenance and activity of the Army, and driven on the same day beyond Skeensborough on the right, and to Hubberton on the left, with the loss of all their Artillery, and five of their armed vessels taken and blown up by the spirited conduct of Captain Carter of the Artillery, with a part of his Brigade of gun boats, a great quantity of amunition, provisions and stores of all sorts, and the greatest part of their baggage. On the 7th, Brigadier General Frazier, at the head of a little more than half the Advanced Corps, came up with near 2000 of the enemy strongly posted, attacked and defeated them with the loss on the enemy's part of their principal officers, 200 killed on the spot, a much larger number taken, and about 200 made prisoners. Major general Reidzel, with the advance guard con-

---

a vessel — the *Royal George* — in readiness to bear him to England. He sailed on the morning of the twenty-third, and reached England the twenty-second of August. He did not return to America. He was made major of the Light Dragoons, September 11, 1781, and attained the army rank of lieutenant-colonel, November 18, 1790, when his name disappears from the army lists. For a more particular account, reference may be had to Hadden's Journal and Orderly Books, p. 242.

sisting of the Chasseurs Company, and 40 grenadiers and Light Infantry, arrived in time to sustain General Frazier, and by his judicious orders and a spirited execution of them, obtained a share for himself and for his troops in the glory of the action.

On the 8th Lieutenant Col° Hill,[169] at the head of the 9th regiment, was attacked near Fort Anne by more than six times his number, and repulsed the enemy with great loss, after a continued fire of three hours. In consequence of this action, Fort Anne was burned and abandoned, and a party of this army is now in possession of the country on the other side. These rapid successes, after exciting a proper sense of what we owe to God, entitle the Troops in general to the warmest praise; and particular distinction is due to Brigdr Genl Frazier, who by his conduct and

[169] John Hill entered the Twenty-fourth Foot, March 15, 1747, as a lieutenant; became adjutant, August 25, 1756; captain-lieutenant, March 9, 1757; captain in the Thirteenth Foot, December 1, 1758; major, October 10, 1765; lieutenant-colonel in the army, September 11th, and of the Ninth Foot, November 10, 1775. Wilkinson's account of the action is somewhat different from this of Burgoyne. He says: "The corps which accompanied General Burgoyne to Skeenesborough, were spread out to keep up and increase the panic produced by the loss of Ticonderoga; the Ninth Regiment, under Lieutenant-Colonel Hill, was sent in pursuit of Colonel Long and his detachment, consisting of the invalids and convalescents, with his regiment about one hundred and fifty strong, making in the whole four or five hundred men. Colonel Long, finding himself pressed, advanced and met Lieutenant-Colonel Hill, and an action ensued, in which the British officer claimed the victory; but it is a fact that the Ninth Regiment had been beaten and was retreat-

bravery, supported by the same qualities in the officers, and soldiers under his command effected an exploit of material service to the King, and of signal honour to the profession of Arms. This Corps have the farther merit of having supported the fatigue of bad weather, without bread and without murmur. Divine service will be performed on Sunday morning at the head of the line, and at the head of the Advanced Corps, and at Sun set on the same day, a Feu de joy will be fired with cannon and small arms at Ticonderoga, Crown Point, the camp at Skeensborough and the camp at Castletown, and the post of Bremen's corps. Sunday, being a day set apart for rejoicing, all working parties are to be remitted, except such as may be necessary for the cleanliness of the camp. Should the weather be fair, the tents are to be struck at 5 in the evening, and the troops to form for the Feu-de-joy an hour before sun set in order

---

ing, and, but for the entire failure of Colonel Long's ammunition, the lieutenant-colonel must have been made prisoner, as well as Captain Montgomery of that regiment, who was wounded and left on the field, when, as General Burgoyne tells us, 'Colonel Hill found it necessary *to change his position* in the heat of action;' but, in truth, when his corps was obliged to retreat, and Colonel Long, for want of ammunition, could not pursue him." It was Lieutenant-Colonel Hill who secreted the colors of the Ninth Regiment in his baggage, contrary to the stipulated terms of surrender, and finally presented them to the king, being rewarded for the act by an appointment on the royal staff, with the army rank of colonel, May 16, 1782. *Vide* British Army Lists, *in loco;* Memoirs of My Own Times, vol. 1, p. 190; Historical Record of the Ninth Foot (Cannon), p. 32.

of Battle. After the Feu de joy the tents are to be pitched again. Captain Gardner is going to England; officers who have letters to send, to leave them at head quarters, before orderly time the 14 inst.

We were obliged to remain a long time at Skeensborough on account of getting horses and wagons from Canada; the Contractor of which, must have realized a great sum, each horse standing Government in about £15 if lost or killed in the service, exclusive of paying the driver, &c. &c., and the King's horses, (so called) from our great park of Artillery (for this part of the service was particularly attended to and the Brass train that was sent out on this expedition was perhaps the finest and probably the most excellently supplied as to officers and men that had ever been allotted to second the operations of an army which did not far exceed the second in number) amounted to a considerable number, indeed the expenses of Government were uncommonly great, as I have heard it computed that every man in our service through the whole of America, including loyalists, women and every other hanger on to the camps, &c, allowing for transports, service and a thousand other etceteras, stood government no less than five shillings a day for each person, and it was thought that at this time, and indeed through the whole war, above 100,000 were daily allowed rations, or provisions. Our heavy baggage &c was mostly then sent to stores appointed at Ticonderoga, as there was no longer any water carriage.

The mare I had made prize of was full able to carry as much baggage as I required, and saved me the expense of purchasing one for that purpose; and I suppose at our next moving we had almost as many horses as men, many officers having 3 or 4, tho it was strongly recommended by the general to take as little baggage as possible, which advice I followed, leaving my bedding behind and making use of a Buffalo skin, with a cloak to cover me at nights. That baggage we never after saw, it being through necessity or accident all destroyed. Many here were of opinion the general had not the least business in bringing the army to Skeensborough, after the precipitate flight of the enemy from Ticonderoga, and tho we had gained a complete victory over them, both at Fort Anne and Hubberton, yet no visible advantage was likely to flow from either except prooving the goodness of our troops at the expense of some brave men. They were also of opinion we should have pushed directly to Fort George,[170] where it was pretty certain they had above 400 wagons, 4 horses in each, with

[170] Fort George was erected in 1757, after the destruction of Fort William Henry and the massacre of a large portion of the garrison by the Indians under Montcalm. It was about a mile south-east of the site of Fort William Henry, which was not rebuilt after its destruction by the French, and stood on an eminence about half a mile from the lake. It is described by Hadden as follows: "*Fort George* which stands near the water at the end of the Lake (George) is a small square Fort faced with Masonry and contains Barracks for about a hundred Men secured from Cannon Shot. This Fort cou'd not stand a Siege, being commanded, & too con-

stores &c and not above 700 men, which would have enabled us to push forward, without waiting for horses from Canada to bring on our heavy artillery, which these discontented persons declared, was much greater than we had the smallest use for. Light field pieces were all we wanted exclusive of the heavy cannon, which was sent out to retake Quebec, in case the enemy had succeeded in their plans the winter of 1775. They also avered that after the late actions, the enemy were struck with such a panic, and so dispersed that by that movement we should not have given them time to collect; which our remaining at Skeensborough gave them full sufficient time to do; but I make not the least doubt, Gen Burgoyne had his proper reasons for so acting though contrary to the opinion of many. The country round Skeensborough swarms with rattle snakes, the bite of which is, I believe, mortal. They alarm the person near by their rattles, which providence has wisely ordered for that purpose, and from whence they take their name.

20. We were joined by a very numerous nation of Indians from the Ottawas, and who surpassed all others I had before seen in size and appearance

---

fined not to be soon reduced by Bombardment. The Rebels before they abandon'd it had endeavour'd to destroy the *defences* and actually blew up the Magazine in the side next the Water, which demolish'd that place." It served principally as a magazine of supplies, and was a connecting link between Ticonderoga and Fort Edward. It was named Fort George in honor of the Duke of York.

when assembled in Congress, which was well worth seeing, they being painted in their usual stile and decked out with feathers of a variety of birds, and skins of wild beasts slain by them, as trophys of their courage; and general Burgoyne, by the help of interpreters, informed them of the cause of the war &c. &c; when they by a groan expressed their approbation of what he had advanced, and the measures he intended to pursue, also their readiness in taking up the hatchet to assist the troops of their father, (King George) which was consented to by the general on a solemn promise from them of not scalping except the dead. They had brought a number of Indian toys, most of which we purchased from them, but were lost with our other baggage as will be hereafter seen.

About this time, a letter addressed to general Burgoyne, burlesqueing his proclamation, (see page 3[171]) appeared, which perhaps may entertain the reader.—

To John Burgoyne Esq Lieut General of his majesty's armies in America, Colonel of the Queens Regiment of Light dragoons, governor of Fort William in North Britain, one of the Representatives of the Commons of Great Britain and commanding an army and fleet employed on an expedition from Canada &c. &c. &c.

Most high, most mighty, most puissant, and sublime general! When the forces under your com-

---

171 *Vide ante* p. 189.

mand arrived at Quebec, in order to act in concert and upon a common principle with the numerous fleets & armies, which already display in every quarter of America the justice & mercy of your King; we, the reptils of America, were struck with unusual trepidation and astonishment. But what words can express the plentitude of our horror, when the Colonel of the Queen's regiment of light Dragoons advanced towards Ticonderoga? The mountains shook before thee, and the trees of the forest bowed their leafy heads. The vast Lakes of the north were chilled at thy presence, and the mighty cataracts stopped their tremendous career and were suspended in awe at thy approach. Judge then, oh! ineffable Governor of Fort William in North Britain, what must have been the terror, dismay, and despair that overspread this paltry continent of America, and us, its wretched inhabitants! Dark and dreary indeed, was the prospect before us, till like the sun in the Horizon, your most gracious and irresistible proclamation opened the doors of mercy and snatched us, as it were, from the jaws of annihilation. We foolishly thought, blind as we were, that your gracious master's fleets and armies were come to destroy us and our liberties; but we are happy in hearing from you, and who can doubt what you assert, that they were called forth for the sole purpose of restoring the rights of the Constitution to a froward, stubborn generation?

And it is for this, oh! sublime, Lieut Genl! that you have given yourself the trouble to cross the wide Atlantic, and with incredible fatigue traversed uncultivated wilds; and we ungratefully refused the profered blessing? To restore the rights of the Constitution, you have called together an amiable host of savages, and turned them loose to scalp our women and children and lay our country waste. This they have performed with their usual skill and clemency, and we remain insensible for the benefit, and unthankful for so much goodness. Our Congress have declared Independence, and our assemblies, as your highness justly observes, have most wickedly imprisoned the avowed friends of that power with which they are at war, and most profanely compelled those whose conscience will not permit them to fight, to pay some small part towards the expenses their country is at in supporting what is called a necessary and defensive war. If we go on thus in our obstinacy and ingratitude, what can we expect, but that you should in your anger give a stretch to the Indian forces under your direction, amounting to thousands, to overtake and destroy us, or what is ten times worse, that you should withdraw your fleets and armies and leave us to our own misery, without completing the benevolent task you have begun in restoring to us the rights of the Constitution.—We submit, we submit most puissant Col[l] of the Queen's regiment of Light Dragoons & Governor of Fort William in North Britain, we offer our heads to the scalping knife, and our bellies to the bayonet. Who can resist the terror of your arms? who can resist the force of your eloquence? The invitation you have made in the consciousness of christianity, your royal master's clemency, and the honour of soldiership we thankfully accept; The blood of the slain, the cries of the injured virgins and innocent children, and the never ceasing sighs and groans of starving wretches, now languishing in the gaols and prison ships of New York, call on us in vain, while your sublime proclamation is sounding in our ears. Forgive us, oh! our country! forgive us dear posterity! forgive us all ye foreign powers! who are anxiously watching our conduct in this important struggle, if we yield implicitly to the persuasive tongue of the most elegant Col[l] of the Queen's regiment of Light dragoons. Forbear then, thou magnanimous Lieut general, forbear to denounce vengeance against us! forbear to give a stretch to those restorers of the Constitution's rights, the Indians under your directions! let not the messengers of wrath & justice await us in the field, and devastation, famine and every concomitant horror, bar our return to the allegiance of a prince, who by his royal will, would deprive us of every blessing of life with all possible clemency. We are domestic; we are industrious; we are infirm and timid; we shall remain quietly at home and not remove our cattle, our corn, or forage, in hopes that you will come at the head of troops, in the full powers of health, discipline, and valour, and take charge of them for yourselves.— Behold our wives and daughters; our flocks and herds; our goods and chattels, are they not at the mercy of our lord and king, and of his lieutenant general, Member of the house of Commons and Governor of Fort William in North Britain?

SARATOGA, *July* 10[172]— 1777 A B. C D E &c.

July 24th. We marched from Skeensborough, and tho but 15 miles to Fort Anne, were two days going it; as the enemy had felled large trees over the river, which there turned so narrow, as not to allow more than one battow abreast, from whence we were obliged to cut a road through the wood, which was attended with great fatigue and labour, for our wagons and artillery. Our heavy cannon went over Lake George, as it was impossible to bring them [over] the road we made, and were to join us near Fort Edward, in case the Enemy were to stand us at that place, it being a good road for cannon and about 16 miles.—Fort Anne is a place of no great strength, having only a block house, which though strong against small arms is not proof against cannon. We saw

[172] On the same day General Burgoyne issued a proclamation to the inhabitants of Castleton and neighboring towns, requesting them "to send deputies, consisting of 10 persons or more from each township, to meet Col. Skeene at Castleton July 15th at 10, A. M., who will give further encouragement to those who complied with the terms of my late manifesto & conditions upon which persons and property of the disobedient may be spared." In reply, General Schuyler, on the 13th issued a counter-proclamation, forbidding these towns to send delegates to meet Burgoyne's commissioner under pain of punishment. *Vide* Collections New Hampshire Historical Society, vol. 2, pp. 148–150.

many of their dead unburied, since the action of the 8th, which caused a violent stench. One officer of the 9th regiment, Lieu^{t} Westrop[173] was then unburied, and from the smell we could only cover him with leaves. At that action, the 9th took their colours, which were intended as a present to their Colonel Lord Ligonier,[174] They were very handsome, a flag

---

173 Richard Westropp had been in the army but a short time, having received his commission of ensign in the Ninth Foot on March 14, 1772, and of lieutenant, January 1, 1774. His regiment took an active part in the campaign of '76, but he passed through it unscathed to meet his fate at Fort Anne. Sergeant Lamb, who saw him fall, says that he was by his side when he was shot through the heart. *Vide* British Army Lists, *in loco;* Journal of Occurrences During the Late American War, p. 143.

174 Edward Ligonier was the son of Colonel Francis Ligonier, who died after the battle of Falkirk, having risen from a bed of sickness to participate in the battle. He was commissioned captain and lieutenant-colonel in the First Foot, August 15, 1759, at which time his regiment was in America, having participated in the successful siege of Louisburg the previous year. The scene of Burgoyne's campaign was familiar to him, as it was upon Lakes George and Champlain that the First Regiment had operated against the French, nearly twenty years before the date here given by Digby. In 1760 Ligonier was in the trying campaign against the Cherokees, and when that was ended, participated in the expedition against Havana in 1762. The hardships in this campaign were very great we are told. Ligonier returned to England in 1763, and on April 21st of that year, was appointed aide de-camp to the king, with the army rank of colonel. Having succeeded to the Irish title of Viscount Ligonier of Clonmel, in 1770, after the death of his uncle, the field marshal, Earl Ligonier, he was made colonel of the Ninth Foot, August 8th, in the following year, shortly after which time he was advanced to the dignity of Earl Ligonier.

of the United States, 13 stripes alternate red and white, [with thirteen stars] in a blue field representing a new constellation. In the evening, our Indians brought in two scalps, one of them an officer's which they danced about in their usual manner. Indeed, the cruelties committed by them, were too shocking to relate, particularly the melancholy catastrophe of the unfortunate Miss McCrea,[175] which affected the general and the whole army with the sincerest regret

---

He became major-general in the army, September 29, 1775, and August 29, 1777, lieutenant-general. He died in 1782, when his titles became extinct. *Vide* British Army Lists, *in loco;* Historical Record of the First Foot, pp. 136–148; Ibid., Ninth Foot, p. 123.

[175] The story of Jane McCrea has been often related, sometimes in most exaggerated forms; even her life has been elaborately written. The generally accepted version is that David Jones, a Tory officer in Burgoyne's army, sent two Indians, one of whom was called Wyandot Panther, to conduct her to the British camp, where she was to be married, and that on the way thither, the Indians disagreeing with respect to a division of the "barrel of rum" to be paid them for their services, Wyandot Panther killed her with a tomahawk. This version is supported by Wilson in his life of Miss McCrea, whom he says was killed by le Loúp, as well as by Neilson, who relates that the Indians exhibited their scalps at a house which they called at, and said that they "had killed Jenny." They had with them Mrs. McNeil — who, it seems, was a cousin of General Fraser — in a state of nudity, and so delivered her to the general, greatly to his embarrassment as well as that of Mrs. McNeil, as his wardrobe was not provided with any thing suitable for a lady to wear. Neilson, commenting upon their treatment of Mrs. McNeil, says: "The inducement to strip and plunder Mrs. McNeil was sufficient to account for the butchery of Miss McCrea." And so it probably was, for the Indians were not

and concern for her untimely fate. This young lady was about 18, had a pleasing person, her family were loyal to the King, and she engaged to be married to a provincial officer, in our Army, before the war broke out. Our Indians, (I may well now call

---

particular whom they murdered, and killed Tories as well as Americans; indeed, the Tories of Argyle flocked to Burgoyne for protection against his savage allies. But we have proof that after all, in this case the Indians were innocent of murder, and that Miss McCrea was killed unintentionally by the Americans. Let us examine this evidence. Miss McCrea had been invited by David Jones to visit the British camp and accompany the several ladies there in an excursion on Lake George. He was troubled about her exposure to danger from the Indians, and intended to press her to marry him at once, that he might be better able to afford her protection. Mrs. McNeil and she were just about to embark under the charge of Lieutenant Palmer and a few soldiers, when, knowing that the Americans were in the vicinity, the lieutenant and his men left them for a few minutes to reconnoitre. While the British soldiers were absent, some of their Indian allies came up and seized Mrs. McNeil and Miss McCrea, and placing the latter upon a horse, hurried away, pursued by a party of Americans, who were close at hand. The Americans fired upon the flying Indians, one of whom, Wyandot Panther, was leading the horse upon which Miss McCrea sat. Mrs. McNeil became separated from Miss McCrea, and did not witness her death, but said afterward that the Americans fired so high as not to injure the Indians, who were on foot. Wyandot Panther, when examined by Burgoyne, affirmed that Miss McCrea was killed by the Americans, who were pursuing him; and General Fraser, at a *post-mortem* investigation, gave it as his opinion that she was thus killed by the Americans "aiming too high, when the mark was on elevated ground, as had occurred at Bunker's (Breed's) hill." But, in addition to this, we now have more positive proof in the testimony of General Morgan Lewis, to the effect that she had three distinct gunshot

them Savages) were detached on scouting parties, both in our front and on our flanks, and came to the house where she resided; but the scene is too tragic for my pen. She fell a sacrifice to the savage passions of these blood thirsty monsters, for the particulars of which, I shall refer the reader to General Burgoyne's letter, dated 3rd September, to General Gates, which he will find on page 263, with his manner of acting on that melancholy occasion. I make no doubt, but the censorious world, who seldom judge but by outward appearances, will be apt to censure Gen Burgoyne for the cruelties committed by his Indians, and imagine he countenanced them in so acting. On the contrary, I am pretty certain it was always against his desire to give any assistance to the savages. The orders from Lord George Germaine [176]

wounds upon her body, and from the additional fact that when her body was removed, a few years ago, to a new burial place, no mark of a tomahawk or injury of any kind was found upon the skull. We may, therefore, look upon the familiar picture of the two savages holding an unattractive-looking female, who does not appear at all disturbed at the sight of the tomahawk about to descend upon her head, as fictitious. *Vide* The Life of Jane McCrea (Wilson), New York, 1853; Burgoyne's Campaign and St. Leger's Expedition, pp. 302–313; Neilson's Account of Burgoyne's Campaign, pp. 68–79; Burgoyne's Orderly Book, pp. 187, 189; Pictorial Field-Book of the Revolution (Lossing), vol. 1, pp. 48, 96, 99, *et passim;* Memoirs of My Own Times, vol. 1, p. 230, *et seq.;* Travels in the Interior Parts of America, vol. 1, pp. 369–372; Journal of Occurrences During the Late American War, pp. 155–157.

[176] Lord George Germaine was the minister for American affairs, which he appears to have managed disgracefully. He

to General Carlton, on Lieutenant General Burgoyne's taking the command of the Army were as follows. "As this plan cannot be advantageously executed without the assistance of Canadians and Indians, his majesty strongly recommends it to your care, to furnish him with good and sufficient bodies of these men, and I am happy in knowing that your influence among them is so great, that there can be no room to apprehend you will find it difficult to fulfill his majesty's intentions." General Burgoyne, afterwards says in parliament: "As to the Indian alliance, he had always at best considered it as a necessary evil. He determined to go to the soldiers of the State, not the executioners. He had been obliged to run a race with the congress in

---

was stiff and imperious, unscrupulous in the gratification of personal resentments, and had been cashiered for cowardice some years before. In Fitzmaurice's Life of William, Earl of Shelburne, we are told that he was a man possessed of "intolerable meanness and love of corruption," and further, that "he wanted judgment in all great affairs, and he wanted heart on all great occasions," was "violent, sanguine and overbearing in his first conception and setting out of plans, but easily checked, and liable to sink into an excess of despondency upon the least reverse without any sort of resource." Fox delighted to compare him to Dr. Sangrado. "For two years," said he, "that a certain noble lord has presided over American affairs, the most violent, scalping, tomahawk measures have been pursued Bleeding has been his only prescription. If a people deprived of their ancient rights are grown tumultuous — bleed them! if they are attacked with a spirit of insurrection — bleed them! if their fever should rise into rebellion — bleed them! cries this state physician; more blood! more blood! still more blood!"

securing the alliance of the Indians. They courted and tempted them with presents, as well as the British. He had in more instances than one controled the Indians &c."

28th. We marched from Fort Anne, but could only proceed about 6 miles, the road being broke up by the enemy and large trees felled across it, taking up a long time to remove them for our 6 pounders, which were the heavyest guns with us. We halted at night on an eminence, and were greatly distressed for water, no river being near, and a report that the enemy had poisoned a spring at a small distance; but it was false, as our surgion tried an experiment on the water and found it good.

After relating how Dr. Sangrado was remonstrated with for the death of so many patients, he gave the doctor's reply, to the effect that, having written a book on the efficacy of such practice, though every patient should die, he must continue for the credit of his book. He was detested by his associates and by the generals who commanded in America. Temple Luttrell abused him in Parliament, without eliciting a reply. He said on one occasion, while Germaine was present, referring to the Burgoyne campaign, "flight was the only safety that remained for the royal army, and he saw one who had set the example in Germany and was fit to lead them on such an occasion;" and Wilkes said: "The noble Lord might conquer America, but he believed it would not be in Germany." This was in allusion to Germaine's disgraceful conduct as an officer in Germany, for which he was dismissed the service. *Vide* The Pictorial History of England (Knight), London, 1841, vol. 1, p. 325; A History of England (Adolphus), London, 1841, vol. 2, p. 496; Life of William, Earl of Shelburne, London, vol. 1, pp. 357–359; Journal of the Reign of George the Third (Walpole), London, 1859, pp. 26, 34.

29th. Moved about 6 or 7 miles farther, and had the same trouble of clearing the road, as the day before. We encamped within a mile of Fort Edward, on the banks of the Hudson river. It was a very good post, and we expected it would have been disputed. There, the road from Fort George then in our possession joined us, and being in possession of that post secured our heavy guns &c coming from Fort George. It was supposed we should not go much farther without them. Our tents were pitched in a large field of as fine wheat as I ever saw, which in a few minutes was all trampled down. Such must ever be the wretched situation of a Country, the seat of war. The potatoes were scarce fit to dig up, yet were torn out of the ground without thinking in the least of the owner.

30th. We moved on farther to a rising ground about a mile south of Fort Edward, and encamped on a beautiful situation from whence you saw the most romantic prospect of the Hudson's river; intersperced with many small islands, and the encampment of the line about 2 miles in our rear. There is a fine plain about the Fort, which appeared doubly pleasing to us, who were so long before buried in woods. On the whole, the country thereabout wore a very different appearance from any we had seen since our leaving Canada, and from that Fort to Albany, about 46 miles, the land improves much, and no doubt in a little time will be thickly settled. The enemy were then encamped about 4 miles from us; but it was not thought they intended to make a stand. At this time a letter appeared addressed to General Burgoyne, I believe found nailed to a tree. There was no name signed, yet it was thought — (how true heaven only knows) — to be wrote by brigadier general Arnold, who opposed our fleet the preceding year on Lake Champlain, and was then second in command under General Gates. He first tells him, not to be too much elated on his rapid progress, as all he had as yet gained was an uncultivated desert, and concludes his letter by desiring him to beware of crossing the Hudson's river, making use of that memorable saying, "Thus far shalt thou go and no farther." We heard by some intelligence from the enemy's camp, that Genl^s St Clair & Schyler[177] were ordered before a com-

[177] Phillip Schuyler was born at Albany on November 22, 1733. His grandfather and father were men of character and wealth. He inherited large estates under the law of primogeniture, but generously divided them with his brothers and sisters. His mother was a woman of unusual attainments, and gave her son a thorough training. His first service was against the French and Indians in 1755. He was with Lord George Howe, with whom he was a great favorite, in the attack on Ticonderoga, in which attack Howe fell, and to Schuyler was assigned the duty of conveying the body of the young nobleman, who was the idol of his companions-in-arms, to Albany. He was a delegate to the Continental Congress in May, 1775, and in June was appointed a major-general. He was assigned to the command of the army in the province of New York, but owing to illness, was obliged to relinquish it to Montgomery. He was most efficient in putting the northern army into a condition of order and discipline; but while engaged in his

mittee of their congress, to account for their reasons of evacuating Ticonderoga. As yet, the fickle Goddess Fortune had smiled upon our arms, and crowned our wishes with every kind of success, which might easyly be seen from the great spirits the Army in general were in; and the most sanguine hopes of conquest, victory &c. &c. were formed of crowning the campaign with, from the general down to the private soldier; but alas! this life is a constant rota-

---

duties, was, in March, 1777, superseded by Gates, owing to the persistent efforts of enemies. He was restored to his command again two months later, and at once proceeded with great vigor to put the fortifications in his department into a thorough state of defense, and his army into a condition to meet the advancing Burgoyne. The fall of Ticonderoga and his own retreat from Fort Edward, gave his opponents an opportunity to effect his displacement, and in August he was again superseded by Gates. His magnanimity and noble patriotism in continuing to devote his wealth and services to the cause of his country, put his enemies to shame. At a court of inquiry, called at his request, he was rewarded by a full acquittal. After this, although pressed by Washington, he refused military command, but rendered efficient aid to the cause. The Baroness Riedesel gives us a glimpse of the noble character of the man, in her interesting letters. She had passed through the terrible scenes which preceded the surrender of Burgoyne, and with her children, approached, with no little fear, the camp of the Americans. What was her surprise and delight to be received with the greatest kindness. We will quote her own description of the scene: "When I approached the tents, a noble-looking man came toward me, took the children out of the wagon, embraced and kissed them, and then, with tears in his eyes, helped me also to alight. 'You tremble,' said he to me; 'fear nothing.' 'No,' replied I, 'for you are so kind, and have been so tender toward my children, that it has inspired me with courage.' He then led me to the

tion of changes; and the man, who forms the smallest hopes, has generally the greatest chance of happiness. In the evening, our Indians had a skirmish with an advance party of the enemy. It was a heavy fire for about half an hour, when the latter fled with loss. During our stay there, many of the country people came to us for protection. Those are styled by the enemy torys, and greatly persecuted if taken after fighting against them.[178]

---

tent of General Gates, with whom I found Generals Burgoyne and Phillips. Burgoyne said to me: 'You may now dismiss all your apprehensions, for your sufferings are at an end.' All the generals remained to dine with General Gates. The man who had received me so kindly came up and said to me: 'It may be embarrassing to you to dine with all these gentlemen; come now with your children into my tent, where I will give you, it is true, but a frugal meal, but one that will be accompanied by the best of wishes.' 'You are certainly,' answered I, 'a husband and a father, since you show me so much kindness.' I then learned that he was the American General Schuyler. The day after this we arrived at Albany, where we had so often longed to be. But we came not as we supposed we should, as victors! We were, nevertheless, received in the most friendly manner by the good General Schuyler, and by his wife and daughters, who showed us the most marked courtesy, as, also, General Burgoyne, although he had — without any necessity it was said — caused their magnificently-built houses to be burned." After the adoption of the Constitution, General Schuyler represented his State as a senator, and maintained a high place in the esteem of the American people. His death occurred at Albany, November 18, 1804.

[178] This is a moderate statement of the fact. Not only were they killed and banished, but Sabine tells us that the Whigs, after the peace, "Instead of repealing the proscription and banishment acts, as justice and good policy required, they

August 9th. We moved on to Fort Miller[179] 9 miles nearer Albany, and which the enemy evacuated some days before. What I could see and learn is, that few of the forts situated on the Hudson River in that part, are proof against cannon; they being built during the last war in order to defend stores and amunition from the inroads of the Indians, who frequently came down in large numbers, plundering and scalping our first settlers residing contiguous

---

manifested a spirit to place the humbled and unhappy loyalists beyond the pale of human sympathy. A discrimination between the conscientious and pure, and the unprincipled and corrupt, was not, perhaps, possible during the struggle; but, hostilities at an end, *mere loyalty should have been forgiven.*" And we are further told that, "throughout this contest, and amidst all those qualities displayed by the Americans, many of those qualities being entitled to high respect and commendation, there was none certainly less amiable than their merciless rancor against those among them who adhered to the royal side." The most severe laws were passed against them, one of which, enacted by the State of New York, declared that "any person being an adherent to the king of Great Britain should be guilty of treason and suffer death." *Vide* Loyalists of the American Revolution (Sabine), Boston, 1864, vol. 1, p. 88; History of England (Mahon), vol. 6, p. 127; History of the American Revolution (Ramsay), vol. 1, p. 295; The Loyalists of America and Their Times (Ryerson), Toronto, 1880, vol. 11, pp. 5, 78, *et passim.*

179 This was one of the forts which was noted during the old French wars, and witnessed the achievements of the troops of Sir William Johnson and Baron Dieskau. The place is frequently denominated in writings relating to the campaign of Burgoyne as Duer's House, from the fact that the house of Judge Duer stood near it, and was occupied by Burgoyne as his head-quarters.

to that river, and were full sufficient to withstand any attack made with small arms. I then heard the very disagreeable news of our regiment (53^{d}) being ordered back to garrison Ticonderoga and Fort George. I was much concerned at it, as in all probability I should not see them again during the war, which must be attended with many inconveniences; but as it was their tour of duty, there was no putting it over tho ever so disagreeable, which it certainly was to every officer in the regiment. We had many sick at this time of fevers & agues so common to the climate. Cap. Wight,[180] to whose company I belonged, was so ill as not to be able to go on with us, and many other officers were seized with those disorders, as the heats then were very severe and violent, particularly in a camp. All sorts of meat were tainted in a very short time, and the stench very prejudicial, and cleanlyness about our camp was a great consideration towards the health of

---

[180] John Wright entered the Fifty-third Foot upon its formation, in 1756, as an ensign, and on January 31, 1758, was commissioned a lieutenant. Throughout the seven years' war, and until 1768, his regiment was stationed at the important fortress of Gibraltar. It was then ordered to Ireland, and on April 13th of that year Lieutenant Wright was promoted to a captaincy. From this time until its embarkation for America, the Fifty-third remained in Ireland. Captain Wright recovered of the illness mentioned by Digby, and was killed at the battle of Stillwater on October 7th. *Vide* British Army Lists, *in loco;* Historical Record of the Fifty-third Foot, p. 2, *et seq.;* Journal of Occurrences During the Late American War, p. 176.

the army. I there received a letter from an officer of ours, who had been wounded at Hubberton, 7th July, in which he informed me that before they were removed to Ticonderoga, the wolves came down in numbers from the mountains to devour the dead, and even some that were in a kind of manner buried, they tore out of the earth; the great stench thro the country being the cause of their coming down, and was enough to have caused a plague.—

10. An express came thro the woods from Genl Clinton,[181] who was supposed to be coming up the river from New York, but did not hear what it

---

[181] Sir Henry Clinton was the son of George Clinton, who was the governor of New York in 1743, and grandson of Francis Fiennes Clinton, the sixth earl of Lincoln. His ancestors were at an early date interested in the colonization of America. He entered the army in 1758 as a captain of the Guards, and saw active service in the seven years' war, rising rapidly by promotion to the rank of major-general, which position he occupied when ordered to America in 1775. In the battle of Bunker Hill, and subsequently that of Long Island, he took a distinguished part. He was severely, and probably justly criticised for his weak efforts in behalf of Burgoyne; but the chief blame fell upon Howe, the commander-in-chief, and upon his recall, Clinton superseded him in the chief command. Being forced to evacuate Philadelphia by the Americans, he headed an expedition against Charleston, South Carolina, which he captured in 1779. The next year Arnold, who had done so much for the American cause, becoming disaffected, joined him, and under his direction aided in an expedition against his former friends, but with little effect. Arnold on this expedition was accompanied by Colonels Dundas and Simcoe, to whom Clinton had secretly given joint commissions, "authorizing them, if they suspected Arnold of sinister in-

contained. Our heavy guns were then shortly expected from Fort George, as moving them was very tedious; a 24 pounder taking many horses to draw it. We had a carrying place to bring over our battows, which was attended with great fatigue and trouble, and were also obliged to make rafts or scows to convey heavy stores &c down the river Hudson.

---

tent, to supersede him and put him in arrest." Great inducements were offered to recruits for the king's forces in New York, as by the following copy of an advertisement will appear:

"ALL ASPIRING HEROES.
Have now an opportunity of distinguishing themselves by joining
THE QUEEN'S RANGER HUZZAS
Commanded by
LIEUTENANT-COLONEL SIMCOE,

Any spirited young man will receive every encouragement, be immediately mounted on an elegant horse, and furnished with clothing, accoutrements &c. to the amount of FORTY GUINEAS, by applying to CORNET SPENCER, at his quarters, No. 1033 Water Street, or his rendezvous, HEWITTS TAVERN near the COFFEE HOUSE, and the defeat at BRANDYWINE, on GOLDEN HILL.

☞ *Whoever brings a Recruit shall instantly receive TWO* GUINEAS. *Vivant Rex et Regina —*"

Clinton's efforts, however, were not successful, and he was superseded by Sir Guy Carleton after the surrender of Cornwallis, whom he had failed to relieve. On his return to England he wrote "A Narrative" of his conduct in America in reply to the observations upon it by Lord Cornwallis, and later, "Observations on Stedman's History of the American War." He was appointed governor of Gibraltar in 1795, but, shortly after his arrival there, died on the 22d of December. *Vide* British Army Lists; Biographical Dictionary (Blake), New York, *in loco;* History of New York (Dunlap), vol. II, p. 201; Journal of Occurrences During the Late American War, pp. 293–333, *et passim;* History of the War of the Independence (Botta), Philadelphia, 1820, vol. 1, pp. 306, 315; vol. 2, pp. 24–26, 307, 370, *et passim;* History of the Siege of Boston (Frothingham), p. 148.

About this time, Cornet Grant[182] of Genl Burgoyne's regm't of Light Dragoons, the 16th, made an unsuccessful attempt to go express to Gen Clinton, and was obliged to return thro the woods, running many risques of falling into their hands, to the very great dissatisfaction of Gen Burgoyne.

11th. A large detachment of German troops consisting of Gen Reidzels dragoons who came dismounted from Germany, a body of Rangers, Indians & voluntiers, with 4 pieces of cannon, went from our camp on a secret expedition; their route was not publicly known, but supposed for to take a large store of provisions belonging to the enemy at Bennington, and also horses to mount the dragoons. During the night there was a most violent storm of Thunder, Lightening, wind & rain. It succeeded a very hot day, and was so severe that the men could not remain in their tents, as the rain poured quite through them. Ours stood it better; our horses tore down the small sheds formed to keep the heat of the sun from them, being so much frightened. About day break it cleared up, and a great heat followed, which soon dried all our cloths &c.

---

[182] James Grant was commissioned a cornet in the Sixteenth Light Dragoons on December 27, 1775, and was taken prisoner, as will be seen farther on in this journal. He appears upon the list of '79, and a man of the same name was commissioned an ensign in the Twenty-seventh Foot on July 7th of that year, and is continued on the army list to 1784; but, owing to uncertainty as to his identity with the object of our search, it is unprofitable to follow his career.

13th. We moved 3 miles and encamped at a post called Batten Kill, a strong situation bordering on the river Hudson, intended for the army to cross over. Our corps crossed the river with a good deal of trouble, and encamped about 2 miles west of it. The troops crossed in battows, which was very tedious, as we had but few. About a mile below, the horses and baggage forded it with some difficulty, the water being high from a great fall of rain, which came on during the preceding night, in consequence of which, the troops were put into barracs built there for 1000 men by Gen Schyler. His house was a small way in our front, and the best we had as yet seen in that part, and much superior to many gentleman's houses in Canada. It was intended we should move the next day to an eminence a little distance, which was reckoned a good post, and where there was plenty of forage for the army.

16th. Our orders for marching were countermanded and others given out for us, to move at 3 o'clock next morning. As I was upon no particular duty, I rode back to the line, who, with Gen Burgoyne were at Fort Miller, and in the evening returned to our camp, crossing over our new bridge of boats, which was almost then finished. At night I mounted an advanced picquet, and had orders to return to camp next morning at Revally Beating, day break. Nothing extraordinary passed during the night, every thing quiet about our post, and on going to return in the morning received orders,— the 17th — to remain, as the corps was not to move that day, and to keep a very sharp look out; on which we naturally supposed something extraordinary had happened. Soon after an engineer came out to us with a number of men to throw up a breast work. Still it looked suspicious; but we were soon made acquainted with the melancholy report, that the detachment, which marched from us on the 11th were all cut to pieces by the enemy at Bennington, their force being much superior. Our 4 pieces of cannon were taken, two 6 pounders & two 3 pounders. I fear the officer who commanded, a German, took post in a bad situation, and was surrounded by the enemy after expending all his amunition. Our Albany voluntiers behaved with great bravery; but were not seconded by the Germans and Savages; and it was much regretted British were not sent in their place.[183] The express also informed

---

[183] This remark of Digby plainly reveals the jealousy which existed on the part of the English toward their German allies — a jealousy which was inexcusable when the relations of both to the war are regarded. That the German auxiliaries performed their duty faithfully, patiently and bravely cannot be questioned; indeed, when we reflect upon all the facts of the case, we can but admire the character which they displayed. It was a piece of great folly on the part of the English general in assigning men equipped as they were, and ignorant of the language, to such a service. Their equipment was ridiculously cumbersome, and rendered them incapable of making any quick movement. But an important fact, related in General Riedesel's Memoirs, should be stated, which shows how they were deceived by supposed loyalists, whom Baum allowed to gather on his

[us] that the enemy was greatly elated in consequence of the above, and were upon the move; but where he could not tell. Our situation was not the best, as from the great fall of rain our bridge was near giving way by the flood, which almost totally cut off our communication with Genl Burgoyne and the line. Our post was also far from a good one, being surrounded and commanded by hills around — Gen Frazier not intending to remain there above a night or two. About 4 in the evening our picquet

---

flanks: "Toward nine o'clock, on the morning of the 16th, small bodies of armed men made their appearance from different directions. These men were mostly in their shirt-sleeves. They did not act as if they intended to make an attack; and Baum, being told by the provincial, who had joined his army on the line of march, that they were all loyalists and would make common cause with him, suffered them to encamp on his side and rear. Shortly after another force of the rebels arrived and attacked his rear. This was the signal for the seeming loyalists, who had encamped on the side and rear of the army, to attack the Germans; and the result was that Baum suddenly found himself cut off from all his detached posts. For over two hours he withstood the sallies and fire of the enemy — his dragoons, to a man, fighting like heroes — but at last, his ammunition being used up, and no reinforcements arriving, he was obliged to succumb to superior numbers and retreat. The enemy seemed to spring out of the ground; indeed, they were estimated at between four and five thousand men. Twice the brave dragoons succeeded in breaking a road through the enemy's ranks; for, upon their ammunition giving out, Baum ordered that they should hang their carbines over their shoulders and trust to their swords. But bravery was now in vain; and the heroic leader, himself severely wounded, was forced to surrender with his dragoons. Meanwhile the Indians and Provincials had taken flight, and sought safety

was relieved by Lord Balcarres and the Battallion of light Infantry, who were to lie on their arms there during the night. Our orders were, to be in readiness to recross the river next morning at day break, and during the night, to remain accoutred and ready to turn out at a moments warning. The rain still continued.

18. Our bridge was carried down by the water, and to complete all, the ford where our horses crossed over the 15th was impassable — The river

---

in the forest." Thus nobly did these poor Germans fight in a cause in which they had no interest, impelled by loyalty to their prince and zeal to uphold the honor of German soldiers. They were in a strange land, and fighting with and for men whose language they did not understand, and who affected superiority over them. Their position was, indeed, a trying one; and that they realized it, may be seen in the following extract from Anburey's letters: "The Germans, to the number of twenty or thirty at a time, will in their conversations relate to each other that they are sure they shall not live to see home again, and are certain that they shall very soon die; would you believe it, after this they mope and pine about, haunted with the idea that,

> 'Nor wives, nor children, shall they more behold,
> Nor friends, nor sacred home.'

Nor can any medicine or advice you can give them divert this settled superstition, which they as surely die martyrs to as ever it infects them. Thus it is that men, who have faced the dangers of battle and of shipwreck without fear (for they are certainly as brave as any soldiers in the world) are taken off, a score at a time, by a mere phantom of their own brain. This is a circumstance well known to every one in the army." *Vide* Memoirs of Major-General Riedesel, vol. 1, p. 130, *et seq.;* Travels Through the Interior Parts of America, vol. 1, p. 161, *et seq.*

being swelled so much. We had a few battows and a large scow for our cannon; so began to cross; but it was a most tedious piece of work, and late at night before every thing was over — when we lay on our arms — not as yet being exact as to the motions of the enemy.

19. We encamped on our former strong post Batten Kill. On this occasion, the Indians in Congress with Mr Luc[184] at their head, with an old

[184] Luc de Chapt de la Corne Saint-Luc was the son of Jean-Louis de la Corne, who achieved a considerable military reputation in Canada. St. Luc for many years had served with the Indians against the English, and had been regarded by them as a dangerous and cruel enemy. When Canada was lost to France, St. Luc determined to return to the land of his fathers, and embarked, October 17, 1761, on the *Auguste* with his entire family and over a hundred of the principal persons of the colony. On the coast of Cape Breton the *Auguste* was wrecked, and St. Luc alone of all the passengers escaped alive. After great hardships he reached Quebec, and finally seeing the uselessness of opposing the English rule, became a British subject; but how faithful to the crown he was may be seen from the fact, that when Montgomery's invasion of Canada appeared to promise success, St. Luc determined to desert with his Indians to the Americans, and secretly wrote to the American general offering his support, which was accepted; but when this acceptance reached St. Luc, the American cause did not promise so well as it promised a short time before, and he concluded to adhere to the English side. For this treachery he was distrusted by Carleton, and Montgomery, when he captured Montreal, refused to include him in the capitulation. Being captured by Montgomery, St. Luc was held a prisoner until the spring of 1777, when he was released, and soon after joined Burgoyne with his savages. He seems to have been as treacherous and cruel as his brutal followers, and as soon as the British were in a critical condition, he deserted them.

Frenchman,[185] who had long resided amongst them, declared their intention of returning to their respective homes, their interpreter informing the [general] (speaking figuratively in the Indian manner) that on

---

Samuel Mott speaks of him as "an arch devil incarnate, who has butchered hundreds, men, women and children of your colonies," and Burgoyne in Parliament thus alluded to him as one secretly practicing against him: "His name is St. Luc le Corne, a distinguished partisan of the French in the last war, and now in the British service as a leader of the Indians. He owes us, indeed, some service, having been formerly instrumental in scalping many hundred British soldiers upon the very ground where, though with a different sort of latitude, he was this year employed. He is by nature, education and practice artful, ambitious and a courtier. To the grudge he owed me for controlling him in the use of the hatchet and scalping-knife, it was natural to his character to recommend himself to ministerial favour by any censure in his power to cast upon an unfashionable general." St. Luc subsequently became a member of the Legislative Council of Canada, and took part in the exciting political questions of the times which succeeded the termination of the war, but did not long survive. He died in the beginning of October, 1784, aged 72 years. *Vide* Documents Relating to the Colonial History of New York, vol. 10, pp. 112, 132, 345, 500, 629, 750, *et passim;* Journal du Voyage de M. Saint-Luc de la Corne, Quebec, 1863; History of Canada (Garneau), vol. 1, pp. 460, 555; vol. 2, pp. 67, 85, 163, 185; American Archives, 4th Series, vol. 4, pp. 973, 1095; Speech of General Burgoyne on a Motion of Inquiry made by Mr. Vyner in the Parliament, May 26, 1778, and, for a very full account, Hadden's Journal and Orderly Books, Appendix No. 17.

185 This was Charles de Langlade, a Frenchman, who had long acted with the Indians, and was familiar with their habits and customs. Anburey calls him *Langdale*, who, he says, "planned and executed, with the nations he is now escorting, the defeat of General Braddock." He had under

their first joining his army, the sun arose bright, and in its full glory; that the sky was clear and serene, foreboding conquest and victory; but that then, that great Luminary was surrounded and almost obscured from the sight by dark and gloomy clouds, which threatened by their bursting to involve all nature in a general wreck and confusion. This the general (tho in his heart he despised them for their fears and might have sentenced Mr Luc by a general Court Martial to an ignominious death for desertion) yet parted with them seemingly without showing his dislike, fearing, perhaps, their going over to the enemy. On which some companies of rangers were ordered to be raised in their place. At this time, many of the inhabitants, who before came into our camp for protection, calling themselves Torys, went from us over to the enemy, who we hoped soon to make pay dear for their late success at Bennington.[186]

---

his command warriors from many tribes — Sioux, Sacs, Foxes, Menominees, Winnebagoes, Ottawas and Chippewas. At the assembling of the tribes, he translated the speeches of the Sioux chiefs into the dialect of the Chippewas, and from the Chippewa dialect into the French tongue. For a memoir, *vide* Collections Wisconsin Historical Society, vol. 7, p. 123; Travels Through the Interior Parts of America, vol. 1, p. 356, *et seq.*

[186] This was a constant danger to the Americans. While a large portion of the people was ready to make any sacrifice, however great, for the cause of liberty, another considerable portion was as ready to join the winning side, whichever it might be. This was realized by the American commanders, and was the cause of much embarrassment to them.

It is scarce to be conceived the many difficulties we had to encounter in carrying on a war in such a country, from the tediousness of removing provisions stores &c, and the smallness of our numbers were much diminished by sending parties back and forward from fort George to our camp.

22nd. A few Germans deserted, one of whom was taken and suffered death.[187] Various were the reports then circulating thro our camp, not of the most pleasing kind, which might easily be perceived on the faces of some of our great men, who I believe began to think our affairs had not taken so fortunate a turn as might have been expected; as to my opinion, it was of very little consequence compared to so many abler judges; certain it was, as an Indian express arrived —

28th — to our camp, that Col. St Leger[188] was obliged to retire with his small army to Oswego, in

---

187 On the 21st of August an order of Burgoyne relating to desertion contained the following: "In regard to Deserters themselves, all out posts, Scouts and working Parties of Provincials and Indians, are hereby promised a reward of twenty Dollars for every Deserter they bring in; and in case any Deserter should be killed in the pursuit, their scalps are to be brought off." The unfortunate man here mentioned was George Hundertmark, "guilty of quitting his Post when Centinel without being regularly relieved, and of Desertion," and was sentenced to be shot to death. *Vide* Burgoyne's Orderly Book, pp. 79, 81, *et seq.*

188 Barry St. Leger was born in 1737, and entered the Twenty-eighth Foot, April 27, 1756, with the commission of an ensign. The following year he went to America and served under Abercrombie; was made captain in the Forty-

his return towards Canada; but I forgot, I should first have mentioned the nature and cause of his expedition. Lieut Col St Leger, 34th regmt, left Canada about the time we did, with a command of near 700 regulars; viz 100 men from the 8th regmt; 100 from the 34th regmt; Sir John Johnston's regmt of New York,[189] 133; and the Hannau Chasseurs, 342, with a body of Canadians and Indians and some small pieces of Cannon. He was to go by Lake Ontario, and to come down the Mohock river on the Back settlements to take fort Stanwix[190] &c, and

---

eighth Foot, and took part in the siege of Louisbourg in 1758. After its capture he accompanied General Wolfe to Quebec, and won distinction there. In July, 1760, he was appointed brigade major, and August 16, 1762, a major of the Ninety-fifth Foot. At the close of the French war, he retired on half pay, but on May 25, 1772, procured an appointment in the army of lieutenant-colonel, and May 20, 1775, received a commission as lieutenant-colonel in the Thirty-fourth Foot. His unfortunate expedition to the Mohawk did not altogether prevent his advancement, as he was made a colonel in the army, November 17, 1780, and a brigadier-general, October 21, 1782. He died in 1789. *Vide* British Army Lists, *in loco;* American Historical Record, vol. 3, p. 435; Colonial History of New York, vol. 8, p. 714; Johnson's Orderly Book, p. 66, and, for an account of his operations in 1777, The Expedition of Lieut.-Col. Barry St. Leger, by William L. Stone, Albany, 1877.

[189] This regiment was known by several names, and very unpleasantly by the Americans on account of its inhumanity. It was called Johnson's Royal Greens on account of the color of its uniform; also as the Queen's Loyal Americans and the Royal Regiment of New York.

[190] This fort was erected in 1758 and called Fort Stanwix, taking its name from General Stanwix, an officer under

to join us at Albany. This was the plan settled by Lord George Germain, as you will see in his letter to Gen Carlton, dated Whitehall March 6th 1777; but why that expedition miscarryed I cannot pretend to say; as the conduct of Col. St Leger [by] common report, which was all I could depend upon, did him every kind of [in] justice in the plan concerted by him for carrying his orders into execution. Our accounts also from Genl Howe, or rather our hearing nothing about his proceedings to the Southward, was another cause of disappointment, as it was but natural to suppose, that had he done nothing very great with so large a body of troops under his command — said to be near 40,000 — we could not easyly penetrate into the enemy's country with one eighth of that number; so that upon mature deliberation, and agreeable to the general's express orders, it was determined by him to drop all sorts of communication with Canada — the Army being too small to afford parties at the different posts between us, and Ticonderoga — and by forcing his way by the greatest exertion possible, fight for the wished for junction with the Southern army; and also to remain on our present ground till provisions stores &c were

General Abercrombie. After the repulse of Abercrombie by the French at Ticonderoga, in which Lord George Howe, the elder brother of General William Howe of Revolutionary fame, was killed, Abercrombie dispatched Stanwix to build this fort near the head waters of the Mohawk, the site of the present town of Rome. It was repaired and strengthened by General Schuyler in 1776 and received his name.

all up previous to so material a movement. In my opinion, this attempt showed a glorious spirit in our General, and worthy alone to be undertaken by British Troops, as the eyes of all Europe, as well as Great Britain were fixed upon us; tho some disatisfied persons with us did not scruple to give it the appellation of *rashness*, and were of opinion, that we should have remained at Fort Edward entrenched, until we heard Genl Clinton was come up near Albany; and then pushed on to co operate with him. Our great design & wish then was to draw on a general engagement, which we hoped would be decisive, as by their unbounded extent of country they might, by avoiding it, protract the war.

September 2nd. Went out with a large forraging party, as was the custom every morning, and marched 9 miles towards the enemy before we could procure any; it then turning very scarce from our remaining so long on that post. We halted at an exceeding good house near the road, which was deserted by its master and family on our approach. The furniture was good, and which I might have appropriated to what use I pleased. About 3 o'clock we returned to our camp with some hay, not without some odd thoughts on the fortune of war, which levels all distinctions of property, and which our present situation pictured strongly.

4th. A drum[mer], who went from our camp as a flag of truce to Genl Gates, returned, and the following letters which passed from Gen Gates to Genl Burgoyne, with his answers and Gates' account of the Bennington affair to their congress, I shall here insert for the amusement of the reader —

To the honourable, the continental congress.

Your excellencies will perceive by the inclosed letters, that the glorious victory at Bennington has reduced the boasting stile of Gen Burgoyne so much, that he begins in some degree to think and talk like other men.

HEAD QUARTERS OF THE KING'S ARMY UPON HUDSON RIVER *August* 30 1777.

SIR.—Major Genl Reidzel has requested me to transmit the inclosed to Lieut Col[l] Baum,[191] whom the fortune of war put into the hands of your troops at Bennington. Having never failed in my attention towards prisoners, I cannot entertain a doubt of your

191 Frederick Baum was lieutenant-colonel of the Brunswick Dragoons, and is spoken of as being a good officer but unfit for this expedition, in which he lost his life; in fact, the troops which he commanded were wholly unfit for the service here assigned them. Stone thus describes the equipment of one of these men: "He wore high and heavy jack boots, with large, long spurs, stout and stiff, leather breeches, gauntlets, reaching high up upon his arms, and a hat with a huge tuft of ornamental feathers. On his side he trailed a tremendous broad sword; a short but clumsy carbine was slung over his shoulder, and down his back, like a Chinese Mandarin, dangled a long queue." It is admitted that Baum and his men fought heroically, but in vain, being overwhelmed by numbers. He lived two days after being wounded, and was buried with military honors August nineteenth.

taking this opportunity to show me a return of civility; and that you will permit the baggage and servants of such officers, your prisoners, as desire it, to pass to them unmolested. It is with great concern, I find myself obliged to add to this application a complaint of the bad treatment the provincial soldiers in the king's service received after the affair at Bennington. I have reports upon oath that some were refused quarter after having asked it. I am willing to believe this was against the order and inclination of your officers; but it is my part to require an explanation, and to warn you of the horrors of retaliation, if such a practice is not in the strongest terms discountenanced. Duty and principle, Sir; make me a public enemy to the Americans, who have taken arms, but I seek to be a generous one, nor have I the shadow of resentment against any individual, who does not induce it by acts derogatory to those maxims upon which all men of honor think alike. Persuaded that a Gentleman of the station to which this lettter is addressed will not be comprised in the exception I have made — I am personally, Sir,

Your most humble servant,

JN° BURGOYNE.

HEAD QUARTERS OF THE ARMY OF THE UNITED STATES *Sep.* 2nd.

SIR. Last night I had the honour of receiving your excellency's letter of the 30th August. I am astonished you should mention inhumanity, or threaten retaliation. Nothing happened in the action of Bennington, but what is common when works are carried by Assault. That the savages of America should in their warfare mangle and scalp the unhappy prisoners, who fall into their hands, is neither new nor extraordinary; but that the famous Lieut General Burgoyne, in whom the fine gentleman is united with the soldier and the scholar, should hire the savages of America to scalp Europeans and the descendants of Europeans; nay more, that he should pay a price for each scalp so barbarously taken, is more than will be believed in England until authenticated facts shall in every gazette convince mankind of the truth of this horrid tale.—Miss McCrea, a young lady lovely to the sight, of virtuous character and amiable disposition, engaged to be married to an officer in your army, was with other women and children taken out of a house near Fort Edward, carried into the woods, and there scalped and mangled in the most shocking manner. Two parents with their six children, [were] all treated with the same inhumanity while quietly residing in their once happy and peaceful dwelling. The miserable fate of Miss McCrea was partly aggravated by her being dressed to receive her promised husband; but met her murderers employed by you. Upwards of one hundred men, women and children have perished by the hands of these ruffians, to whom it is asserted, you have paid the price of blood. Inclosed are letters from your wounded officers, prisoners in my hands, by whom you will be informed of the generosity of their Conquerers. Such cloathing, necessaries, attendants &c. which your excellency pleases to send to the prisoners shall be carefully delivered. I am, sir, your most

Humble servant

H. GATES.[192]

SIR. I received your letter of the 2d inst, and in consequence of your complying with my proposal, have sent the baggage, servants &c of those officers, who are prisoners in your hands. I have hesitated, sir, upon answering the other paragraphs of your letter. I disdain to justify myself against the rhapsodies of fiction, and calumny, which from the first of this contest, it has been an unvaried American policy to propagate; but which no longer impose upon the world. I am induced to deviate from this rule in the present instance, lest my silence should be construed an acknowledgement of the truth of your allegation, and a pretence be thence taken for exercising future barbarities by the American troops. Upon this motive, and upon this alone, I condescend to inform you, that I would not be conscious of the

[192] After General Gates had written this letter to Burgoyne, he called General Lincoln and his aide-de-camp, Wilkinson, to hear it read. Upon being pressed for an opinion respecting it, his hearers suggested that it might be considered somewhat too personal, to which the old general replied with his usual profane bluntness: "——, I don't believe either of you can mend it," and abruptly terminated the consultation.

acts, you presume to impute to me, for the whole continent of America, tho. the wealth of worlds were in its bowels and a paradise on its surface. It has happened, that all my transactions with the Indian nations last year and this, have been open, clearly heard, distinctly understood and accurately minuted by very numerous, and in many parts, very prejudiced audiences. So diametrically opposite to truth is your assertion that I have paid a price for scalps, that one of the first regulations established by me at the great Council in May, and repeated and enforced, and invariably adhered to since, was that the Indians should receive compensation for prisoners, because it would prevent cruelty, and that not only such compensations should be witheld, but a strict account demanded for scalps. These pledges of Conquest— for such you well know they will ever esteem them— were solemnly and peremptorily prohibited to be taken from the wounded and even the dying, and the persons of aged men, women and children, and prisoners were pronounced sacred even, in assaults.— Respecting Miss McCrea; her fall wanted not the tragic display you have laboured to give it, to make it as sincerely abhorred and lamented by me, as it can possibly be by the tenderest of her friends. The fact was no premeditated barbarity, on the contrary, two chiefs who had brought her off for the purpose of security, not of violence to her person, disputed who should be her guard, and in a fit of savage passion in the one from whose hands she was snatched, the unhappy woman became the victim. Upon the first intelligence of the events, I obliged the Indians to deliver the murderer into my hands, and tho to have punished him by our laws and principles of justice would have been perhaps unprecedented, he certainly should have suffered an ignominous death, had I not been convinced, by circumstances and observation beyond the possibility of a doubt, that a pardon under the terms I prescribed and they accepted, would be more efficatious than an execution to prevent similar mischiefs. The above instance excepted, your intelligence respecting cruelties of the Indians is absolutely false. You seem to threaten me with European publications, which affect me as little as any other threats you could make, but in regard to American publications, whether the charge against me, (which I acquit you of believing), was pencilled from a gazette or for a gazette, I desire and demand of you, as a man of honour, that should it appear in print at all, this answer may follow it. I am Sir,

Your humble servant,

JN°. BURGOYNE.

6th. We were pretty credibly informed by accounts which came from the enemy, and were depended upon, that in the action near Bennington, 16th August, we had killed, wounded, prisoners and missing—including wounded in our hospitals, who escaped—near 1000 men. It was then expected we should shortly move, as the magazines of provisions and other stores were mostly up, and our new bridge over the Hudson river was near finished. Our removal from that post was also very necessary, in respect of procuring forage, which began then to turn very scarce; indeed, I wonder we did so well, as it was amazing the great quantity of hay, Indian corn &c we were obliged to provide for so great a number of cattle. Potatoes and all other vegetables were long before consumed, and very few fresh provisions to be got then. A few of our wounded officers and men from the hospitals of Ticonderoga joined the army; also captain Wight and others, who suffered from fever and such disorders, came up. The weather then began to turn cold in the mornings and evenings, which was but badly calculated for the light cloathing of the army, most of our winter apparel being sent from Skeensborough to Ticonderoga in July. Many officers had also sent back their tents and markees, of which I was one, and in their place substituted a soldier's tent, which were then cold at nights though a luxury to what we after experienced

10th. About 11 o'clock, an express arrived with intelligence that the enemy were on the move, and had advanced from their camp at Half Moon to Still water, a few miles nearer us, but they might have saved themselves that trouble, as we should soon have been up with them. He also informed [us] that in consequence of that unfortunate affair at

Bennington, they were joined by some thousands of Militia, who in all probability would have remained neuter had we proved successful. From these accounts we threw up more works to protect our camp till ready to move towards them; after which we should be as liable to an attack in our rear as front, and the waiting to secure every store &c against such an attack, caused our being so long on that post

11th. We received orders to be in readiness to cross the Hudson river at a moment's warning; but all that day was a continued fall of heavy rain, which continued till the 13th, when the morning being very fine, the army passed over the Bridge of boats and encamped on the heights of Saratoga. We encamped in three columns in order of Battle. The duty here turned very severe, such numbers being constantly on either guards or picquets; during that day and the next we had many small alarms, as parties of theirs came very near our camp; but a few companies soon sent them off.

15th. Moved about 3 miles nearer the enemy, and took post on a strong position late in the evening, and had just time to pitch our camp before dark; about 11 at night we received orders to stand to our arms, and about 12 I returned to my tent and lay down to get a little rest, but was soon alarmed by a great noise of fire, and on running out saw Major Ackland's tent and markee all in a blaze, on which I made the greatest haste possible to their assistance, but before I could arrive, Lady Harriot Ackland, who was asleep in the tent when it took fire, had providentially escaped under the back of it; but the major was much burned in trying to save her.[193] What must a woman of her rank, family and fortune feel in her then disagreeable situation; liable to constant alarms and not knowing the moment of an

[193] Anburey has the following account of this occurrence: "Our situation, as being the advanced post of the army, was frequently so very alert that we seldom slept out of our cloaths. In one of these situations a tent, in which Major Ackland and Lady Harriet were asleep, suddenly caught fire; the major's orderly sergeant, with great danger of suffocation, dragged out the first person he got hold of, which was the major. It providentially happened that in the same instant Lady Harriet, without knowing what she did, and perhaps not perfectly awake, made her escape, by creeping under the walls in the back part of the tent, and upon recovering her senses, conceive what her feelings must be when the first object she beheld was the major, in the midst of the flames, in search of her! The sergeant again saved him, but the major's face and body was burnt in a very severe manner; every thing they had with them in the tent was consumed. This accident was occasioned by a favorite Newfoundland dog, who being very restless, overset the table on which a candle was burning, (the major always had a light in his tent during the night, when our situation required it) and it rolling to the walls of the tent, instantly set them on fire." The almost romantic attachment of Burgoyne's two officers, Major Acland and General Riedesel and their lovely and devoted wives, relieves in a striking manner the horrors of the campaign, so strongly contrasted is it with the suffering and selfishness which everywhere prevailed. Here were two gentle and refined women amid the wreck and ruin of war, and always very near to the portals of death, living an almost idyllic life of unselfish devotion and love to their husbands, and of charity and self-sacrifice to those about them. Truly it is a spectacle worthy of contemplation!

attack; but from her attachment to the major, her ladyship bore everything, with a degree of steadiness, and resolution, that could alone be expected from an experienced veteran.

16th. A detachment with about 2000 men with 6 pieces of cannon attended Gen Burgoyne on a reconnoitering party towards the enemy. We remained out till near night, and fired our evening gun at sun set to make them imagine we had taken post so much nearer them; and afterwards returned to our camp with the gun. We heard Gen Gates had been there the preceding day attended by a corps of riflemen. It was then pretty certain and generally believed, and indeed wished for, that we should shortly have a decisive engagement,— I say wished for, as they never would allow us to go into winter quarters, till we had gained some great advantage over them; should that be the case, many of the country people would join us, but not till then — they choosing to be on the strongest side.

17th. The whole moved about 9 in the morning, and tho we were marching till near night, we came but 3 miles nearer them — we going a great circuit thro thick woods, for such is all that country — in order to keep possession of the heights, we lay on our arms not having light or time to pitch our tents.

18th. About 11 in the morning, we heard the report of small arms at a small distance. It was a party of the enemy, who surprised some unarmed men foraging not far from our camp. They killed & wounded

13, and then retreated[194] on our sending a party to oppose them; and during that day and night we were very watchful and remained under arms.

19th. At day break intelligence was received, that Colonel Morgan,[195] with the advance party of the

[194] A number of men belonging to the British camp were endeavoring to get some potatoes in a field near by for their mess when surprised by the Americans. Anburey says that they might easily have been taken prisoners, and states the number killed and wounded to have been near thirty. He remarks that "such cruel and unjustifiable conduct can have no good tendency, while it serves greatly to increase hatred, and a thirst for revenge." *Vide* Travels Through the Interior Parts of America, vol. 1, p. 409.

[195] Daniel Morgan has been claimed to be a native both of Pennsylvania and of New Jersey, but his biographer, Graham, decides that he was born in Hunterdon county, New Jersey, in the winter of 1736. His parents were Welsh, and his early life one of hardship. At the age of seventeen he ran away from home and found employment as a farm laborer in Virginia. He was a wagoner in the Braddock expedition and noted for his great strength and daring. While in the frontier service the next year, he was beaten with five hundred lashes for striking a British lieutenant in return for a blow which the officer bestowed upon him with his sword, under the severity of which punishment he would have succumbed had not his constitution been of iron. The terrible marks of this beating, which "cut his flesh to ribbons," he bore to his grave. He was commissioned an ensign in 1758, and, after a rough life of a few years, married and settled down as a farmer in Virginia. When the news of the battle of Lexington reached him, he mustered a picked company of riflemen and marched with them to Cambridge, a distance of six hundred miles, in twenty-one days. It was in the dusk of evening when Morgan met General Washington, who was riding out to inspect the camp. As they met, Morgan touched his broad-brimmed hat and said: "General—from the right bank of the Potomac." Hastily dismount-

enemy, consisting of a corps of rifle men, were strong about 3 miles from us; their main body amounting to great numbers encamped on a very strong post about half a mile in their rear; and about 9 o'clock we began our march, every man prepared with 60 rounds

ing, Washington "took the captain's hand in both of his and pressed it silently. Then passing down the line, he pressed, in turn, the hand of every soldier, large tears streaming down the noble cheeks as he did so. Without a word he then remounted his horse, saluted, and returned to the camp." In Arnold's campaign against Canada, Morgan was an active spirit, and was taken a prisoner in the attack upon Quebec. It is said that he wept when he realized the hopelessness of the campaign. While in confinement he was offered a colonel's commission to join the British, but repelled the offer with indignation. After being exchanged, he joined the army of defense and did noble service in the battles which preceded the surrender of Burgoyne. At the close of the battle which decided this event, it is said that Gates approached him with a proposition to desert Washington and support his pretensions to the chief command, but was indignantly repelled by Morgan, who replied: "I will serve under no other man but Washington." For this reply Gates revenged himself by not mentioning his name in his report of the battle in which he rendered such distinguished service. After the surrender of Burgoyne, he served in the South, and achieved honor at the battle of the Cowpens, for which he was awarded a gold medal by Congress. At the close of the war he retired to his Virginian farm, which he named *Saratoga;* but, upon the breaking out of the whisky insurrection in western Virginia, in 1794, he was called to command the militia for its suppression, and soon after was elected to Congress. Before the close of his term he retired, prostrated by sickness. Washington, however, continued to consult him, although he was incapacitated for service. He died at Manchester, Virginia, July 6, 1802. *Vide* The Life of Daniel Morgan (Graham); also, A Sketch of Morgan by John Esten Cooke.

of cartridge and ready for instant action. We moved in 3 colums, ours to the right on the heights and farthest from the river in thick woods. A little after 12 our advanced picquets came up with Colonel Morgan and engaged, but from the great superiority of fire received from him — his numbers being much greater — they were obliged to fall back, every officer being either killed or wounded except one,[196] when

196 The sharpshooters of Morgan caused great havoc in the British ranks. Lamb says: "Several of the Americans placed themselves in high trees, and, as often as they could distinguish a British officer's uniform, took him off by deliberately aiming at his person." Anburey describes most graphically the terrible scenes of the day following this battle: "Our army," he says, "abounded with young officers, in the subaltern line, and in the course of this unpleasant duty (the burial of the dead), three of the 20th regiment were interred together, the age of the eldest not exceeding seventeen.—In the course of the last action, Lieutenant Hervey, of the 62nd, a youth of sixteen, and nephew of the Adjutant-General of the same name, received several wounds, and was repeatedly ordered off the field by Colonel Anstruther; but his heroic ardor would not allow him to quit the battle, while he could stand and see his brave lads fighting beside him. A ball striking one of his legs, his removal became absolutely necessary, and while they were conveying him away, another wounded him mortally. In this situation the surgeon recommended him to take a powerful dose of opium, to avoid a seven or eight hours' life of most exquisite torture; this he immediately consented to, and when the Colonel entered the tent with Major Harnage, who were both wounded, they asked whether he had any affairs they could settle for him? his reply was, 'that being a minor, every thing was already adjusted;' but he had one request, which he had just life enough to utter, 'Tell my uncle I died like a soldier.' Where will you find in ancient Rome heroism superior!" This mode of war-

the line came up to their support and obliged Morgan in his turn to retreat with loss. About half past one, the fire seemed to slacken a little; but it was only to come on with double force, as between 2 & 3 the action became general on their side. From the situation of the ground, and their being perfectly acquainted with it, the whole of our troops could not be brought to engage together, which was a very material disadvantage, though everything possible was tried to remedy that inconvenience, but to no effect, such an explosion of fire I never had any idea of before, and the heavy artillery joining in concert like great peals of thunder, assisted by the echoes of the woods, almost deafened us with the noise. To an unconcerned spectator, it must have had the most awful and glorious appearance, the different Battalions moving to relieve each other, some being pressed and almost broke by their superior numbers. This crash of cannon and musketry never ceased till darkness parted us, when they retired to their camp, leaving us masters of the field; but it was a dear bought victory if I can give it that name, as we lost many brave men, The 62nd had scarce 10 men a company left, and other regiments suffered much, and no very great advantage, honor excepted, was gained by the day. On its turning dusk we

---

fare, in which the officers were singled out by accurate marksmen for death, was new to the British and deemed by them cruel. *Vide* Journal of Occurrences During the Late American War, p. 159; Travels Through the Interior Parts of America, vol. 1, p. 423, *et seq.*

were near firing on a body of our Germans, mistaking their dark clothing for that of the enemy. General Burgoyne was every where and did every thing [that] could be expected from a brave officer,[197] & Brig gen. Frazier gained great honour by exposing himself to every danger. During the night we remained in our ranks, and tho we heard the groans of our wounded and dying at a small distance, yet could not assist them till morning, not knowing the position of the enemy, and expecting the action would be renewed at day break. Sleep was a stranger to us, but we were all in good spirits and ready to obey with cheerfulness any orders the general might issue before morning dawned.

20th. At day break we sent out parties to bring in our wounded, and lit fires as we were almost froze with cold, and our wounded who lived till the morning must have severely felt it. We scarce knew how the rest of our army had fared the preceding day, nor had we tasted victuals or even water for some time before; so sent parties for each. At 11 o'clock, some of our advanced sentrys were fired upon by

[197] Lamb, who was present, speaks of this in his journal, and others comment upon Burgoyne's coolness and courage in battle — placing himself in the fore front of danger, a conspicuous object for the American sharpshooters, against whose bullets he seemed to bear a charmed life. His presence among his troops was in marked contrast to the action of Gates, who remained in the rear and witnessed no part of this or the previous battle; in fact, we are told by Wilkinson, what seems almost incredible: "*That not a single general officer was on the field of battle the* 19*th Sept.* until the evening, when General Learned was ordered out."

their rifle men, and we thought it the prelude to another action; but they were soon silenced. It was Gen Phillips and Fraziers opinion we should follow the stroke by attacking their camp that morning; and it is believed, as affairs after turned out, it would have been better for the army to have done so; why it was not attended, to I am not a judge; tho I believe Gen Burgoyne had material objections to it, particularly our hospitals being so full and the magazines not properly secured to risque that movement.[198] About 12 the general reconnoitered our

---

[198] Wilkinson gives us a conversation held by him with General Phillips, in which the latter fully explains the reason why Burgoyne did not attack Gates on the twentieth. Said Phillips: "After the affair of the 19th September terminated, General Burgoyne determined to attack you the next morning on your left, with his whole force; our wounded, and sick, and women had been disposed of at the river; the army was formed early on the morning of the 20th, and we waited only for the dispersion of the fog, when General Fraser observed to General Burgoyne, that the grenadiers and light infantry who were to lead the attack, appeared fatigued by the duty of the preceding day, and that if he would suspend the operation until the next morning, he was persuaded they would carry the attack with more vivacity. Burgoyne yielded to the proposition of Fraser; the orders were countermanded, and the corps returned to camp; and as if intended for your safety and our destruction, in the course of the night, a spy reached Burgoyne with a letter from General Sir Henry Clinton, advising him of his intended expedition against the highlands, which determined Burgoyne to postpone the meditated attack of your army, and wait events; the golden, glorious opportunity was lost — you grew stronger every day, and on the 7th of October overwhelmed us." This is a very different account from Digby's. *Vide* Memoirs of My Own Times, vol. 1, p. 251, *et seq.*

post and contracted the extent of ground we then covered to a more secure one nearer the river, which we took up in the evening — our left flank near the Hudson river to guard our battows and stores, and our right extending near two miles to heights west of the river, with strong ravines, both in our front and rear, the former nearly within cannon shot of the enemy. On our taking up this ground, we buried numbers of their dead. Their loss must have been considerable, as the fire was very severe. Contiguous to our ground was a fine field of Indian corn, which greatly served our horses, who had but little care taken of them the last 2 days, and many were killed the 19th. At night, half stood to their arms, and so relieved each other, in which time of watch we could distinctly hear them in the wood between us felling trees ; from which we supposed they were fortifying their camp, which by all accounts, and the situation of the country, we had reason to believe was very strong

21st. Their morning gun, from its report, seemed almost as near as our own, and soon after we heard them beating their drums frequently for orders. At 12 we heard them huzzaing in their camp, after which they fired 13 heavy guns, which we imagined might be signals for an attack; and which would be the most fortunate event that we could have wished, our position being so very advantageous. Soon after we found it was a Feu-de-joy, but for what cause we could not tell,[199] In the evening, an express was sent thro the woods to Gen Clinton, informing him that if he could not advance nearer to Albany, by which movement many troops then opposing us would be drawn off to stop his progress, we should be obliged to return to Ticonderoga by 12th October at farthest, as our provisions would not allow of our remaining there beyond that period. At 6 in the evening we encamped, It rained very heavy, and the general often expressed his desire that the men would take some rest — being greatly harassed after their great fatigue — to make them the better able to bear what might follow. The night was constant rain, and we lay accoutred in our tents

22nd. Formed a bridge of boats across the Hudson, on the left flank of our line. A spy from the enemy was taken near our camp, and we had reason to suppose there were many others around. He informed that they had a report Gen Burgoyne was killed on the 19th, which must have arose from Capn Green,[200]

---

[199] This *feu-de-joie* was probably caused by the reception of the news of the partially successful expedition against Ticonderoga in the rear of Burgoyne's army. On the eighteenth, Colonel Brown attacked Ticonderoga and captured a portion of the Fifty-third Regiment in the old French lines and released about a hundred prisoners, which were held by the British. He also took an armed vessel stationed to defend the carrying place, with several officers. Digby does not recognize the fact that one gun was fired for each of the colonies.

[200] Charles Green was born December 18, 1749, at Gibraltar, where his father was stationed with his regiment. At

one of the aid de camps, being wounded and falling from his horse near the general. About noon there was a confused report of Gen Clinton's comeing up the river, and it must be owned Gen Burgoyne was

---

the early age of eleven he became a gentleman cadet in the Royal Artillery, and an ensign in the Thirty-first Foot at the age of sixteen. November 23, 1769, he was made a lieutenant — his regiment being then in Florida — and served against the Charibs in 1772-3. In May he returned to England and was appointed adjutant of his regiment, and became, in 1774, a captain-lieutenant by purchase. He served in the campaign of '76, and, at the beginning of the campaign of '77, was made aide-de-camp to Major-General Phillips. After recovering from the wound which Digby here mentions, he returned in March, 1778, to England, and became aide-de-camp to Lieutenant-General Oughton. He rejoined his regiment in Canada, in 1780, and was appointed major of brigade the following year. He became major of the Thirty-first by purchase in 1788. In 1793 he was made lieutenant-colonel of a battalion, and the next year was transferred to the Thirtieth Foot, which he accompanied to Corsica, where he remained until 1796, when he received the appointment of coast governor of Grenada, which office he retained until 1801, when he returned to England, and, in January, 1797, was promoted to a colonelcy. In October, 1798, he received a further promotion to the rank of brigadier general, and for some time commanded in Ireland. He was raised to the honor of knighthood, May 3, 1803, and in the spring of 1804 conducted an expedition against Surinam, and, after its capture, administered the civil government there for a year, when, owing to broken health, he returned to England, and was further honored by being created a baronet, December 5, 1805. In May, 1807, he was placed in command of the garrison at Malta, which position he retained a year, and, in 1809, was raised to the rank of lieutenant-general, and, in 1819, to that of general. He died at Cheltenham, England, in 1831. *Vide* British Army Lists, *in loco;* Annual Biography and Obituary, vol. 16, p. 439.

too ready to believe any report in our favour. Orders were given for our cannon to fire 8 rounds at mid night from the park of Artillery. It was done with a view of causing the enemy to draw in their out posts expecting an attack, at which time 2 officers in disguise were sent express to Gen Clinton with messages to the same effect as was sent the 21st. The intention answered, as they stood to their works all that night which was constant rain.

23rd. It was said we were to strengthen our camp and wait some favourable accounts from Gen Clinton, and accordingly began to fell trees for that purpose. I visited our hospitals, which were much crowded, and attended the Auctions of our deceased officers, which for the time caused a few melancholy ideas, though still confirmed me in believing that the oftener death is placed before our eyes the less terrible it appears. All kinds of supplies and stores from Canada were then entirely cut off, as the communication was dropped, and the variety of reports and opinions circulating were curious and entertaining, as I believe our situation was rather uncommon; it was such at least as few of us had before experienced. Some few thought we should be ordered to retreat suddenly under cover of some dark night, but that was not thought probable, as it would be cruel to leave the great numbers of sick and wounded we had in such a situation; we also were certain our general would try another action before a retreat was thought on. Others said we waited either to receive a reinforcement from Ticonderoga or Gen Clinton, which last might have some weight, but as to the former, we knew there were too few troops there to be able to spare us any. Others again thought when the enemy saw us determined to keep our ground and heard of Gen Clinton's movements, they would draw off part of their great force to oppose him; but that was not thought very probable by their receiving so large reinforcements daily to their camp. On the whole, I believe most people's opinions and suppositions were rather founded on what they wished, than on any certain knowledge of what would happen; time only, that great disposer of all human events, could alone unfold to us what was to come. Our few remaining Indians appeared very shy at going out on any scouting parties, indeed, I always took them for a people, whose very horrid figure had a greater effect on their enemy than any courage they possessed, as their cruel turn often assured me they could not be brave, Humanity & pity for the misfortunes of the wretched, being invariably the constant companions of true courage; theirs is savage and will never steadily look on danger. We there got some news papers of the enemy taken from [a] deserter, in which there was an account of the 19th, by a M^{r}. Wilkinson, adjutant genl. to their army, very partially given, saying we retreated the 19th from the field of battle, which was absolutely false as we lay that night on the same ground we fought on, as a proof of which, we buried their dead the morning of the 20th—they not venturing near. He concludes with a poor, low expression, saying, "On the 20th the enemy lay very quietly licking their sores."[201]

24th. At day break they fired on our German picquet and killed 3 men, but this alarm gave us no unnecessary trouble, as we were always under arms an hour before day and remained so till it was completely light. During the night it rained heavy, and on the 26th, many bodies not buried deep enough in the ground appeared, (from the great rain), as the soil was a light sand, and caused a most dreadful smell. We still continued making more works. A report [was] circulated [that] Ticonderoga was taken, but not believed. I shall here insert Gen Gates' orders to his troops which we received by a deserter—

HEAD QUARTERS OF THE ARMY OF THE UNITED STATES *September* 26. 1777.

"The public business having so entirely engaged the attention of the General, that he has not been

[201] The letter here referred to by Digby was addressed by Wilkinson to Colonel Vischer, who was at Albany on the twentieth of September, and was published in the papers of the day. In it he said: "The concurrent testimony of the prisoners and deserters of various characters, assures us, that General Burgoyne who commanded in person was wounded in the left shoulder, that the 62nd regiment was cut to pieces, and that the enemy suffered extremely in every quarter where they were engaged. As General Burgoyne's situation will shortly constrain him to a decisive action, reinforcements should be immediately pushed forward to our assistance, as our numbers are far from being equal to an insurance of victory, and every bosom must anticipate the consequences of a defeat. The enemy have quietly licked their sores this day."

properly at leisure to return his grateful thanks to Gen. Poors[202] & Gen Learned's[203] Brigades, to the

---

[202] Enoch Poor was the son of Thomas and a grandson of Daniel Poor, who was one of the pioneers in the settlement of Andover, Massachusetts, in which town Enoch was born in 1736. After receiving his education, he removed to Exeter, New Hampshire, and engaged in commercial pursuits. When the sound of the guns fired at Lexington reached his ears, he hastened to cast in his lot with the patriots, and was appointed colonel of the Second New Hampshire Regiment. After the evacuation of Boston his regiment was ordered to New York, and later joined in the invasion of Canada. On February 21, 1777, he was appointed a brigadier-general, and did valuable service in the campaign of that year which resulted so gloriously for the cause of Independence. After witnessing the surrender of Burgoyne, General Poor accompanied his command to the Delaware, where he ably supported General Washington in his operations in that quarter, and shared with him the hardships of Valley Forge. He greatly distinguished himself at the battle of Monmouth, and later in an expedition against the Indians of the Six Nations. In August, 1780, General Poor was placed in command of a brigade under Lafayette, by whom he was greatly esteemed. Unfortunately, while in this command, he had a quarrel with a French officer and was killed by him in a duel, September 8, 1780. Washington, when he announced his death to Congress, spoke of him as "an officer of distinguished merit, who, as a citizen and a soldier, had every claim to the esteem of his country."

[203] Ebenezer Learned was born at Framingham, Massachusetts, in 1728, and served as a captain in the French war of 1756–1763. After the battle of Lexington, which fired the military ardor of the country, Learned marched with the Third Massachusetts Regiment, of which he had been made colonel, to Cambridge, which place he reached on the day after the battle. When the army was ordered to New York, Learned, who had contracted disease in the service, retired, by permission of Congress, in May, 1776; but, recovering his health again, offered his services to his country, and was

regiment of rifle men, to the corps of light infantry and to Col° Marshall's[204] regiment for their valiant behaviour in the action of the 19th inst, which will for ever establish and confirm the reputation of the arms of the United States; notwithstanding the General has been so late in giving this public mark of honour and applause to the brave men, whose valour has so eminently served their country, he assures them the just praise he immediately gave to the Honorable, the Continental Congress, will remain a lasting record of their honour and renown.

By the account of the enemy; by their embarrassed circumstances; by the desperate situation of their affairs, it is evident they must endeavour by one rash stroke to regain all they have lost, that failing, their utter ruin is inevitable. The General therefore intreats his valiant army, that they will, by the exactness of their discipline, by their alertness to

---

appointed a brigadier-general on April 2, 1777, and he soon after joined the army, which was concentrating on the Hudson to repel the advance of the British invaders from Canada. He participated in the campaign which terminated so successfully for the patriots, but, his health again failing, he was obliged to retire permanently from military service on March 24, 1778. He was made a pensioner December 7, 1795, and died April 1, 1801, at Oxford, Massachusetts.

[204] Thomas Marshall was born at Boston, Massachusetts, in 1718. He was a captain in the Ancient and Honorable Artillery Company in 1763 and the four following years, and was made major of a regiment in 1765, and lieutenant-colonel in 1767. He was in command of the Tenth Massachusetts Regiment at the time here spoken of by Digby. He died at Weston, Massachusetts, November 18, 1800.

fly to their arms on all occasions, and particularly by their caution not to be surprised, secure that victory, which Almighty Providence (if they deserve it) will bless their labour with."

27th. We received the unwelcome news that a letter from Gen Clinton to Gen Burgoyne (it was not an answer to his of the 21st) had fallen into the hands of the enemy. On the express being taken he swallowed a small silver bullet in which the letter was, but being suspected, a severe tartar emetic was given him which brought up the ball.[205] We also heard they were in possession of Skeensboro' and had a post both there and at Hubberton. We also received accounts of their making an attack upon Ticonderoga and taking prisoners part of the 53rd regiment; but this was not properly authenticated. In the evening our few remaining Indians left us.

28th. A large detachment was ordered out to forage for the army, which was greatly wanting, as all our grass was ate up and many horses dying for want. We brought in some hay without any skirmish, which we expected going out.

29th. About day break our picquet was fired on from the wood in front, but the damage was trifling. I suppose seldom two armies remained looking at each other so long without coming to action. A man of

---

[205] It will be seen that Digby gives the version of this affair which is consonant with the evidence relating to it, which has been preserved. He says that the message taken was from Clinton to Burgoyne, and not from Burgoyne to Clinton, as stated by Fonblanque. *Vide ante*, note 26.

theirs in a mistake came into our camp in place of his own, and being challenged by our sentry, after recollecting himself, "I believe," says he, "I am wrong and may as well stay where I am." That he might be pretty certain of.

30th. We had reason to imagine they intended to open a battery on our right; they also fired three morning guns in place of two, which caused us to expect a reinforcement, which was soon confirmed by a deserter who came over to us. That evening 20 Indians joined us from Canada; our horses were put on a smaller allowance

October 2nd. Dispatches were received from Brigadier General Powell, who commanded at Ticonderoga with his account of their attempt on that place, and being at length repulsed with loss they retreated over the mountains.

3rd. Dispatches from Ticonderoga were taken by the enemy coming thro the woods directed by an Indian.

4th. Our picquet was fired upon near day break, but as our own posts were strong, and we all slept with our clothes on; it was but little minded. Here the army were put on a short allowance of provisions, which shewed us the general was determined to wait the arrival of general Clinton, (if possible), and to this the troops submitted with the utmost cheerfulness.

5th. A small party of our sailors were taken by the enemy, also about 20 horses, that strayed near their lines. The weather continued fair and dry since 26th September.

6th. I went out on a large forage for the army, and took some hay near their camp. On our return we heard a heavy fire and made all the haste possible with the forage. It was occasioned by some of our ranger's falling in with a party of theirs; our loss was trifling. At night we fired a rocket from one of our cannon at 12 o'clock, the reason I could never hear for doing so. In general it is a signal between two armies at a small distance, but that could not have been our case. During the night there were small alarms and frequent popping shots, fired by sentrys from our different outposts.

7th. Expresses were received from Ticonderoga, but what the purport of them were I could never learn. A detachment of 1500 regular troops with two 12 pounders, two howitzers and six 6 pounders were ordered to move on a secret expedition and to be paraded at 10 o'clock, though I am told, Major Williams[206] (Artillery) objected much to the removal of the heavy guns; saying, once a 12 pounder is removed from the Park of artillery in America

---

[206] Griffith Williams became a gentleman cadet in 1744, and was commissioned a lieutenant-fireworker, April 6, 1745. March 1, 1755, he was advanced to the position of first lieutenant; January 1, 1759, of captain-lieutenant, and February 12, 1760, of captain. He was promoted to a majority in the army, February 17, 1776. In the battle of October seventh he "kept a battery in action until the artillery horses were all destroyed, and his men either killed or wounded; being unable to get off their guns, he was surrounded and taken."

(meaning in the woods) it was gone. From some delay, the detachment did not move till near one o'clock, and moved from the right of our camp ; soon after which, we gained an eminence within half a mile of their camp, where the troops took post ; but they were sufficiently prepared for us, as a deserter from our Artillery went over to them that morning and informed them of our design. This I have since heard, and it has often surprised me how the fellow could be so very exact in his intelligence, as were I taken prisoner, I could not (had I ever so great a desire) have informed them so circumstantially. About 3 o'clock, our heavy guns began to play, but the wood around being thick, and their exact knowledge of our small force, caused them to advance in great numbers, pouring in a superiority of fire from Detachments ordered to hang upon our flanks, which they tried if possible to turn. We could not receive a reinforcement as our works, General Hospital Stores, provisions &c would be left defenceless, on which an order was given for us to retreat, but not before we lost many brave men. Brigadier General Frazier was mortally wounded which helped to turn the fate of the day. When

He was subsequently exchanged, and became a major in the artillery, March 21, 1780; lieutenant-colonel, January 9, 1782, and colonel of the Second Battalion, December 1, 1783. He commanded a battery at the siege of Gibraltar, and upon his return, was in command at Woolwich, where he died March 18, 1790, after a service of nearly half a century. *Vide* Kane's Artillery List and British Army Lists, *in loco;* History of the Royal Artillery (Duncan), vol. 1, pp. 288, 315.

General Burgoyne saw him fall, he seemed then to feel in the highest degree our disagreeable situation. He was the only person we could carry off with us. Our cannon were surrounded and taken — the men and horses being all killed — which gave them additional spirits, and they rushed on with loud shouts, when we drove them back a little way with so great loss to ourselves, that it evidently appeared a retreat was the only thing left for us. They still advanced upon our works under a severe fire of grape shot, which in some measure stopped them, by the great execution we saw made among their columns; during which, another body of the enemy stormed the German lines after meeting with a most shameful resistance, and took possession of all their camp and equipage, baggage &c &c, Col° Bremen fell nobly at the head of the Foreigners, and by his death blotted out part of the stain his countrymen so justly merited from that days behaviour.[207] On our retreating,

[207] From a careful study of the action of the German soldiers in this and other battles of the campaign of '77, there seems to be no sufficient ground for this statement. The German soldiers on all occasions fought bravely and with astonishing persistence, when it is considered how little they were interested in the success or failure of the cause for which they were imperiling their lives. In this case they were posted to defend the British right flank behind a breastwork of rails extending about two hundred yards across a field. The rails were piled horizontally and supported by pickets driven into the ground. The space between this breastwork and the great redoubt was occupied by the Canadian loyalists, who thus protected the German left flank. While Arnold was making his furious attack on the great

which was pretty regular, considering how hard we were pressed by the enemy, General Burgoyne appeared greatly agitated as the danger to which the lines were exposed was of the most serious nature at that particular period. I should be sorry from my expression of *agitated*, that the reader should imagine the fears of personal danger was the smallest cause of it. He must be more than man, who could undisturbed look on and preserve his natural calmness, when the fate of so many were at stake, and entirely depended on the orders he was to issue. He said but little, well knowing we could defend the lines or fall in the attempt. Darkness interposed, (I believe fortunately for us) which put an end to the action.

---

redoubt, a large portion of these Canadians were absent from their post, some aiding in the defense of the great redoubt, and at this critical moment Learned appeared with his brigade and drove those who remained from their position, leaving the German left flank wholly exposed. It was then that Arnold came upon the scene from his attack on the great redoubt, and taking in the situation at a glance, seized Learned's brigade, and rushing through the open space in the British lines left by the retreat of the Canadians, fell upon the unprotected left flank and rear of the Germans with a fury which forced them to retreat, leaving their general dead on the field. This left the key of the position in the hands of the Americans. Undoubtedly this was disastrous to Burgoyne; but that the Germans acted cowardly in the matter, we have no evidence to prove. On the other hand, we have the concurrent testimony of English officers that they were brave men, although in this case they have been criticised by several writers, we think, without a full knowledge of all the facts. The courage of the men engaged in this campaign — English, Germans or Americans — cannot be justly impugned.

General Frazier was yet living, but not the least hopes of him. He that night asked if Gen[l] Burgoynes army were not all cut to pieces, and being informed to the contrary, appeared for a moment pleased, but spoke no more. Capt[n] Wight (53 Grenadiers), my captain, was shot in the bowels early in the action. In him I lost a sincere friend. He lay in that situation between the two fires, and I have been since informed lived till the next day and was brought into their camp. Major Ackland was wounded and taken prisoner with our Quarter master General,[208] and Major Williams of the Artillery. Sir

[208] John Money was a native of Norwich, England, and was commissioned an ensign in the Norfolk militia in 1760, at which date he was twenty years of age. The next year he took part in the battle of Felinghausen as a volunteer, and March 11, 1762, was made a cornet in the Sixth Dragoons; February 10, 1770, he was commissioned a captain in the Ninth Foot. He participated in the campaign of '76, and on July seventeenth of that year was made deputy quartermaster-general. Digby rightly speaks of him as quartermaster-general, as at this time he was acting as such. During this and the previous campaign, he distinguished himself on several occasions. Having been exchanged, he served on the staff of General Cornwallis, and on November 17, 1780, was promoted to a majority in the army, and September 28, 1781, took this position in the Ninth Foot. He was further promoted to the rank of lieutenant-colonel in the army, November 18, 1790, colonel, August 21, 1795, major-general, June 18, 1798, lieutenant-general, October 30, 1805, and general, June 4, 1814. During this time he was on half pay as a major of the Ninety-first Foot, and was the author of several works of a military character. He died on his estate, called Crown Point, near Norwich, on March 26, 1817. *Vide* British Army Lists, *in loco;* The Georgian Era,

Francis Clerk fell, Aid de camp to the general,[209] with other principal officers. Our Grenadier Company out of 20 men going out, left their Captain and 16 men on the field. Some here did not scruple to say, General Burgoyne's manner of acting verified the rash stroke hinted at by General Gates in his orders of the 26th; (see page 281) but that was a harsh and severe insinuation, as I have since heard his intended design was to take post on a rising ground, on the left of their camp,—the 7th— with the detachment, thinking they would not have acted on the offensive, but stood to their works, and on that night our main body was to move, so as to be prepared to storm their lines by day break of the 8th; and it appears by accounts since, that Gen Gates would have acted on the defensive, only for the advice of Brigadier General Arnold, who assured him from his knowledge of the troops, a vigorous sally would inspire them with more courage than waiting behind their works for our attack, and also their knowledge of the woods would contribute to ensure the plan he proposed. During the night we were employed in moving our cannon Baggage &c nearer to the river. It was done with silence, and fires were kept lighted to cause them not to suspect we had retired from

---

vol. 2, p. 97; Hadden's Journal and Orderly Books, pp. xlvii, xlix, 90, 225; Journal of Occurrences During the Late American War, pp. 142, 176; Remembrancer of Public Events, vol. 11, p. 28.

209 *Vide ante*, note 126.

our works where it was impossible for us to remain, as the German lines commanded them, and were then in possession of the enemy, who were bringing up cannon to bear on ours at day break. It may easily be supposed we had no thought for sleep, and some time before day we retreated nearer to the river. Our design of retreating to Ticonderoga then became public.

8th. Took post in a battery which commanded the country around, and the rest of the army surrounding the battery and under cover of our heavy cannon. About 8 in the morning we perceived the enemy marching from their camp in great numbers, blackening the fields with their dark clothing. From the height of the work and by the help of our glasses, we could distinguish them quite plain. They brought some pieces of cannon and attempted to throw up a work for them, but our guns soon demolished what they had executed. Our design was to amuse them during the day with our cannon, which kept them at a proper distance, and at night to make our retreat, but they soon guessed our intentions, and sent a large body of troops in our rear to push for the possession of the heights of Fort Edward. During the day it was entertaining enough, as I had no idea of artillery being so well served as ours was. Sometimes we could see a 12 pounder take place in the centre of their columns, and shells burst among them, thrown from our howitzers with the greatest judgment. Most of their shot were directed at our bridge

View of the **West Bank** *of the* **Hudson's River** *3 Miles above Still Water,* **upon which** *the* **Army** *under the command of* **Lt. General Burgoyne,** *took post on the 20th Sepr. 1777.*
(*Shewing* **General Frazer's** *Funeral.*)

This sketch was made by Sir Francis Carr Clerke, who was fatally wounded on the seventh of October.

of boats, as no doubt they imagined we intended to retreat that way; but their guns were badly served. About 11 o'clock general Frazier died, and desired he might be buried in that battery at evening gun fireing. So fell the best officer under Burgoyne, who from his earliest years was bred in camps, and from the many engagements he had been in, attained a degree of coolness and steadiness of mind in the hour of danger, that alone distinguishes the truly brave man. At 12 o clock some of their balls fell very near our hospital tents, pitched in the plain, and from their size, supposed to attract their notice, taking them perhaps for the general's quarters, on which we were obliged to move them out of the range of fire, which was a most shocking scene,—some poor wretches dying in the attempt, being so very severely wounded. At sun set general Frazier was buried according to his desire, and general Burgoyne attended the service, which was performed I think in the most solemn manner I ever before saw; perhaps the scene around, big with the fate of many, caused it to appear more so, with their fireing particularly at our battery, during the time of its continuance.[210] About 11 at night, the army began their retreat, General Reidzel commanding the Van guard, and Major

[210] We have several accounts of this sad scene. Madame Riedesel is especially graphic in her delineation of it, and, as her memoirs are not accessible to most readers, we may be permitted to copy from them: "I had just sat down with my husband at his quarters to breakfast. General Frazier and, I believe, General Burgoyne were to have dined with me on

General Phillips the rear, and this retreat, though within musket shot of the enemy and encumbered with all the baggage of the army, was made without loss. Our battallion was left to cover the retreat of the whole, which from numberless impediments did

---

that same day. I observed considerable movement among the troops. My husband thereupon informed me, that there was to be a reconnoissance, which, however, did not surprise me, as this often happened. On my way homeward, I met many savages in their war dress, armed with guns. To my question where they were going, they cried out to me, 'War! War!' which meant that they were going to fight. This completely overwhelmed me, and I had scarcely got back to my quarters, when I heard skirmishing, and firing, which by degrees, became constantly heavier, until, finally, the noises became frightful. It was a terrible cannonade, and I was more dead than alive. About three o'clock in the afternoon in place of the guests who were to have dined with me, they brought into me upon a litter poor General Frazier (one of my expected guests), mortally wounded. Our dining table, which was already spread, was taken away and in its place they fixed up a bed for the general. I sat in the corner of the room trembling and quaking. The noises grew continually louder. The thought that they might bring in my husband in the same manner was to me dreadful and tormented me incessantly. The general said to the surgeon, 'Do not conceal any thing from me. Must I die?' The ball had gone through his bowels, precisely as in the case of Major Harnage. Unfortunately, however the general had eaten a hearty breakfast, by reason of which the intestines were distended, and the ball, so the surgeon said, had not gone, as in the case of Major Harnage, between the intestines but through them. I heard him often amidst his groans, exclaim 'Oh, fatal ambition! Poor General Burgoyne! My poor wife'! Prayers were read to him. He then sent a message to General Burgoyne, begging that he would have him buried the following day at six o'clock in the evening, on the top of a hill which was a sort of a

not move until near 4 o'clock in the morning of the 9th, and were then much delayed in breaking up the bridges in our rear. This was the second time of their being destroyed that season—the first by the enemy to prevent our pursueing them. What a great

---

redoubt. I knew no longer which way to turn. The whole entry and the other rooms were filled with the sick, who were suffering with the camp sickness, a kind of dysentery. Finally, toward evening, I saw my husband coming, upon which I forgot all my sufferings, and thanked God that he had spared him to me. He ate in great haste with me and his adjutant behind the house. We had been told that we had gained an advantage over the enemy, but the sorrowful and downcast faces which I beheld, bore witness to the contrary, and before my husband again went away, he drew me one side, and told me that every thing might go very badly, and that I must keep myself in constant readiness for departure; but by no means to give any one the least inkling of what I was doing. I therefore pretended that I wished to move into my new house the next morning, and had every thing packed up. My Lady Ackland occupied a tent not far from our house. In this she slept, but during the day was in the camp. Suddenly one came to tell her that her husband was mortally wounded, and had been taken prisoner. At this she became very wretched. We comforted her by saying that it was only a slight wound, but as no one could nurse him as well as herself, we counseled her to go at once to him, to do which she could certainly obtain permission, ——— She was the loveliest of women. I spent the night in this manner—at one time comforting her and at another looking after my children whom I had put to bed. As for myself, I could not go to sleep, as I had General Frazier and all the other gentlemen in my room, and was constantly afraid that my children would wake up and cry, and thus disturb the poor dying man, who often sent to beg my pardon for making me so much trouble. About three o'clock in the morning, they told me that he could not last much longer. I had desired to be apprised of the approach of this

alteration in affairs! Our hospitals full of sick and wounded were left behind, with a letter from general Burgoyne to general Gates, in which he tells him he makes no doubt of his care to the sick and wounded, conscious of his acting in the same manner himself

---

moment. I accordingly wrapped up the children in the bed coverings and went with them into the entry. Early in the morning, at eight o'clock, he expired. After they had washed the corpse they wrapped it in a sheet and laid it on a bedstead. We then again came into the room, and had this sad sight before us the whole day. At every instant, also, wounded officers of my acquaintance arrived, and the cannonade again began. A retreat was spoken of but there was not the least movement made toward it. About four o'clock in the afternoon, I saw the new house which had been built for me in flames: the enemy, therefore, were not far from us. We learned that General Burgoyne intended to fulfill the last wish of General Frazier, and to have him buried at six o'clock, in the place designated by him. This occasioned an unnecessary delay, to which a part of the misfortunes of the army was owing. Precisely at six o'clock the corpse was brought out, and we saw the entire body of generals with their retinues on the hill assisting at the obsequies. The English chaplain, Mr. Brudenel, performed the funeral services. The cannon balls flew continually around and over the party. The American general, Gates, said that if he had known that it was a burial he would not have allowed any firing in that direction. Many cannon balls also flew not far from me, but I had my eyes fixed upon the hill, where I distinctly saw my husband in the midst of the enemy's fire, and therefore I could not think of my own danger. The order had gone forth that the army should break up after the burial, and the horses were already harnessed to our calashes. I did not wish to set out before the troops. The wounded Major Harnage, although he was so ill, dragged himself out of bed, that he might not remain in the hospital, which was left behind protected by a flag of truce. As soon as he observed me in the midst of danger, he had my children

had the fortune of war placed it in his reach. During our march, it surprised us their not placing troops on the heights we were obliged to pass under, as by so doing, we must have suffered much. We came up with the general and the line about 9 in the morning at Davagot,[211] seven miles from the enemy. It then began to rain very hard and continued so all day. We halted till near 3 in the evening, which surprised many; about which time, a large body of the enemy were perceived on the other side the river, and supposed to be on their way to Fort Edward in order to obstruct our crossing at that place, on which we were immediately ordered to march after burning all unnec-

---

and maid servants put into the calashes, and intimated to me that I must immediately depart. As I still begged to be allowed to remain, he said to me, 'Well then your children at least must go, that I may save them from the slightest danger.' He understood how to take advantage of my weak side. I gave it up, seated myself inside with them, and we drove off with them at eight o'clock in the evening. The greatest silence had been enjoined, fires had been kindled in every direction: and many tents left standing, to make the enemy believe that the camp was still there. We traveled continually the whole night. Little Frederica was afraid and would often begin to cry. I was, therefore, obliged to hold a pocket handkerchief over her mouth, lest our whereabouts should be discovered. At six o'clock in the morning a halt was made, at which every one wondered. General Burgoyne had all the cannon ranged and counted, which worried all of us, as a few more good marches would have placed us in security." *Vide* Letters and Journals of Madame Riedesel, pp. 116–123.

[211] This place is now called Coveville. The old name is said to have been derived from dovecote, on account, perhaps, of having been a haunt for wild pigeons.

essary baggage, camp equipage and many wagons and carts, which much delayed our line of march. Here Lady Harriot Ackland was prevailed to go to the enemy, or I might rather say, it was her wish to do so, her husband, the major, being a prisoner. She was conducted to general Gates by a chaplain,[212] and received, I am informed, by him with the greatest politeness possible; indeed he must have been a brute to have acted otherwise.[213] We waded the Fish

[212] Rev. Edward Brudenel was the chaplain to the artillery, and is the person to whom Fonblanque erroneously marries Lady Acland after the major's death. His bravery was marked at this terrible funeral by his "steady attitude and his unaltered voice, though frequently covered with dust which the shot threw up on all sides of him." He subsequently became the rector of a parish in Lincolnshire, and died in London, June 25, 1805. *Vide* note to Hadden's Journal, p. 106.

[213] The account of the manner in which Lady Acland received the news of her husband's dangerous condition, namely, that he was mortally wounded and a prisoner in the enemy's hands is related by the Baroness Riedesel and quoted in note 210. She resolved to go to him, and applied to Burgoyne for permission, who says: "Though I was ready to believe that patience and fortitude in a supreme degree were to be found, as well as every other virtue, under the most tender forms, I was astonished at this proposal. After so long an agitation of spirits, exhausted not only for want of rest, but absolutely want of food, drenched in rains for twelve hours together, that a woman should be capable of such an undertaking as delivering herself to an enemy probably in the night, and uncertain of what hands she might fall into, appeared an effort above human nature. The assistance I was enabled to give was small indeed. I had not even a cup of wine to offer her; but was told she had found, from some kind and fortunate hand, a little rum and dirty water. All I could furnish to her was an open boat

Kiln near Schylers house, about 8 o'clock that night, — the enemy having destroyed the Bridge some days

---

and a few lines, written upon dirty and wet paper, to General Gates, recommending her to his protection. In this open boat, accompanied by Chaplain Brudenel, her maid and husband's body servant, who was wounded, at night-fall and in the midst of an icy storm, she set out on her dangerous undertaking. It was ten o'clock when they reached the outpost, and Lady Acland hailed it herself. Major Dearborn was in command, and the party were conducted to his quarters, — a log cabin on the shore of the lake. Here they were detained until sunrise, but Lady Acland's mind was partially relieved from anxiety by the announcement that her husband was not in danger from his wounds." Wilkinson says: "I visited the guard before sunrise, her boat had put off and was floating down the stream to our camp, where General Gates, whose gallantry will not be denied, stood ready to receive her with all the tenderness and respect to which her rank and condition gave her a claim; indeed the feminine figure, the benign aspect, and polished manners of this charming woman, were alone sufficient to attract the sympathy of the most obdurate; but if another motive could have been wanting to inspire respect, it was furnished by the peculiar circumstances of Lady Harriet, then in that most delicate situation, which cannot fail to interest the solicitudes of every being possessing the form and feelings of a man." Lady Acland is always spoken of as a woman of charming refinement. General Gates, in a letter to his wife, said: "She is the most amiable, delicate piece of quality you ever beheld." She was greatly beloved in the army for her kind attentions to the sick and wounded, often denying herself such little comforts as came to her in order to bestow them upon the suffering. A widow for thirty seven years, she died, July 21, 1815. *Vide* Memoirs of My Own Times, vol. 1, pp. 284, 377; Journal of Occurrences During the Late American War, pp. 185–189; Historical Magazine, vol. 4, p. 9; Political and Military Episodes, pp. 297–302; Memoirs of Madame Riedesel, p. 120; Campaign of General John Burgoyne (Stone), Appendix 7.

before — and took post soon after on the heights of Saratoga, where we remained all night under constant heavy rain, without fires or any kind of shelter to guard us from the inclemency of the weather. It was impossible to sleep, even had we an inclination to do so, from the cold and rain, and our only entertainment was the report of some popping shots heard now and then from the other side the great river at our Battows.[214]

10th. Preparations were made early in the morning to push for the heights of Fort Edward, and a detachment of artificers we sent under a strong escort to repair the bridges and open the road to that place. The 47th regiment, Captain Frazier's marksmen and MacKay's provincials[215] were ordered for that service;

[214] Madame Riedesel gives an interesting account of the distressing condition of affairs at this period in Burgoyne's army. *Vide* Her Letters and Journal, pp. 124–134.

[215] Samuel McKay was an ensign in the Sixty-second Foot, December 30, 1755, and was promoted to the rank of lieutenant, December 6, 1756, at which time he was in America. He served through the French war, and at its conclusion, in 1763, retired upon half pay. He was in command of a body of Canadian volunteers at Fort St. John when it was captured by Montgomery in September, 1775, and was made a prisoner. He was sent to Hartford, and while there on parole, attempted to escape, but was recaptured and roughly handled by his captors. He was confined in jail, it was thought, securely, but succeeded in making his escape; and making his way to Canada, raised a company of volunteers, with which he joined St. Leger's expedition. He went safely through the campaign of '77, and died in the summer of 1779. *Vide* British Army Lists, *in loco;* American Archives, 4th Series, vol. 4, p. 248; 5 Ibid., vol. 5, p. 452; Ibid., vol. 6, pp. 563, 574, 601, 633; 5th Series, vol. 1, p. 133.

but about 11 o clock, intelligence was received that the enemy were surrounding us, on which it was resolved to maintain our post, and expresses were sent to recall the 47th regiment &c. We burned Schyler's house to prevent a lodgement being formed behind it,[216] and almost all our remaining baggage, rather

[216] Digby doubtless gives the correct version of this affair. Burgoyne was charged with having destroyed property unnecessarily, but denied it in Parliament in the following words: "I am ignorant of any such circumstance; I do not recollect more than one accident by fire. I positively assert there was no fire by order or countenance of myself, or any other officer except at Saratoga. That district is the property of Major General Schuyler of the American troops; there were large barracks built by him, which took fire the day after the army arrived upon the ground in their retreat, and I believe I need not state any other proof of that matter being merely accident, than that the barracks were then made use of as my hospital, and full of sick and wounded soldiers. General Schuyler had likewise a very good dwelling house, exceeding large storehouses, great saw mills and other out buildings, to the value altogether of perhaps ten thousand pounds; a few days before the negotiations with General Gates, the enemy had formed a plan to attack me; a large column of troops were approaching to pass the small river, preparatory to a general action, and were entirely covered from the fire of my artillery by these buildings. Sir, I know that I gave the order to set them on fire; and in a very short time that whole property I have described, was consumed. But to shew that the person most deeply concerned in that calamity, did not put the construction upon it which it has pleased the honourable gentleman to do, I must inform the house, that one of the first persons I saw, after the convention was signed was General Schuyler. I expressed to him my regret at the event which had happened, and the reasons which had occasioned it. He desired me to think no more of it; said that the occasion justified it, according to the principles and rules of war, and he should

than it should fall into their hands. Here again the discontented part of the army were of opinion that our retreat was not conducted so well as it might have been, and that in place of burning our bridge of boats over the Hudson, which we left on fire on our retreating the night of the 8th, from whence it was evident to the enemy which side of the river we intended to keep on, and would oblige us to ford the Hudson opposite to where they had a force; consequently would be attended with a disadvantage. We should have crossed our bridge on the night of the 8th to gain the Fort Edward side of the river, and would have nothing to delay our march—we moving so many hours before they were apprized of our motions. They also declared our halting so long at Davagot, the 9th within 7 miles of the enemy, was the cause of our being surrounded, as even then we had time to have pushed on, and the day being so constant rain was in our favour, as had we attempted to ford the river at Saratoga, the small arms of the enemy, as well as ours must have been so wet, that but few would go off, and they knew our superiority at the bayonet. They also said that even the 10th by spiking our cannon and destroying all our baggage &c a paltry consideration in comparison, in our circumstances—we might have made our retreat good to Fort George,

---

have done the same upon the same occasion, or words to that effect." *Vide* Speech of General Burgoyne on a Motion of Inquiry made by Mr. Vyner in Parliament, May 26, 1778.

saving the troops and Musquetry: but even then it was not certain that vessels were prepared to convey us over the lake; in which case it would have been a worse post than Saratoga for the army. These were the opinions of unsatisfied and discontented men, who never approved of anything that turned out contrary to their expectations. Had Burgoyne been fortunate, they would not have dared to declare them; as he was unsuccessful, they set him down guilty. However, all thoughts of a retreat were then given over, and a determination [made] to fall nobly together, rather than disgrace the name of British troops; on which we immediately changed our ground a little, and under the protection of that night, began to entrench ourselves, all hands being ordered to work. We were called together and desired to tell our men that their own safety, as well as ours, depended on their making a vigorous defence; but that I was sure was an unnecessary caution,— well knowing they would never forfeit the title of Soldiers. As for the Germans, we had but a poor opinion of their spirit since the night of the 7th. Certain our situation was not the most pleasing; but we were to make the best of it, and I had long before accustomed and familiarized my mind to bear with patience any change that might happen. The men worked without ceasing during the night, and without the least complaining of fatigue, our cannon were drawn up to the embrasures and pointed ready to receive them at day break.

11th. Their cannon and ours began to play on each other. They took many of our Battows on the river, as our cannon could not protect them. We were obliged to bring our oxen and horses into our lines, where they had the wretched prospect of living but a few days, as our grass was all gone, and nothing after but the leaves of the trees for them; still they continued fireing into us from Batteries they had erected during the night, and placed their riflemen in the tops of trees; but still did not venture to storm our works. At night we strengthened our works and threw up more.

12th. Our cattle began to die fast and the stench was very prejudicial in so small a space. A cannon shot was near taking the general, as it lodged quite close to him in a large oak tree. We now began to perceive their design by keeping at such a distance, which was to starve us out. I believe the generals greatest wish, as indeed it ought to be, was for them to attack us, but they acted with much greater prudence, well knowing what a great slaughter we must have made among them: they also knew exactly the state of our provisions, which was [sufficient for] but 4 or 5 days more, and that upon short allowance. In the evening, many of our Canadian drivers of wagons, carts and other like services, found means to escape from us. At night, I ventured to take a little sleep which had long been a stranger to me, and tho but a short time could be spared between our watches, yet [I] found myself much refreshed.

We were all in pretty good health, though lying in wet trenches newly dug must be very prejudicial to the constitution, and tho it might not affect it for the time, yet rheumatism afterwards would be the certain consequence.

13th. Their cannon racked our post very much; the bulk of their army was hourly reinforced by militia flocking in to them from all parts, and their situation, which nearly surrounded us, was from the nature of the ground unattackable in all parts; and since the 7th the men lay constantly upon their arms,— Harassed and fatigued beyond measure, from their great want of rest. All night we threw up Traverse[217] to our works, as our lines were enfiladed or flanked by their cannon.

14th. A council of war was called, and a flag of truce sent to the enemy by Major Kingston,[218] and the

---

[217] A traverse, in military parlance, is a breastwork thrown up to protect a line of works against an enfilading or reverse fire.

[218] Robert Kingston was commissioned an ensign in the Eleventh Foot, September 3, 1756, and a lieutenant, January 26, 1758. August 8, 1759, he exchanged into Burgoyne's regiment, the Sixteenth Light Dragoons, and served in the Portugal campaign, in which Burgoyne achieved renown. For his meritorious services he was advanced to the grade of captain, April 27, 1761; was made major, July 15, 1768, and served with his regiment until 1774, when he went on half pay until April 17, 1776. He accompanied Burgoyne on his return to America in the spring of 1777, as deputy adjutant-general, and August 29, 1777, became a lieutenant-colonel in the army, and after the death of Sir Francis Clerke took that lamented officer's position of sec-

following message delivered by him to Gen Gates from Gen Burgoyne. "I am directed to represent

---

retary to General Burgoyne. He it was who conducted the negotiations leading to the surrender. On approaching the advanced post between the armies he was met by Wilkinson, the adjutant of Gates, and conducted blindfolded to the tent of the American general. Wilkinson says that at this time "he appeared to be about forty; he was a well-formed, ruddy, handsome man, and expatiated with taste and eloquence on the beautiful scenery of the Hudson's river and the charms of the season. When I introduced him into General Gates' tent and named him, the gentlemen saluted each other familiarly with 'General Gates, your servant;' and Kingston, 'how do you do?' and a shake of the hand." Having read to Gates this communication from Burgoyne, Wilkinson says: "To my utter astonishment, General Gates put his hand to his side pocket, pulled out a paper, and presented it to Kingston, observing: '*There, sir, are the terms on which General Burgoyne must surrender.*' The major appeared thunderstruck, but read the paper, whilst the old chief surveyed him attentively through his spectacles." We are informed that he at first declined to take back to Burgoyne the terms of Gates, but finally thought better of it and consented to do so upon the cogent reason given by Gates, "*that as he had brought the message he ought to take back the answer.*" Kingston was commissioned lieutenant-colonel of the Eighty-sixth Foot, September 30, 1779; was subsequently appointed lieutenant-governor of Demarara, and was in command when that island was surrendered to the French, February 3, 1782. He was promoted to a colonelcy in the army on the twentieth of the following November, and served for seven years as a commissioner on the claims of loyalists in the American war. He was made a major-general, October 12, 1793, but his name does not appear on the list of the following year. *Vide* British Army Lists, *in loco;* Memoirs of My Own Times, vol. 1, pp. 299–313; The Remembrancer of Public Events, vol. 14, p. 333; The Loyalists of America and their Times (Ryerson), Toronto, 1880, vol. 2, pp. 166–182.

to you from Gen Burgoyne, that after having fought you twice, he has waited some days in his present situation determined to try a third conflict against any force you could bring to attack him; he is apprized of the superiority of your numbers, and the disposition of your troops to impede his supplies and render his retreat a scene of carnage on both sides. In this situation he is impelled by humanity and thinks himself justified by established principles and precedent of state and of war, to spare the lives of brave men upon honourable terms. Should Major General Gates be inclined to treat upon that idea, Gen Burgoyne would propose a cessation of arms during the time necessary to communicate the preliminary terms, by which in any extremity he and his army mean to abide." It was then generally believed by their not attacking us, and our speedy want of provisions, that terms were the only resource left us. What could be thought of else in our truly distressed situation? They, of course, would not risque an action in such circumstances, which was the only hope left us, as by their declining it, we must in consequence, fall a prey to want and hunger which then stared us fully in the face. On the return of the flag, Gen Gates sent in the following propositions, to which I shall insert Gen Burgoynes replys and those which it was impossible for us to accept, were our situation ever so desperate, are in my opinion most spiritedly answered by General Burgoyne.

GENERAL GATES' PROPOSITIONS.

1. "Gen Burgoyne's army being exceedingly reduced by repeated defeats, by desertion, sickness &c. &c. their provisions exhausted, their military stores tents and baggage taken or destroyed, their retreat cut off and their camp invested, they can only be allowed to surrender prisoners of war."

Reply, "Lieut General Burgoyne's, army however reduced, will never admit that their retreat is cut off, while they have arms in their hands."

2. "The officers and soldiers may keep their baggage belonging to them, the Generals of the United States, never permit individuals to be pillaged"

3. "The troops under his excellency Gen Burgoyne will be conducted by the most convenient route to New England, marching by easy marches and sufficiently provided for by the way."

4. "The officers will be admitted on parole, may wear their side arms, and will be treated with the liberality customary in Europe, so long as they, by proper behaviour continue to deserve it; but those who are apprehended having broke their parole (as some British officers have done) must expect to be close confined"—

Reply, "There being no officers in this army under or capable of being under, the description of breaking parole, this article needs no answer."

5. "All public stores, Artillery, Arms, amunition, carriages horses &c must be delivered to commissaries appointed to receive them."

Reply "All public stores may be delivered, arms excepted."

6. "These terms being agreed to and signed, the troops under his excellency Gen Burgoyne's command may be drawn up in their encampment, when they will be ordered to ground their arms and may thereupon be marched to the river side to be passed over on their way towards Bennington"

Reply "This article inadmissible in any extremity. Sooner than this army will consent to ground their arms in their encampment, they will rush on the enemy determined to take no quarter"

Signed 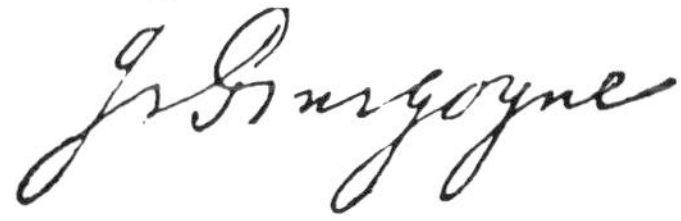

7. "A cessation of arms to continue until sun set to receive general Burgoynes answer"

Signed — 

CAMP AT SARATOGA. *October* 14th 1777.

These propositions being laid before the council of war consisting of all the field officers of the army and captains commanding corps — for deaths had reduced us so much — we deemed unhonourable to be accepted. This gave the greatest satisfaction possible to Gen Burgoyne, who wished, if possible, to avoid any terms; still persisting [in] a faint glimmering of hope, from either the arrival of Gen Clinton or some other unforseen and providential manner, of our being extricated from the many difficulties that then surrounded us. At night another council of war was called, and terms as high on our side sent, supposing a medium would be struck.

15th. A cessation of arms was agreed upon till 2 o'clock at Noon, during which we walked out of our lines into the plain by the river and between both armies, when near the period of the cessation being over, we stood to our works, more watchful of a surprise than at any other time. Col. Sutherland[219] near

[219] Nicholas Sutherland was commissioned an ensign in the Sixty-second Foot, June 14, 1755, and was promoted to the rank of lieutenant in the Seventy-seventh Foot, January 8, 1757, and of captain-lieutenant, September 15, 1758, at which time his regiment was in America. He took part in the siege, which resulted in the surrender of Fort Du Quesne, and the next year was in an expedition against the Cherokees, in which he was wounded. He became a captain, December 31, 1761, and the next year took part in an expedition against Martinico and Havana. He was on half pay from 1763 till March 14, 1765, when he entered the Twenty-first Foot, then about to embark for America, as captain. He became major in this regiment by purchase, February 21, 1772, and returned shortly after to England, where the Twenty-first was stationed until the spring of 1776, when it was ordered again to America, and after General Nesbit's death he was advanced, November 5, 1776, to that officer's place of lieutenant-colonel. In the negotiations for the surrender of Burgoyne, he was an important figure, as will be seen from the following: The terms had been practically arranged, October fifteenth, and Captain Craig, at half-past ten o'clock, had written to Wilkinson, the aid-de-camp of Gates, that they had received Burgoyne's approbation and concurrence. Owing to the news of Clinton's

two returned with the flag, and brought accounts that General Gates seemed almost willing to come into our terms; but soon after a report circulated that General Clinton was coming up the river, tho at a great distance, which Burgoyne eagerly catched at, and to make it stronger, Gates so easily complying with our proposals confirmed it to him; on which he expressed his desire to withdraw the treaty if possible, but luckily for the army, he was overruled

---

advance, before alluded to, Burgoyne desired to break the agreement, which only required the signatures of the party to complete it. The next day Gates, finding that Burgoyne was delaying to complete the agreement, finally gave him two hours to decide in, at the expiration of which time hostilities were to recommence. Says Wilkinson: "The two hours had elapsed by a quarter, and an aid-de-camp from the general had been with me to know how matters progressed. Soon after I perceived Lieutenant-Colonel Sutherland opposite to me and beckoned him to cross the creek; on approaching me he observed: 'Well, our business will be knocked in the head after all.' I enquired why? He said: 'The officers had got the devil in their heads and could not agree.' I replied gaily: 'I am sorry for it, as you will not only lose your fusee* but your whole baggage.' He expressed much sorrow, but said he could not help it. At this moment I recollected the letter Captain Craig had written me the night before and taking it from my pocket I read it to the colonel, who declared he had not been privy to it; and added, with evident anxiety: 'Will you give me that letter?' I answered in the negative, and observed: 'I should hold it as a testimony of the good faith of a British commander.' He hastily replied: 'Spare me that letter, sir, and I pledge you my honour I will return it in fifteen minutes.' I penetrated the motive and willingly handed it to him; he sprang off with it, and directing his course to the British camp, ran

---

* Which he had owned thirty-five years and had desired me to except from the surrendered arms and save for him as she was a favorite piece.

in opinion, as the report of Clinton was entirely groundless, and we had then but two days provisions.

In the morning our money chest was distributed among the army: still, the general delayed signing the treaty and nothing was done; cannonading and small arms commenced afresh, upon the report of the treaty being broke up, but after many flags passing and repassing, the terms were at last mutually agreed to, and to be signed that evening by both generals viz.—

ARTICLES OF CONVENTION [220] BETWEEN LIEUT GENERAL BURGOYNE AND MAJOR GENERAL GATES.

1. The troops under Lieutenant General Burgoyne to march out of their camp with the honours of war,

---

as far as I could see him. In the meantime I received a peremptory message from the general to break off the treaty if the convention was not immediately ratified. I informed him by the messenger that I was doing the best I could for him and would see him in half an hour. Colonel Sutherland was punctual to his promise and returned with Captain Craig, who delivered me the convention signed by General Burgoyne. I then returned to head-quarters, after eight hours' absence, and presented to General Gates the important document that made the British army conventional prisoners to the United States." Lieutenant-Colonel Sutherland returned to England on parole several months after the surrender, and died there July 18, 1781. *Vide* British Army Lists, *in loco;* Memoirs of My Own Times, vol. 1, p. 316, *et seq.;* Historical Record of the Twenty-first Foot, p. 25, *et seq.;* Burgoyne's Orderly Book, p. 17.

[220] This document was originally headed Articles of Capitulation, but the word *capitulation* was objected to by Burgoyne and *convention* substituted therefor, to save in some

and the Artillery out of the entrenchments to the verge of the river, where the old fort stood, where the arms and artillery are to be left—the arms to be piled by word of command by their own officers.

2. A free passage to be granted to the army under Lieut Gen Burgoyne to Great Britain, on condition

---

measure his wounded pride. This occasioned a laugh among some of his critics, as it was so much in accord with the acts of those at this time in authority, who in all their doings laid great stress upon preserving the national dignity. The following, among many of a like strain, written after the surrender, and printed in a London journal, well illustrates the manner in which the opponents of the government viewed the course of those who were managing the war:

"ETIQUETTE."

What though America doth pour
Her millions to Britannia's store,
(Quoth Grenville) that won't do; for yet,
Though it risk all and nothing get,
Taxation is the etiquette.

The tea destroy'd; the offer made,
That all the loss should be repaid;
North asks not justice, nor the debt,
But he must have the etiquette.

At Bunker's Hill the cause was tried;
The earth with British blood was dy'd;
Our army, though 'twas soundly beat
(We hear) bore off the etiquette.

The bond dissolv'd, the people rose;
Their rulers from themselves they chose,
Their Congress then at nought was set;
Its *name* was not the etiquette.

Though 'twere to stop the tide of blood,
Their titles must not be allow'd—
(Not to the chiefs of armies met,)
"*One*" Arnold was the etiquette.

The Yankees at Long Island found
That they were nearly run aground;
Howe let them 'scape when so beset-
He will explain that etiquette.

of not serving again in North America during the present contest; and the port of Boston is assigned for the entry of transports to receive the troops whenever general How shall so order.

3 Should any chartel take place by which the army under Lieut Gen Burgoyne, or any part of it may be exchanged, the foregoing article to be void, as far as such exchange shall be made.

4. The army under Lieut general Burgoyne to march to Massachusets bay by the easiest, most convenient and expeditious route, and to be quartered in, near, or as convenient as possible to Boston,

---

His aides-de-camp to Britain boast
Of battles *Yankee* never lost;
But they are *won* in the Gazette —
That saves the nation's etiquette.

Clinton, his injured honour saw;
Swore he'd be tried by martial law,
And kick Germaine whene'er they met;
A *riband* saved that etiquette.

Though records speak Germaine's disgrace,
To quote them to him face to face,
(The Commons now are *si honnête*,)
They voted not the etiquette.

Of Saratoga's dreadful plain —
An army ruin'd — why complain?
To pile their arms as they were let,
Sure they came off with etiquette.

Cries Burgoyne, 'They may be reliev'd;
That army still may be retriev'd,
To see the King, if I be let,'
'No Sir! 'Tis not the etiquette.'

God save the King! and should he choose
His people's confidence to lose,
What matters it? They'll not forget
To serve him still through etiquette.

Vide Journal of the Reign of George the Third (Walpole), London, 1859, vol. 2, p. 275, *et seq.*

that the march of the troops may not be delayed, when transports arrive to receive them.

5 The troops to be supplied on their march and during their being in quarters, with provisions by general Gates' orders; at the same rate of rations as the troops of his own army; and if possible, the officer's horses and cattle to be supplied with forage at the usual rate.

6 All officers to retain their carriages, batt horses and other cattle, and no baggage to be molested or searched — Lieut General Burgoyne giving his honour that there are no public stores secreted therein: major general Gates will of course take the necessary measures for the due performance of this article, Should any carriages be wanted during the march for the transportation of officer's baggage, they are, if possible, to be supplied by the country at the usual rates.

7 Upon the march and during the time the army shall remain in quarters in the Massachusets Bay, the officers are not, as far as circumstances will admit, to be separated from their men; the officers to be quartered according to their rank, and are not to be hindered from assembling their men for roll calling and other necessary purposes of regularity.

8 All corps whatever of General Burgoyne's army, whether composed of sailor's, battow-men, artificers, drivers, independent companies and followers of the army of whatever country, shall be included in the fullest sense and utmost extent of the above articles,

and comprehended in every respect as British subjects.

9. All Canadians and persons belonging to the Canadian establishment, consisting of sailors, battow men, artificers, drivers, independent companies and any other followers of the army, who come under no particular description, are to be permitted to return there; they are to be conducted immediately by the shortest route to the first British post on Lake George, and are to be supplied with provisions in the same manner as the other troops, and are to be bound by the same condition of not serving during the present contest in North America.

10. Passports to be immediately granted for three officers not exceeding the rank of captains, who shall be appointed by Lieut Gen Burgoyne to carry dispatches to Sir Willm Howe, Sir Guy Carlton and to Great Britain by the way of New York; and Major Gen Gates engages the public faith that these dispatches shall not be opened. These officers are to set out immediately after receiving their dispatches, and are to travel the shortest route and in the most expeditious manner.

11 During the stay of the troops in Massachusets Bay, the officers are to be admitted on Parole, and are to be permitted to wear their side arms.

12 Should the army under Lieut General Burgoyne find it necessary to send for their clothing and other baggage to Canada, they are to be permitted to do

it in the most convenient manner, and the necessary passports granted for that purpose.

13 These articles are to be mutually signed and exchanged tomorrow morning at nine of the clock, and the troops under Lieut Gen. Burgoyne are to march out of their entrenchments at 3 o clock this afternoon.

CAMP AT SARATOGA, 16th *October* 1777

Signed —

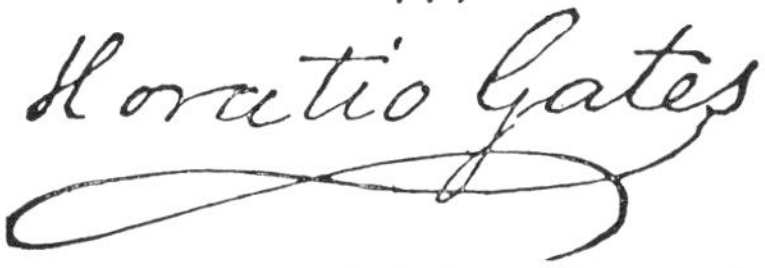

Major General.

In place of marching from our encampment that evening as expressed in the convention, it was deferred till the next morning. In the mean time, we made preparations for so long a march — about 200 miles — and the wet, rainy season just coming on. I had not destroyed all my baggage, tho' indeed most of it was gone at the general conflagration ; but as to the horses who outlived our late scene of every imaginable distress, they exhibited a most wretched picture of poverty and want, made up of nothing but skin and bone, and it may naturally be supposed, rather unfit for such a journey.

17 A day famous in the annals of America.[221]

Gen Burgoyne desired a meeting of all the officers early that morning, at which he entered into a detail

[221] Verily, as Digby remarks, the seventeenth of October was a day memorable in the annals of America ; for the

of his manner of acting since he had the honour of commanding the army; but he was too full to speak; heaven only could tell his feelings at the

---

surrender of Burgoyne's army has been regarded by historians from that day to this as the turning point in that conflict which freed a people from thraldom to aristocracy and made possible a true republie. Under date of December 2, 1777, Walpole says: "At night came an express from General Carleton, informing that he had learnt by deserters, and believed, that the Provincials had taken Burgoyne and his whole army prisoners. The King fell into agonies on hearing this account, but the next morning, at his levee to disguise his concern, affected to laugh and to be so indecently merry, that Lord North endeavoured to stop him;" and under date of the fifteenth, thirteen days later, he records the reception of the official account from the hands of Captain Craig. Upon this a public fast was appointed, which stirred up the wits all over the kingdom. As an example Walpole gives us the following effusion upon the several generals who conducted the war in America:

> " First General Gage commenced the war in vain;
> Next General Howe continued the campaign,
> Then General Burgoyne took the field, and last,
> *Our forlorn hope* depends on *General Fast*."

Walpole also wrote, under date of February 27, 1778: "The Fast was observed — a ridiculous solemnity, as the nation was to beg a blessing on their arms, when the war was at an end, or at least suspended for sixteen months if the Americans pleased."

The following was a

"REFLECTION ON THE FAST."

Psalm xxvi, v. 6.

> " With *cruel hearts* and *bloody hands*,
> The Ministry were stain'd,
> A Fast was publish'd thro' these lands
> That they might all be clean'd,
> But, oh! what blunders, time affords,
> Thro' want of *grace* and *sense*,
> They wash'd them in — *a form* of *words*
> Instead of *Innocence*."

time. He dwelled much on his orders to make the wished for junction with General Clinton, and as to how his proceedings had turned out, we must (he said), be as good judges as himself. He then read over the Articles of Convention, and informed us the terms were even easier than we could have expected from our situation, and concluded with assuring us, he never would have accepted any terms, had we provisions enough, or the least hopes of our extricating ourselves any other way. About 10 o'clock, we marched out, according to treaty, with drums beating & the honours of war, but the drums seemed to

---

The London *Morning Post* had the following:

"OUR COMMANDERS

Nov. 2, '77.

Gage nothing did and went to pot;
Howe lost one town and other got;
Guy nothing lost and nothing won,
Dunmore was homeward forced to run,
Clinton was beat, and got a garter,
And bouncing Burgoyne catch'd a Tartar,
Thus all we gain for millions spent
Is to be laughed at, and repent."

But the following reads almost like an American production. It is entitled:

"THE HALCYON DAYS OF OLD ENGLAND. A BALLAD.

What honours were gaining by taking their forts,
Destroying batteaux and blocking up ports;
Burgoyne would have worked them — but for a mishap,
By Gates and one Arnold he's caught in a trap.
Sing tantarara, etc.

But Howe was more cautious and prudent by far,
He sailed with his fleet up the great Delaware.
All summer he struggled and strove to undo them
But the plague of it was that he could not get to them."

Vide Journal of the Reign of George the Third, vol. 2, pp. 76, 170, 186, 214, *et passim.*

have lost their former inspiriting sounds, and though we beat the Grenadiers march, which not long before was so animating, yet then it seemed by its last feeble effort, as if almost ashamed to be heard on such an occasion. As to my own feelings, I cannot express them. Tears (though unmanly) forced their way, and if alone, I could have burst to give myself vent. I never shall forget the appearance of their troops on our marching past them; a dead silence universally reigned through their numerous columns, and even then, they seemed struck with our situation and dare scarce lift up their eyes to view British Troops in such a situation. I must say their decent behaviour during the time, (to us so greatly fallen) meritted the utmost approbation and praise.[222] The meeting between Burgoyne and Gates was well

---

[222] Walpole sarcastically observes, while reflecting upon the surrender and the word "dictated," as applied to its terms by Burgoyne: "The terms were singularly gentle and the Provincials, while the prisoners deposited their arms, kept out of sight, not to insult their disgrace." The grief of the British soldiers was as profound as the joy of the Americans. Every rhymester in the land was ready to join in the chorus, no matter how rough his voice might be, and many of the strains sound strangely to modern ears. As an example, we quote from a volume of the poems of Rev. Wheeler Case, printed in 1778, and thought worthy of a reprint in 1852:

"The hero *Gates* appears in sight,
His troops are clothed in armor bright;
They all as one their banners spread,
With *Death* or Victory on their head.

"O horrid place! Oh dreadful gloom!
I mourn for want of *elbow room*,
My tawny soldiers from me fled,
Have now returned to scalp my head."

worth seeing. He paid Burgoyne almost as much respect as if he was the conqueror, indeed, his noble air, tho prisoner, seemed to command attention and respect from every person. A party of Light dragoons were ordered as his guard, rather to protect his person from insults than any other cause. Thus ended all our hopes of victory, honour, glory &c &c &c. Thus was Burgoyne's Army sacrificed to either the absurd opinions of a blundering ministerial power; the stupid inaction of a general, who, from his lethargic disposition, neglected every step he might have taken to assist their operations,[223] or lastly,

[223] The failure of General Howe to co-operate with Burgoyne excited widespread astonishment and made him, as well as his brother, the earl, very unpopular, as will be seen from the following letter written from New York to England, December 10, 1777: "If you was in this town you would be surprised to find the Howes so unpopular; they have been so here all this campaign. The total loss of General Burgoyne's army can only be imputed to them.—To possess the lakes and the North river, and by that means to separate the northern and southern colony, seems to have been the expectation of the King, Ministers, Parliament and Nation. Had General Howe gone up the North River, instead of acting to the southward that line of separation would have been formed in July. General Burgoyne's army would have been saved, and both armies, conjunctly or separately, might have acted against New England, which would have been striking at the heart of the rebellion.—General Howe, in his retreat from the Jerseys, in his embarkation, in his stay aboard the transports before he sailed, in his voyage to the mouth of the Delaware, where he played at bopeep with the rebels, and in his circumbendibus to Chesapeak Bay, expended nearly three months of the finest time of the campaign; and all this to go out of his way, to desert his real business, and to leave Burgoyne with 6,000 regulars to fall a

perhaps, his own misconduct in penetrating so far, as to be unable to return, and tho I must own my

---

sacrifice." On his return to England he was assailed on every side and endeavored to meet his critics by a defense in which he asserted that he had received no positive orders to co-operate with Burgoyne. This, however, was not deemed sufficient, but it is now known, that by the carelessness of Lord George Germaine, the minister of George the Third, for American affairs, the orders intended for Howe were not forwarded to him, as will be seen from the following, taken from the Life of the Earl of Shelburne: "The inconsistent orders given to Generals Howe and Burgoyne, could not be accounted for except in a way which it must be difficult for any person who is not conversant with the negligence of office to comprehend. Among many singularities, he had a particular aversion to being put out of his way on any occasion; he had fixed to go into Kent or Northamptonshire at a particular hour, and to call on his way at his office to sign the despatches, all of which had been settled, to both these Generals. By some mistake, those to General Howe were not fair copied, and upon his growing impatient at it, the office, which was a very idle one, promised to send it to the country after him, while they dispatched the others to General Burgoyne, expecting that the others could be expedited before the packet sailed with the first, which, however, by some mistake sailed without them, and the wind detained the vessel which was ordered to carry the rest. Hence came General Burgoyne's defeat, the French declaration and the loss of thirteen colonies. It might appear incredible if our own Secretary and the most respectable persons in office had not assured me of the fact; what corroborates it is that it could be accounted for in no other way. It requires as much experience in business to comprehend the very trifling causes which have produced the greatest events, as it does strength of reason to develope the design." *Vide* A View of the Evidence relating to the conduct of the American War under Sir William Howe, Lord Viscount Howe and General Burgoyne, London, 1779, p. 82, *et seq.;* Life of William, Earl of Shelburne, vol. 1, p. 358, *et seq.*

partiality to him is great, yet if he or the army under his command are guilty, let them suffer to the utmost extent, and by an unlimited punishment, in part blot out and erase if possible, the crime charged to their account.

No doubt the reader has seen general Burgoyne's letter dated Albany 20th October 1777 to Lord George Germain, in which he gives the fullest account of the army under his command, being reduced so much by repeated distresses and unsuccessful attempts to enter into a convention with Major General Gates commanding the Continental army on the 17th October at Saratoga. He there gives his reasons for acting on every occasion in the most particular manner, which I hope, and sincerely wish, will fully acquit him to the world of any censure the misfortunes of his army might (as mankind in general are apt to condemn the unsuccessful) throw on him. The reader may also, with the greatest show of reason, imagine it a presumption in me not to copy his journal for that time and destroy my own, admitting of a comparison little in my favour; but let him recollect my first design in putting the above passages to paper, it was as expressed in my preface, for the eye of a friend who, I flattered myself,— for we are by nature vain,— would receive as much satisfaction from the manner I have expressed my thoughts and feelings at the different times, of material changes and alterations in our affairs, (and there has been many) as the bare recital of facts, which are so well known at present to the world.

RETURN OF THE KILLED AND WOUNDED & PRISONERS DURING THE CAMPAIGN 1777.—

Return of the Killed, wounded and prisoners of the British troops under the Command of his excellency Lieut. General Burgoyne in the course of the Campaign 1777—(I have not attempted to correct errors in this table —J. P. B.)

RANK IN THE ARMY		Officers			Sergeants			Drummers			Rank & file			Total of each regiment
CASUALTIES.	Regmt.	Killed	Wounded	Prisoners	Killed	Wounded	Prisoners	Killed	Wounded	Prisoners	Killed	Wounded	Prisoners	
British line six Regiments	9	4	10	3	2	6	3	0	0	1	24	47	67	167
	20	3	9	5	1	4	1	1	2	1	48	86	78	209
	21	5	3	2	1	4	1				37	83	65	201
	24	2	4	0	5	4	0	0	3	0	32	59	50	198
	47	0	1	1	3	0	2	1	0	1	13	13	20	55
	62	7	7	2	0	7	5	1	0	3	74	129	139	374
Eight Companies of light Infantry and Grenadiers belonging to the Regiments left to garrison Canada and its frontiers	29	1	2	0	0	1	0	0	0	0	13	38	1	56
	31	0	0	0	0	0	0	0	0	0	2	7	4	13
	34	0	4	0	2	1	0	0	0	0	13	45	4	79
	53	1	3	0	0	1	0	0	0	0	7	11	11	34
Royall regiment of Artillery........		2	4	3	1	0	1	0	0	0	21	32	21	85
Detachment of 33rd regiment		0	0	0	0	0	1	0	0	0	0	9	9	19
Engineers		0	0	1	0	0	0	0	0	0	0	0	0	1
16 Dragoons		0	0	1	0	0	0	0	0	0	0	0	0	1
Foot guards		1	0	0	0	0	0	0	0	0	0	0	0	1
Total Killed wounded and prisoners..														1429

BRITISH OFFICERS KILLED, WOUNDED AND PRISONERS DURING THE CAMPAIGN 1777

Royal regiment of Artillery.

Killed, Captain Jones[224] & 2^d^ Lieut. Clieland.[225]

[224] Thomas Jones entered the Military Academy at Woolwich as a cadet, March 18, 1755, and, on December twenty-

Wounded. Captains Bloomfield,[226] Green, 31st regt —aid-de-camp. to Major Gen Phillips — Lieutenants Howarth,[227] Smith,[228] Volunteer Sutton.[229]

---

seventh following, was commissioned lieutenant-fireworker; second lieutenant in the Royal Artillery, April 2, 1757; first lieutenant, January 1, 1759; captain-lieutenant, October 23, 1761, and captain, January 1, 1771. He participated in the siege of Belleisle in 1761, and embarked for America in 1773. When Arnold and Montgomery made their attack upon Quebec, Captain Jones was active in opposing them, and at the conclusion of the campaign of '76, returned with Burgoyne to England, where he was married during the winter. He returned in June of the next year, and was killed at the battle of Freeman's Farm, September nineteenth. His intrepidity and ability were frequently spoken of by writers of the time. *Vide* British Army Lists, *in loco;* History Royal Artillery, vol. 1, pp. 229, 304, 135; A State of the Expedition, p. 79, Appendix 49, and Hadden's Journal and Orderly Books, pp. 50, 98, 109, 164, *et passim.*

225 Molesworth Clieland received his commission of second lieutenant in the First Battalion Royal Artillery on March 15, 1771. The artillery formed a most important part of Burgoyne's army, and owing to its extent and the splendor of its equipment, caused much criticism among his enemies, who claimed that it was disproportionate to his infantry. It did however most effective service; but owing to the nature of the country, great labor was required in moving it, and the men in charge were subjected to severe toil and hardship. Lieutenant Clieland was the first officer of the artillery to fall. He was killed at Skenesborough on July sixth. *Vide* British Army Lists, *in loco;* Journal of Occurrences, etc., p. 174.

226 Thomas Blomefield entered the Royal Military Academy at Woolwich on February 9, 1758, before he had completed his fourteenth year, and exhibited such remarkable talents as to secure a commission in the First Battalion of the Royal Artillery as lieutenant-fireworker on January 3, 1759. When only fifteen years of age, at the

Prisoners, Major Williams, Lieutenants Howarth and York.[230]

---

bombardment of Havre de Grace by Admiral Rodney, he commanded a bomb vessel with ability. He was made second lieutenant, August 1, 1762, and participated in the capture of Martinique and Havana. He was promoted to the rank of first lieutenant in the Second Battalion, May 28, 1766, and captain-lieutenant, January 29, 1773. Shortly after his arrival in Canada, on June 3, 1776, he was made major of brigade to Major-General Phillips. He performed most important service in the construction of floating batteries during the campaign of that year, and at the close of the campaign returned to England. In the spring of 1777 he returned to Canada and participated in Burgoyne's expedition. Madame Riedesel thus speaks of his wound: "One day I undertook the care of Major Plumpfield, adjutant of General Phillips, through both of whose cheeks a small musket ball had passed, shattering his teeth and grazing his tongue. He could hold nothing whatever in his mouth. The matter from the wound almost choked him, and he was unable to take any other nourishment, except a little broth, or something liquid. We had Rhine wine. I gave him a bottle of it, in hopes that the acidity of the wine would cleanse his wound. He kept some continually in his mouth; and that alone acted so beneficially, that he became cured, and I again acquired one more friend. Thus in the midst of my hours of care and suffering, I derived a joyful satisfaction, which made me very happy." He was among the paroled officers at Cambridge, and returned to England in the spring of 1779. His subsequent commissions in the Royal Artillery and army were as follows: Captain, January 19, 1780; major in the army, March 19, 1783, and in the artillery, September twenty-fifth of the same year; a lieutenant-colonel, December 5, 1793; colonel in the army, January 26, 1797, and in the artillery, November 12, 1800; a major-general, September 25, 1803, and colonel commandant of the Ninth Battalion, June 1, 1806. He commanded the artillery at the siege of Copenhagen with great success, for which he received the thanks of Parliament and a

Battalion of Light Infantry consisting of 10 *Companies Commanded by Earl Balcarres,*

9th Company; Lieut Wright.[231]

20th Company;

---

baronetcy, which honor was conferred upon him, November 14, 1807. His last promotion was to the rank of lieutenant-general, July 25, 1810. His death took place at his home at Shooter's Hill, in Kent, August 24, 1822. *Vide* British Family Antiquity (Playfair), London, 1811, vol. 7, p. 833, *et seq.;* Burke's Peerage and Baronetage, *in loco;* British Army Lists, *in loco;* A State of the Expedition, p. 67; History of the Royal Artillery (Duncan), vol. 1, pp. 174, 177, 379; vol. 2, pp. 158, 167; Letters and Journals of Madame Riedesel, p. 132.

[227] Edward Howarth was commissioned a second lieutenant in the Royal Artillery, on June 17, 1772, and was one of the most brilliant of that youthful band of officers who accompanied Burgoyne to America in 1776. He was wounded and taken prisoner at Saratoga in the final battle of the campaign. Concerning him Anburey relates the following curious incident: "Your friend Howarth's wound, I hear, is in his knee; it is very singular, but he was prepossessed with an idea of being wounded, for when the orders came for the detachment's going out, he was playing picquet with me, and after reading the orders, and that his brigade of guns were to go, he said to me, 'God bless you A——, farewell, for I know not how it is, but I have a strange *presentiment* that I shall either be killed or wounded.' I was rather surprised at such an expression, as he is of a gay and cheerful disposition, and cannot but say, that during the little time I could bestow in reflection that day, I continually dwelt upon his remark, but he is now happily in a fair way of recovery." On July 7, 1779, Howarth was promoted to the rank of first lieutenant in the artillery, and on December 1, 1782, of captain-lieutenant and captain. He occupied the position of quartermaster for eleven years; namely, from April 4, 1783, to March 1, 1794, at which latter date he attained the army rank of major. On January 1, 1798, he

21st Company;
24th Company;

---

was promoted to the army rank of lieutenant-colonel and brevet-major-general; and July 16, 1799, was made a major in the artillery. He was further promoted to a lieutenant-colonelcy in the artillery, April 18, 1801; a colonelcy, December 29, 1805; major-general in the army, June 4, 1811; lieutenant-general in the army August 12, 1819, and colonel commanding in the artillery, August 6, 1821. General Howarth served under Wellington in the Peninsular war with great distinction, commanding the artillery as brigadier-general at the battles of Talavera, Busaco and Ferantes d'Onore, and for the ability he displayed, was in 1814, honored with the Knight Grand-Cross of the Order of Bath. In 1824, he was further rewarded with the Knight Grand-Cross of the Royal Hanoverian Guelphic Order, a medal and two clasps. Owing to failing health he was obliged to vacate his command, and retiring to his country seat at Birnstead, Surrey, he died on March 5, 1827. He had been in almost constant service for over half a century. *Vide* British Army Lists, *in loco;* History of the Royal Artillery, vol. 1, pp. 226, 381; Hadden's Journal and Orderly Books, pp. xlviii, lvi.

228 William P. Smith became a cadet in Woolwich, April 1, 1768, and a second lieutenant in the Royal Artillery, March 15, 1771. He was wounded in the battle of October 7, and was among the convention prisoners. He subsequently received the following promotions: First lieutenant, July 7, 1779; captain-lieutenant, Febrnary 28, 1782, and captain of the Sixth Company of the Second Battalion, May 24, 1790; major in the army, March 1, 1794, and in the artillery, April 25, 1796; lieutenant-colonel in the army, January 1, 1798, and in the artillery, January 8, 1799. His last commission was that of colonel in the artillery, July 20, 1804. His death took place July 23, 1806. *Vide* British Army Lists, *in loco;* History of the Royal Artillery, vol. 1, p. 181.

229 Of Volunteer Sutton we can find no particulars. He is mentioned by Lamb in his list of wounded officers, and we

27th Company; Wounded, Captn Craig.
62d Company; Wounded, Lieut Jones.[232]

---

may infer had seen military service. At the dawn of day on the sixth of July, General Fraser pursued Colonel Francis, and overtaking him, would have met with a disastrous defeat but for the timely arrival of Riedesel with his Germans. Sutton was wounded in this action. If he survived his wound, he must have returned to Canada, as he is nowhere again mentioned, and his name does not appear among the convention prisoners.

[230] John H. York became a cadet at Woolwich, May 1, 1768, and a second lieutenant in the Royal Artillery, March 15, 1771. He was taken prisoner October seventh. At what time he was exchanged is unknown. He was promoted as follows, viz.: to the rank of first lieutenant, July 7, 1779; captain-lieutenant, April 6, 1782, and captain in the Third Company, Fourth Battalion, May 26, 1790; a major in the army, March 1, 1794, and in the artillery, December 9, 1796; a lieutenant-colonel in the army, January 1, 1798, and in the artillery, July 16, 1799. His last commission was that of colonel in the artillery, July 20, 1804, and he was shortly after, November 1, 1805, drowned on the South American coast. *Vide* British Army Lists, *in loco;* History of the Royal Artillery, vol. 1, pp. 257, 315.

[231] James Wright received his first commission as ensign in the Ninth Foot, March 23, 1764, while that regiment was doing service in Florida. In 1769 the Ninth returned home and was assigned to garrison duty in Ireland. He was commissioned a lieutenant, September 1, 1771, and accompanied his regiment to Canada in 1776, taking part in the campaign of that year. He was killed in the final battle at Saratoga. *Vide* British Army Lists, *in loco;* Historical Record Ninth Foot.

[232] John Jones received his commission of ensign in the Sixty-second Foot on December 9, 1767, and was promoted to the rank of lieutenant, September 1, 1771. His regiment

29th Company; Killed, Lieut Douglass.[233] Wounded, Lieut. Battersby.[234] Prisoner, Ensign Johnston.[235]

31st Company;

---

arrived in Canada in the spring of 1776, and he, therefore, took part in the campaign of that year. He was wounded at Hubbardton in the action of July seventh, and his name disappears from the army lists after 1781. *Vide* British Army Lists, *in loco;* Historical Record Sixty-second Foot.

[233] James Douglas was commissioned a lieutenant in the army on April 8, 1773, and received his appointment of ensign in the Twenty-ninth Foot on June 30, 1774. He was promoted to a lieutenancy in his regiment, February 27, 1776, and was wounded in the action of July seventh. He was being borne from the field after his wound, when a shot passed directly through his heart, killing him instantly. His place was filled by Ensign Dowling of the Forty-seventh Foot, on the fourteenth, by order of the commanding general. *Vide* British Army Lists, *in loco;* Travels Through the Interior Parts of America, vol. 1, p. 339; Burgoyne's Orderly Book, p. 55.

[234] James Battersby entered the Twenty-ninth Foot, February 2, 1770, as an ensign, at which time this regiment was stationed in Boston and won unpleasant notoriety in the "massacre" of the fifth of March following. He was promoted to a lieutenancy, December 16, 1773, and in February, 1776, embarked at Chatham with his regiment for the seat of war in America. He was wounded in the action of October seventh, and was one of the convention prisoners. He was promoted to a captaincy, February 16, 1778, while a prisoner. His name appears on the army lists for the last time in 1784. *Vide* British Army Lists, *in loco;* Historical Record Twenty-ninth Foot; Journal of Occurrences During the Late American War, p. 176.

[235] William Johnson was commissioned an ensign in the Twenty-ninth Foot on March 29, 1776. Of his subsequent fate we know nothing. His name was borne on the army lists of 1780 for the last time.

34th Company; Wounded, Capn Harris.[236]

53d Company; Wounded, Major Earl Balcarres. Lieutenants Houghton & Cullen.[237]

---

[236] John Adolphus Harris entered the Thirty-fourth Foot under an ensign's commission, January 11, 1760, and was promoted to the rank of lieutenant, January 28, 1762. At this time the Thirty-fourth was in the West Indies, and Lieutenant Harris participated in the siege of Havana, and after the peace accompanied his regiment to Florida, where it remained until 1768, when it was assigned to garrison duty in Ireland. On November 28, 1771, he was promoted to a captaincy, and in 1776, the Thirty-fourth having been assigned to duty in America, he took part in the campaign of that year. He was wounded at Hubbardton in the action of July seventh. Anburey thus speaks of him in a letter home, dated July seventeenth: "I omitted to mention to you, that your old friend Captain H——, was wounded at the battle of Huberton, early in the action, when the grenadiers formed to support the light infantry. I could not pass by him as he lay under a tree, where he had scrambled upon his hands and knees, to protect him from the scattering shot, without going up to see what assistance could be afforded him, and learn if he was severely wounded. You who know his ready turn for wit, will not be surprised to hear, though in extreme agony, that with an arch look, and clapping his hand behind him, he told me, if I wanted to be satisfied, I must ask that, as the ball had entered at his hip, and passed through a certain part adjoining; he is now at Ticonderoga, and from the last account, is recovering fast." Owing to the severity of his wound, he was unable to take part in the subsequent movements of the campaign, and so was not among the captured officers. After his return to England, he became major of the Eighty-fourth Foot, or Royal Highland Emigrants, First Battalion, October 22, 1779, and lieutenant-colonel of the Sixtieth Foot, or Royal Americans, January 16, 1788. He was afterward commissioned in the army as follows: Lieutenant-colonel, February 26, 1795; major-general, January 1, 1798; lieutenant-general, January 1, 1805, and general, June 4, 1814. His name appears upon

20th Regmt. Killed, Lieutenants Lucas,[238] Cooke,[239] Obines.[240] Wound. Lieut. Col^l. Lynd,[241] Captains Wemys,[242] Doulin,[243] Stanley,[244] Farquar;[245] Lieuten-

---

the army lists for the last time in 1826. *Vide* British Army Lists, *in loco;* Historical Record Thirty-fourth Foot; Travels Through the Interior Parts of America, vol. 1, p. 361, *et seq.*

[237] William Cullen entered the Fifty-third Foot as an ensign while that regiment was doing garrison duty in Ireland, August 31, 1774, and was promoted to a lieutenancy, March 2, 1776, just before the departure of his regiment for America. He was wounded July seventh, in the action with the troops of Colonel Francis, and probably returned to Ticonderoga, as he was not among the captives of Burgoyne's army. The Fifty-third Regiment was stationed in Canada for several years after the close of the war, and during this time Lieutenant Cullen was commissioned a captain, his commission bearing date September 13, 1781. He seems to have become weary of his long sojourn in America and retired on a captain's half pay in 1784. *Vide* British Army Lists, *in loco;* Historical Record, Fifty-third Foot; Journal of Occurrences During the Late American War, p. 175.

[238] Thomas Lucas entered the Twentieth Foot upon the eve of its embarkation for America, having received his commission of lieutenant therein, March 1, 1776. He passed through the perils of the campaign of that year to meet his death in the battle of Freeman's Farm, September nineteenth.

[239] John Cooke entered the Twentieth Foot as an ensign while it was stationed in Ireland, March 14, 1774, and when his regiment was about to proceed to the relief of Carleton at Quebec, he was promoted to the rank of lieutenant, March 3, 1776. He ended his brief career at the battle of Freeman's Farm, on September nineteenth.

[240] Hamlet Obins entered the British army as a cornet in the Third Light Dragoons, January 1, 1766, and was promoted to a lieutenancy in the Sixteenth Light Dragoons,

ants Dowlin,[246] Ensig[n] Connel.[247] Prisoners; Stanley, Farquar. Cap[n] Dowlin, Ensign Connel.

Burgoyne's regiment, February 18, 1769, in which regiment he remained until the breaking out of the war in America, when he was transferred to the infantry and commissioned a lieutenant in the Twentieth Foot, March 9, 1776. He fell in the battle of October seventh, which decided the fate of Burgoyne's army. *Vide* British Army Lists, *in loco;* Journal of Occurrences During the Late American War, p. 176.

[241] John Lind entered the Thirty-fourth Foot, December 12, 1755, and the next year was with his regiment at Fort St. Phillip, where it sustained a siege. He was commissioned a captain, January 12, 1760, and took part in the expedition against Belleisle during that year. In 1762 he participated in the expedition against the Spanish West Indies, and at the successful close of the war accompanied his regiment to Florida, where he remained until 1768, when his regiment was ordered home and went into garrison in Ireland. On November 28, 1771, he was made major of his regiment, and January 16, 1776, was transferred to the Twentieth Foot and promoted to the rank of lieutenant-colonel. In the spring of that year he accompanied his regiment to America and took part in the campaign under Carleton. The next year he followed the fortunes of Burgoyne to the battle of Freeman's Farm, where he was wounded, but remained with his command and was among the surrendered officers at Saratoga a few weeks later. He was raised to the army rank of colonel, November 20, 1782, and was made a major-general, October 12, 1793. He died May 1, 1795. *Vide* Historical Record of the Thirty-fourth Foot; do. Twentieth Foot; British Army Lists, *in loco;* Gentleman's Magazine for 1795.

[242] Francis Weymis was commissioned a lieutenant in the Twentieth Foot, September 26, 1757, at which time his regiment formed part of the expedition under Lieutenant-General Sir John Mordant, against Rochfort, which resulted in the capture and destruction of the fortifications on the Isle

21st Regmt; Killed, Lieutenants Curray,[248] Mc-Kinzy,[249] Turnbull,[250] Robertson.[251] Wounded, Lieut. Rutherford;[252] Prisoner, Lieut Rutherford,

---

d'Aix, on the western coast of France. The French, in the summer of 1759, sent an army into Germany with which country England was in alliance, and the regiment to which Lieutenant Weymis belonged was ordered to Germany to form part of the forces under Prince Ferdinand, of Brunswick. The service performed by the British troops in the German service was severe, and when the Twentieth returned to England in 1763, it received the thanks of Parliament for its conduct. From this date until 1769, a period of six years, Lieutenant Weymis was with his regiment at Gibraltar. On the 25th of May, 1772, he was promoted to the regimental and army rank of captain. After the campaign in America of 1776, Lieutenant Weymis passed the following winter at the Isle aux Noix, and was wounded in the battle of the nineteenth of September. He was among the convention prisoners, and upon his return home at the close of the war was promoted to the rank of major, March 19, 1783. His name disappears from the army lists after 1787. *Vide* British Army Lists, *in loco;* Historical Record Twentieth Foot, pp. 15–23; Journal of Occurrences During the Late American War, p. 175.

243 Richard Dowling first appears on the army lists as adjutant of the Twentieth Foot, January 8, 1768, while that regiment was doing garrison duty at Gibraltar, where it remained until 1774, when it proceeded to Ireland, and was there stationed until the spring of '76. Adjutant Dowling was commissioned a captain in his regiment, July 7, 1775, and accompanied it to America the following spring. He was wounded in the battle of September nineteenth, and taken prisoner, from which time he disappears from view. His name continued upon the army lists until April 1, 1780, when his place was filled by Thomas Storey. *Vide* British Army Lists, *in loco;* Historical Record Twentieth Foot, pp. 15–23; Journal of Occurrences During the Late American War, p. 176.

24th Regmt: Killed, Lieut. Col. Frazier, Major Grant. Wounded, Major Agnew,[253] Captains Blake,[254] Strangways,[255] Lieut. Doyle.[256]

---

[244] John Stanly entered the Twentieth Foot as a lieutenant, September 7, 1772, while the regiment was stationed at Gibraltar. He was promoted to a captaincy about the time of its departure for America, March 9, 1776. He was wounded and taken prisoner at Freeman's Farm, and his name appears for the last time on the army lists in 1783.

[245] William Farquar was commissioned a lieutenant in the Forty-seventh Foot, September 25, 1759, after that regiment's brilliant service in the siege and capture of Louisbourg and the fall of Quebec. In 1763 he entered upon half pay, but re-entered the service, and obtained a lieutenancy, May 3, 1765, in the Fifty-sixth Foot, which was at that time on duty at Gibraltar. He received a captain's commission in the Twentieth Foot, May 13, 1776. He was wounded and taken prisoner in the battle of September nineteenth. At what time he was exchanged we are not informed. He was promoted to a majority in the army, March 19, 1783. His name disappears from the army lists after 1794. *Vide* Historical Record Forty-seventh Foot; do. Fifty-sixth Foot; British Army Lists, *in loco.*

[246] James Dowling was first commissioned an ensign in the Forty-seventh Regiment, June 18, 1775, the day after the battle of Bunker Hill, in which the Forty-seventh was engaged. He accompanied his regiment to Canada in the spring of the next year. Lieutenant Douglass of the Twenty-ninth Foot having been killed in the action of July seventh, Burgoyne promoted Ensign Dowling to the vacant lieutenancy, July 14, 1777. He was wounded in the performance of his duty, October seventh, and seems to have escaped capture thereby. His name disappears from the army lists after 1787. *Vide* British Army Lists, *in loco;* Burgoyne's Orderly Book, p. 55; Journal of Occurrences During the Late American War, p. 176.

47th Regmt; Killed, Lieuts Reynels,[257] Harvey,[258] Stewart,[259] Ensigns Taylor,[260] Phillips,[261] Young,[262] Adjutant Fitzgerald.[263] Wounded; Lieut. Col°. Ans-

---

[247] Morgan Connel was commissioned an ensign in the Twentieth Foot, April 6, 1776. He was wounded in the battle of October seventh and taken a prisoner. We have no further account of him.

[248] Samuel Currie received his first commission in the British army, which was that of a second lieutenant in the Twenty-first Foot, on March 14, 1766. At this date his regiment was stationed in Western Florida, and remained there until 1770, when it was ordered to Canada, and, on February 21, 1772, he was promoted to the rank of first lieutenant. Shortly after he returned to England, where the Twenty-first was in garrison until the spring of '76, when Lieutenant Currie accompanied it to Quebec, and shortly after his arrival in Canada, viz., on July 4, 1776, he received the appointment of assistant commissary of General Gordon's brigade. He lost his life in the battle of September nineteenth. *Vide* British Army Lists, *in loco;* Historical Record Twenty-first Foot; Journal of Occurrences During the Late American War, p. 175.

[249] Kenneth Mackenzie entered the British military service as an ensign in the Thirty-third Foot, August 26, 1767, and was promoted to a lieutenancy, February 27, 1771. On August 16, 1775, he was transferred to the Twenty-first Foot, and the following spring accompanied his regiment to America. He was made a first lieutenant on May 7, 1776, and participated in the campaign of that year. He ended his life in the performance of a soldier's duty on the battlefield of September nineteenth. *Vide* British Army Lists, *in loco;* Historical Record Thirty-third Foot; Journal of Occurrences During the Late American War, p. 175.

[250] George Turnbull received his commission of second lieutenant in the Twenty-first Foot on May 3, 1776, and was probably one of those youthful officers, of which there were

truther,[264] Major Harnage,[265] Captain Bunbury,[266] Ensigns, Blackee,[267] Harvey.[268] Prisoners: Lieut. Naylor,[269] Ensign De Antroch.[270]

---

so many in Burgoyne's army, who lost their lives in the disastrous campaign of 1777. He was killed October seventh near Stillwater.

[251] John James Roberton entered the British army as a second lieutenant of Royal Engineers, July 13, 1774. He was attached to the right wing of the army by an order of June 27, 1777, his duty being to strengthen the right of the camp under the direction of Brigadiers Powell and Hamilton. The last mention made of him in Burgoyne's Orderly Book is on September seventh, when he was assigned to the duty of repairing the roads between the camp at Duer's House and Fort Edward. On the nineteenth he was killed.

[252] Richard Rutherford entered the Twenty-first Foot as a second lieutenant, February 26, 1776. He was wounded in the battle of September nineteenth, and as his name is dropped from the army list of 1779, we may infer that he did not recover from his wounds.

[253] William Agnew was commissioned a lieutenant in the Twenty-fourth Foot, September 3, 1756, and a captain-lieutenant, May 15, 1763. Having served in Germany, his regiment was transferred to Gibraltar, and he subsequently accompanied it to America in the spring of 1776. He was made major of the Twenty-fourth, July 14, 1777, in place of Major Grant, who was killed on the seventh of that month. He was wounded in the battle of Freeman's Farm, September nineteenth. He became lieutenant-colonel of his regiment, February 15, 1782, but his name is not borne upon the lists of the next year. *Vide* British Army Lists, *in loco;* Historical Record Twenty-fourth Foot; Journal of Occurrences During the Late American War, p. 175.

[254] John Blake was made an ensign of the Twenty-fourth Foot, May 23, 1761, and lieutenant, June 12, 1766. He was promoted to a captaincy, July 7, 1775. He was

Engineers, Prisoner, Lieut. Dunford.[271]

Foot Guards: Killed, Sir Francis Clark, aid-de-camp to General Burgoyne,

---

wounded in the battle of the nineteenth of September, and did not rejoin his regiment, as his name is not in the list of surrendered officers. He appears at the head of the list of captains on the list of 1788. *Vide* British Army Lists, *in loco;* Historical Record Twenty-fourth Foot.

[255] Hon. Stephen Digby Strangways was the second son of Stephen Fox and Elizabeth, the only daughter and heir of Thomas Strangways Horner, Esq. His father was raised to the peerage, March 11, 1741, as Lord Ilchester, of Ilchester, in Somersetshire, and subsequently, on June 5, 1756, was made Earl of Ilchester. Stephen Digby Strangways was born on December 3, 1751, and was the brother of Lady Harriet Acland. He entered the British military service as a cornet in the Royal Irish Dragoons, August 5, 1767, at the age of sixteen years; but, preferring the infantry service, exchanged into the Twenty-fourth Foot, and obtained a captaincy, April 17, 1769. He participated in the campaign of 1776, and was wounded in the battle of October seventh, but was with the army when it surrendered. He was made major of the Twentieth Foot, December 1, 1778, and attained no higher rank in the army. *Vide* Burke's Peerage and Baronetage, *in loco;* British Army Lists, *in loco;* Historical Record Twenty-fourth Foot; Hadden's Journal and Orderly Books, p. liv.

[256] William Doyle was of an ancient Irish family noted in military annals. He entered the British infantry service as an ensign in the Twenty-fourth Foot, July 16, 1774, and was promoted to a lieutenancy, November 27, 1776, at the close of Carleton's successful campaign, in which he took part. He was among the officers who surrendered at Saratoga. He was raised to the rank of captain, July 31, 1787, major in the army, May 6, 1795, and lieutenant-colonel, July 22, 1797. He exchanged into the Sixty-second Foot, and was made its lieutenant-colonel, August 16, 1804. He was promoted to the army rank of colonel, October 30, 1805; major-

16th Dragoons. Prisoner, Cornet Grant.[272]

N. B I could not get an exact account of the loss of the German troops commanded by Gen Reidzel,

---

general, June 4, 1811, and lieutenant-general, August 12, 1819. *Vide* British Army Lists, *in loco;* Burgoyne's Orderly Book, p. 178.

[257] Thomas Reynell was the son of Sir Thomas Reynell of Laleham, Middlesex county, and his wife, who so faithfully followed him through the terrible scenes of the campaign with Mrs. Riedesel, Acland and Harnage, until the fatal nineteenth of September, when he received his death wound, was Anne, the daughter of Samuel Coutty, Esq., of Kinsale. Mrs. Reynell was left with three small children, the oldest of whom was less than six years of age, and the youngest an infant. The oldest of these children, Richard Littleton Reynell, born April 30, 1772, settled in America, where he was married and lived until his death, September 4, 1829, at which time he enjoyed the title of baronet. His brother, Samuel, who was born October 31, 1775, and was hardly two years of age at his father's death, died unmarried, and the title descended to Thomas, the youngest brother. Thomas Reynell, the subject of this brief sketch, entered the British military service as an ensign in the Sixty-second Foot, December 8, 1767, and was advanced to the rank of lieutenant, May 3, 1770. He sailed with his regiment from the Cove of Cork, April 8, 1776, and took part in the campaign of Carleton of that year. Anburey thus relates the incidents of his death: "You will readily allow that it is the highest test of affection in a woman, to share with her husband the toils and hardships of the campaign, especially such an one as the present. What a trial of fortitude the late action must have been, through a distressing interval of long suspence! The ladies followed the route of the artillery and baggage, and when the action began, the Baroness Reidesel, Lady Harriet Ackland, and the wives of Major Harnage and Lieutenant Reynell, of the Sixty-second Regiment, entered a small uninhabited hut, but when the action became general and bloody, the Sur-

but believe it was pretty near equal to that of the British.

---

geons took possession of it, being the most convenient for the first care of the wounded; in this situation were these ladies four hours together, where the comfort they afforded each other was broke in upon, by Major Harnage being brought in to the surgeons deeply wounded! What a blow must the next intelligence be, that informed them that Lieutenant Reynell was killed!" Madame Riedesel gives us further particulars of the trying scenes of that day: "The wife of Major Harnage, a Madame Reynels the wife of the good lieutenant who the day previous had so kindly shared his broth with me, the wife of the commissary, and myself, were the only ladies who were with the army. We sat together bewailing our fate, when one came in, upon which they all began whispering, looking at the same time exceedingly sad. I noticed this, and also that they cast silent glances toward me. This awakened in my mind the dreadful thought that my husband had been killed. I shrieked aloud, but they assured me that this was not so, at the same time intimating to me by signs, that it was the lieutenant — the husband of our companion — who had met with misfortune. A moment after she was called out. Her husband was not yet dead, but a cannon ball had taken off his arm close to his shoulder. During the whole night we heard his moans, which sounded fearfully through the vaulted cellars. The poor man died toward morning." The cellar of the house in which these ladies found shelter during this dreadful night is still shown to the curious. Both Lamb and Digby are in error as to the regiment of which he was a member. Lamb makes him of the Twenty-fourth, and Digby of the Forty-seventh. *Vide* Burke's Peerage and Baronetage and British Army Lists, *in loco;* Travels Through the Interior Parts of America, vol. 1, p. 426; Letters and Journals of Madame Riedesel, p. 129, *et seq.*

[258] Stephen Harvey became a lieutenant in the army, August 15, 1775, and was assigned to the Sixty-second Foot with a lieutenant's commission therein, February 29, 1776, and accompanied his regiment to America a few

Battalion of Grenadiers consisting of ten Companies Commanded by Major Ackland.

9th Company; Killed, Captain Stapleton,[273] Lieu-

weeks later. Lamb thus records his fate: "Nor should the heroism of Lieutenant Hervey, of the 62nd regiment, a youth of sixteen, and nephew to the adjutant general of the same name be forgotten. It was characterized by all that is gallant in the military character. In the battle of the 19th September, he received several wounds, and was repeatedly ordered off the field by Lieutenant-Colonel Anstruther, but his heroic ardor would not allow him to quit the battle while he could stand, and see his brave comrades fighting beside him. A ball striking one of his legs, his removal became absolutely necessary, and while they were conveying him away, another wounded him mortally. In this situation, the surgeon recommended him to take a powerful dose of opium, to avoid a seven or eight hours' life of most exquisite torture. This he immediately consented to, and when the colonel entered the tent, with Major Harnage, who were both wounded, they asked whether he had any affairs they could settle for him? His reply was, that being a minor, every thing was already adjusted; but he had one request, which he retained just life enough to utter: 'Tell my uncle, I died like a soldier ——.'" Anburey gives the same relation and adds: "Where will you find in ancient Rome heroism superior!" *Vide* British Army Lists, *in loco;* Journal of Occurrences During the Late American War, p. 179.

[259] Archibald Stuart was a lieutenant in the army under a commission dated October 10, 1759; but we have no further account of him until June 23, 1775, when we find him a lieutenant of Invalids at Hull. He was commissioned a lieutenant of the Sixty-second Foot on the eve of its departure to relieve Quebec. He fell in the battle of October seventh.

[260] George Taylor received his commission as an ensign in the Sixty-second Foot on March 2, 1776, and was in the campaign of that year under Carleton. He was one of those

tenant Huggart;[274] Wounded, Captain Swetman,[275] Lieutenant Rowe,[276]

---

youthful officers who had but just commenced a promising military career, which was brought to an untimely end during this campaign. He fell at the battle of Freeman's Farm, September nineteenth, in which battle the Sixty-second suffered severe loss.

[261] Levinge Cosby Phillips was commissioned an ensign in the Sixty-second Foot, December 20, 1776. Wilkinson thus alludes to him: "The morning after the action I visited the wounded prisoners who had not been dressed, and discovered a charming youth not more than 16 years old, lying among them; feeble, faint, pale and stiff in his gore; the delicacy of his aspect and the quality of his clothing attracted my attention, and on enquiry I found he was an Ensign Phillips; he told me he had fallen by a wound in his leg or thigh, and as he lay on the ground was shot through the body by an army follower, a murderous villain, who avowed the deed, but I forgot his name; the moans of this hapless youth moved me to tears; I raised him from the straw on which he lay, took him in my arms and removed him to a tent, where every comfort was provided and every attention paid to him, but his wounds were mortal, and he expired on the 21st; when his name was first mentioned to General Gates, he exclaimed, 'just Heaven! he may be the nephew of my wife," but the fact was otherwise. Let those parents who are now training their children for the military profession; let those misguided patriots, who are inculcating principles of education subversive of the foundations of the republic, look on this picture of distress, taken from the life, of a youth in a strange land, far removed from friends and relations co-mingled with the dying and the dead, himself wounded, helpless and expiring with agony, and then should political considerations fail of effect, I hope, the feelings of affection and the obligations of humanity, may induce them to discountenance the pursuits of war, and save their offspring from the seductions of the plume and the sword, for the more solid and useful avocations of civil life; by which alone peace and virtue and the republic can be preserved,

20th Company; Wounded, Major Ackland, twice; Prisoners, Major Ackland.

---

and perpetuated." *Vide* British Army Lists, *in loco;* Memoirs of My Own Times, vol. 1, p. 246.

262 Henry Young received his commission of ensign in the Sixty-second Foot on November 21, 1776, and this was his first campaign. Of the several officers of tender years in Burgoyne's army, all connected with families of repute, whose lives were sacrificed by a wretched king and a besotted aristocracy in the support of a bad cause, we have touching notices in the journals of the survivors who participated in the great contest. Madame Riedesel thus refers to the last hours of Ensign Young: "A few days after our arrival, I heard plaintive moans in another room near me, and learned that they came from Young, — who was lying very low. I was the more interested in him, since a family of that name had shown me much courtesy during my sojourn in England. I tendered him my services, and sent him provisions and refreshments. He expressed a great desire to see his benefactress, as he called me. I went to him, and found him lying on a little straw, for he had lost his camp equipage. He was a young man, probably eighteen or nineteen years old; and, actually, the own nephew of the Mr. Young whom I had known, and the only son of his parents. It was only for this reason that he grieved; on account of his own sufferings he uttered no complaint. He had bled considerably, and they wished to take off his leg, but he could not bring his mind to it, and now mortification had set in. I sent him pillows and coverings, and my women servants a mattress. I redoubled my care of him, and visited him every day, for which I received from the sufferer a thousand blessings. Finally, they attempted the amputation of the limb, but it was too late, and he died a few days afterward. As he occupied an appartment close to mine, and the walls were very thin, I could hear his last groans through the partition of my room." *Vide* British Army Lists, *in loco;* Letters and Journals of Madame Riedesel, p. 114.

21st Company; Killed, Lieut Don;[277] wounded Captn. Ramsey,[278] Lieut. Fetherston;[279] Prisoners, Captn Ramsey.

---

[263] George Tobias Fitzgerald was appointed adjutant of the Sixty-second Foot, October 26, 1775, and fell at Saratoga on October eleventh.

[264] John Anstruther, of the noble Scotch family of Anstruther of Balcaskie, entered the Twenty-sixth Foot as ensign, May 2, 1751, and was advanced to the rank of lieutenant in the Eighth Foot, August 28, 1756. The dates of his subsequent commissions are as follows: captain-lieutenant, September 25, 1761; captain, July 23, 1762; major, November 5, 1766; lieutenant-colonel in the Sixty-second Foot, October 21, 1773. He served in the campaign of 1776, and was wounded in the action of September nineteenth, and also in that of October seventh. After the surrender he was paroled, and returned home in 1778. He was promoted to a colonelcy in the army, November 17, 1780, but does not seem to have had a command after his return to England. His name disappears from the army lists after 1782. *Vide* British Army Lists, *in loco;* Historical Record Sixty-second Foot.

[265] Henry Harnage was of an ancient English family, and, at the age of seventeen, received his first commission in the military service as an ensign in the Fourth Foot, June 7, 1756, and, on September twenty-ninth of the following year, was advanced to a lieutenancy therein. He was promoted, May 4, 1767, to a captaincy in the Sixty-second Foot, the second battalion of his regiment having received that number, and, December 21, 1775, to a majority. He was wounded in the battle of September nineteenth in the bowels, almost precisely in the same manner as was General Fraser; but, said the surgeon, "the general had eaten a hearty breakfast, by reason of which the intestines were distended, and the ball, —— had not gone, as in the case of Major Harnage, between the intestines, but through them." In spite of this severe wound, he was on the battle-field of October seventh, when he was again wounded. When the army retreated on the

24th Company;

47th Company; Prisoner, Lieutenant England.[280]

next night, we are told by Madame Riedesel that "he dragged himself out of bed, that he might not remain in the hospital, which was left behind, protected by a flag of truce," and, although suffering from his wound, he did not forget to attend to the protection of her and her children. He was made a lieutenant-colonel in the army, November 17, 1780, while he was on the way to London with dispatches from Sir Henry Clinton, and was commissioned to the same rank in the One Hundred and Fourth Foot, March 18, 1782, in which year his name appears on the army lists for the last time. *Vide* British Army Lists, *in loco;* Letters and Journals of Madame Riedesel, p. 114.

266 Abraham Bunbury was commissioned a lieutenant in the Sixty-second Foot, September 17, 1773, and received the rank of captain in the army, December 21, 1775. He does not appear to have had a command during Burgoyne's campaign. He was wounded in the battle of October seventh, and, as his name does not appear in the list of officers paroled at Cambridge, we may infer that he was taken with other wounded men back to Canada. His name appears upon the army lists for a number of years, but he held no command in the army.

267 Henry Blacker was commissioned as an ensign in the Sixty-second Foot, December 21, 1775, and was acting in that capacity when the surrender at Saratoga took place, as his name so appears in the parole of Burgoyne's officers, December 13, 1777. He was, however, commissioned to a lieutenancy under the date of October eighth. He was promoted to a captaincy, October 26, 1786.

268 George Hervey was commissioned an ensign in the Sixty-second Foot, April 6, 1776, and was wounded in the action of September seventeenth. He, however, was in the battle of October seventh, and was among those who signed the parole after the surrender.

269 Wm. Pendred Naylor was commissioned an ensign in the Sixty-second Foot, March 12, 1774, and accompanied

62nd Company; Wounded, Captn. Shrimpton.[281]
29th Company; Wounded, Lieut Steel.[282]

---

his regiment to America in the spring of 1776. After the close of the campaign of that year, Ensign Naylor was promoted to a lieutenancy, November 21, 1776, which rank he held when taken prisoner in the battle of October 7, 1777. His name continued to be borne upon the army lists until 1783, when it disappeared.

[270] Henry Danterroche was made an ensign in the Sixty-second Foot on November 21, 1776, after the close of the campaign of that year. He was taken prisoner in the battle of October seventh, and does not appear to have subsequently advanced beyond the grade of ensign. His name appears upon the army lists for the last time in 1786.

[271] Andrew Durnford was commissioned as an ensign in the Royal Engineers, July 28, 1769, and was advanced to the rank of lieutenant, March 6, 1775. He was taken prisoner in Colonel Baum's unfortunate attack on Bennington. At what time he was exchanged we do not know, but find him acting as assistant deputy quartermaster-general in New York and Georgia from 1779 to the close of the war. He was commissioned a captain-lieutenant and captain in the Engineers, October 1, 1784, and a major in the army, May 6, 1795. His name does not appear in the army lists after 1799.

[272] James Grant entered the Sixteenth Light Dragoons as cornet, December 27, 1774, and was transferred to the Twenty-first Dragoons, December 27, 1775. He was one of the men selected by Burgoyne to bear dispatches through the American lines to Clinton, but was not successful, and returned to the British camp. He was subsequently taken prisoner, but was paroled and returned to England. On October 20, 1779, he was promoted to the army rank of lieutenant, and, on January 7, 1780, exchanged into the Sixty-first Foot as an ensign. On the following twenty-sixth of April he was made a lieutenant, but we can trace his career no farther, as his name disappears from the army lists after 1782.

31st Company.

34th Company; Wounded, Captain Forbes.[283]

53rd Company; Killed, Captain Wight.

---

[273] Francis Samuel Stapleton entered the Ninth Foot as an ensign, September 4, 1762, while that regiment was engaged in its arduous and successful campaign in the island of Cuba, and the next year accompanied the regiment to Florida, which territory Spain had ceded to Great Britain in exchange for Cuba, which it had lost in the war. In the autumn of 1769 the Ninth arrived in Ireland, and on December 12, 1770, while it was in garrison there, Ensign Stapleton was raised to the rank of lieutenant, and on May 21, 1773, was promoted to a captaincy in his regiment. He participated in the operations by which the Americans were expelled from Canada in 1776, and fell mortally wounded in the action of the 7th July, 1777. *Vide* British Army Lists, *in loco;* Historical Record Ninth Foot; Journal of Occurrences During the Late American War, p. 174.

[274] James Haggart received his first commission of second lieutenant of marines, May 25, 1775, and was killed in the battle of July 7, 1777. Anburey relates that upon the very first attack of the Light Infantry a ball destroyed both of his eyes.

[275] George Swettenham was commissioned a lieutenant in the army, February 28, 1760, and of the Ninth Foot, August 8, 1764, while that regiment was stationed in Florida under the command of Lieutenant-General Whitemore. In 1769 he returned to Ireland with his regiment, where it remained until the breaking out of the war in America. On March 2, 1776, he was promoted to a captaincy, and was wounded at the battle of Freeman's Farm. He was among the paroled officers of the surrendered army. His regiment returned to England at the close of the war, in 1783, and was stationed in Scotland in 1784 and 1785, and in the latter year his name disappears from the army lists. *Vide* British Army Lists, *in loco;* Historical Record Ninth Foot; Burgoyne's Orderly Book, p. 178.

British Line.

9th Regiment; Killed, Lieutenant Westrop; Wounded, Captn. Mt. Gomery,[284] Lieutenants Ste-

---

[276] John Rowe entered the service as an ensign in the Ninth Foot, December 12, 1770, while this regiment was in Ireland, and was advanced to a lieutenancy, October 19, 1772. He was wounded in the action of July seventh, and does not appear to have been with his regiment after this date. He was superseded September 20, 1777.

[277] John Don received his commission of second lieutenant in the Twenty-first Foot, August 28, 1771, and of first lieutenant, February 23, 1776. Anburey thus speaks of his death in the action of the nineteenth of September: "Shortly after this we heard a most tremendous firing upon our left, where we were attacked in great force, and the very first fire, your old friend, Lieutenant Don, of the 21st regiment, received a ball through his heart. I am sure it will never be erased from my memory; for when he was wounded, he sprung from the ground, nearly as high as a man." *Vide* British Army Lists, *in loco;* Travels Through the Interior Parts of America, vol. 1, p. 414.

[278] Hon. Malcolm Ramsay entered the Twenty-first Foot as ensign on May 18, 1761, and appears on the same date to have been made a second lieutenant. The Twenty-first was at this time engaged in the successful expedition against Belleisle, on the coast of France, and, after the capture of that place, proceeded to Mobile. Lieutenant Ramsay was promoted to the rank of first lieutenant, January 16, 1765; captain-lieutenant, October 6, 1769, and captain, December 25, 1770. In 1772 his regiment was ordered home, where it remained until the spring of 1776, when it sailed for Canada to relieve Carleton. Captain Ramsay was wounded, September nineteenth, at the battle of Freeman's Farm, and so severely as not to be able to share in the subsequent perils of the campaign. He was probably in Canada at the time of the surrender of Burgoyne, where we find him, December 21, 1777, commissioned a major in the Eighty-third Foot. He was made lieutenant-colonel of the Eighty-

velly,[285] Murray,[286] Prince,[287] Ensign D Salon,[288] Adjutant, Fielding;[289] Prisoners, Captn. Mt Gomery, Money — Ensign D Salons and Surgeon [Shelly]

---

third, and deputy adjutant-general in New Brunswick, August 24, 1781. His name appears on the army lists for the last time as "lieutenant-colonel late Eighty-third Foot" in 1794. *Vide* British Army Lists, *in loco;* Historical Record Twenty-first Foot; Journal of Occurrences During the Late American War, p. 175.

[279] Wm. Featherstone was commissioned a second lieutenant in the Twenty-first Foot, May 17, 1762, and a lieutenant, November 18, 1768. The regiment was during this time stationed at Mobile, where it remained until 1772, when it returned to England. Early in the spring of 1776 it was ordered back to America to relieve Carleton, and Lieutenant Featherstone participated in the campaign of that year. He was commissioned a captain lieutenant with rank of captain in the army, September 12, 1777. He was wounded in the battle of October seventh, and we infer, was conveyed to Canada, as his name does not appear upon the list of officers who surrendered at Saratoga. His name is borne upon the army lists as captain until 1794, when it disappears. *Vide* British Army Lists, *in loco;* Historical Record Twenty-first Foot.

[280] Poole England received his first commission as ensign in the Forty-seventh Foot, November 6, 1769, and on April 16, 1773 — the year in which his regiment embarked for America — he was promoted to a lieutenancy. He participated in the battle of Bunker Hill — in which action he was wounded — and, when Boston was evacuated, accompanied his regiment to Canada. He was fort major at Ticonderoga, September 6, 1777, and was taken prisoner, but liberated on parole. His name is not found on the army lists later than 1783.

[281] John Shrimpton was commissioned a lieutenant in the Sixty-second Foot, June 3, 1761, and, on the twenty-second of the following October, received the same rank in the

army, and was advanced to the rank of captain-lieutenant and captain, September 17, 1773. He was wounded on the seventh of July in the following manner: "After the action was over, and all firing had ceased for near two hours, upon the summit of the mountain I have already described, which had no ground anywhere that could command it, a number of officers were collected to read the papers taken out of the pocketbook of Colonel Francis, when Captain Shrimpton, of the 62nd regiment, who had the papers in his hand, jumped up and fell, exclaiming, 'he was severely wounded;' we all heard the ball whiz by us, and turning to the place from whence the report came, saw the smoke; as there was every reason to imagine the piece was fired from some tree, a party of men were instantly detached, but could find no person, the fellow, no doubt, as soon as he had fired, had slipt down and made his escape." Anburey again speaks of him shortly after: "Major (sic) Shrimpton, who I told you was wounded upon the hill, rather than remain with the wounded at Huberton, preferred marching with the brigade, and on crossing this creek, having only one hand to assist himself with, was on the point of slipping in, had not an officer, who was behind him caught hold of his cloaths, just as he was falling. His wound was through his shoulder, and as he could walk, he said he would not remain to fall into the enemy's hands, as it was universally thought the sick and wounded must." Captain Shrimpton recovered sufficiently to participate in the subsequent scenes of the campaign of 1777, and was one of the surrendered officers who signed the parole at Cambridge. He returned to England and became tower major at the Tower of London in 1787, but we lose sight of him the following year. *Vide* British Army Lists, *in loco;* Travels Through the Interior Parts of America, vol. 1, pp. 231, *et seq.*, 342.

[282] Thomas Steele entered the Twenty-ninth Foot as an ensign, June 21, 1769, and was advanced to the rank of lieutenant therein, November 3, 1773. The Twenty-ninth Regiment was in America during this period, but returned to England in 1774, where it was in garrison for two years, when it was ordered back to America to assist in the war there. Lieutenant Steele was wounded in the action of July seventh, but not, it would appear, seriously enough to

prevent him from participating in the subsequent events of Burgoyne's campaign, as we find him at the close of it among the surrendered officers. The army lists do not bear his name later than 1784.

[283] Gordon Forbes entered the Thirty-third Foot as an ensign under a commission bearing date August 27, 1756, and was advanced to the rank of lieutenant in the Seventy-second Foot — the second battalion of the Thirty-third, which had been renumbered — on October 2, 1757. On October 17, 1762, he was promoted to a captaincy, and during the two following years, served in the expedition against the Spanish settlements in the West Indies. On his return to England, he exchanged into the Thirty-fourth Foot, April 12, 1764, and accompanied his regiment to Louisiana, which Spain had just ceded to Great Britain. The Thirty-fourth returned to England in 1773, and was ordered to America in the spring of 1776. At the close of the successful campaign against the Americans in that year, Captain Forbes was promoted, on November eleventh, to a majority, and transferred to the Ninth Foot, with which regiment he gallantly served in the campaign of the following year. He was wounded in the action of the nineteenth of September, and was among the officers who surrendered in the following month. He returned to England in 1778, and was made lieutenant-colonel of the One Hundred and Second Foot, September 24, 1781. On October 12, 1787, — having been on half pay during the four previous years — he was made lieutenant-colonel of the Seventy-fourth Foot, and, November 18, 1790, colonel in the army. On April 18, 1794, not having had a regimental command for a period of five years, he was appointed colonel of the One Hundred and Fifth Foot, and, on October third, was made a major-general in the army. On January 24, 1787, — the One Hundred and Fifth having been disbanded during the preceding year — he was made colonel of the Eighty-first, but was transferred to the Twenty-ninth Foot on August eighth following. He was promoted to the rank of lieutenant-general, January 1, 1801, and of general, January 1, 1812. His death took place January 17, 1828. *Vide* British Army Lists, *in loco;* Hadden's Journal and Orderly Books, pp. xlvii, 162–164.

[284] Wm. Stone Montgomery. See note 167, *ante*, p. 221.

[285] Joseph Stevelly was commissioned an ensign in the Ninth Foot, January 1, 1774, and was promoted to the rank of lieutenant, December 19, 1776. He was wounded at Fort Anne, July ninth, but was with his regiment at the time of the surrender. His name is not borne on the army lists after 1781.

[286] James Murray was commissioned an ensign in the Ninth Foot, September 26, 1772, and a lieutenant, March 2, 1776. He served through Carleton's campaign, and was wounded the following year in the attack on Fort Anne, July ninth. Anburey, in writing home, speaks of him as "our pleasant Hibernian friend," and describes the rough manner in which he comforted his fellow sufferers who had met with the same misfortune which had befallen him. Murray was among the officers who were paroled at Cambridge after the surrender. He served as the quartermaster of his regiment until the close of the war, having acted in that capacity for a period of fourteen years — namely, from January 14, 1770, to the close of 1783. He was advanced to the rank of captain, March 31, 1787. In 1789 he retired from the service upon half pay. *Vide* British Army Lists, *in loco;* Travels Through the Interior Parts of America, vol. 1, p. 350, *et seq.*

[287] William Prince entered the Ninth Foot as an ensign, March 14, 1772, and was advanced to a lieutenancy, July 7, 1775. He was wounded at the battle of Freeman's Farm, September nineteenth, but not sufficiently to prevent him from remaining with his regiment, hence he was among the officers who surrendered at Saratoga a few weeks later. He was promoted to a captaincy, April 5, 1781, but does not appear to have attained any higher rank. His name is borne on the army lists for the last time in 1785.

[288] Baron Alexander Salons was commissioned an ensign in the Ninth Foot, September 2, 1776. By an order of August thirteenth he was assigned to service in Captain Fraser's corps, and, three days later, while in performance of his duty, was wounded at the battle of Bennington. He was sent back with the wounded to Canada, and, after his

return to England, was made a captain in the Eighty-fifth, which was assigned to duty in Jamaica. The climate of Jamaica wrought great havoc in the regiment, and it is said that in a short time nine-tenths of the men of the regiment were dead or on the sick list. In 1783 his name disappears from the army lists.

[289] Isaac Fielding received his commission as adjutant in the Ninth Foot, November 24, 1775. He was wounded at Fort Anne, July ninth, but had recovered from his wound sufficiently to take part in the final scenes of the campaign; hence he was among the officers who surrendered at Saratoga. We have no account of his subsequent career, as his name disappears from the army list after 1780.

Return of the army of the United States under the command of H. Gates, Major General, 17th *October* 1777.

Brigadiers	12.	
Colonels	44.	
Lieut Colonels	43.	
Majors	49.	
Captains	344.	
First lieuten^{ts}	332.	
Second lieut^{s}	326.	
Ensigns	345.	
Chaplains	5.	
Adjutants	42.	
Quarter masters	44.	
Paymasters	30.	
Surgeons	37.	
Surgeons mates	43.	
Sergeants	1392.	
Drummers	636.	
Rank & file	13,216.	
Sick present	622.	
Sick absent	731.	
At Fort Edward	3875.	on command.
On Furlough	180.	
	22348.	

Signed — Horatio Gates

Major General.

Return of the British Troops under the Command of Lieut Genl Burgoyne 17 October 1777.

Generals staff	10.
Lieut Col^{s}	4.
Majors	6.
Captains	40.
Lieutenants	59.
Ensigns	36.
Chaplains	4.
Adjutants	5.
Q^{r}. masters	3.
Surgeons	7.
Mates	7.
Sergeants	162.
Drummers & fifers	135.
Rank & file fit for duty	2365.
Sick	361.
Musicians	36.
Batt men	139.
	3379.

Signed J. Burgoyne

Lieut. General.

Return of the German troops under the Command of Lieut. General Burgoyne, 17th October 1777.

Officiers	132.
Bat officiers	197.
Chusurgiers	19.
Soldats	1792.
Tambours	72.
Total Germans	2202.

Riedesel

General Major.

Total provincial army		22348.
British	3379	5581.
Germans	2202	
Difference of armies................		16767.

*General Burgoyne's speech to the Indians in Congress, Bouquet June 21 1777 and their answer.

Brave Chiefs and Warriors.

"The great King, our common father and the patron of all who seek and deserve his protection, has considered with satisfaction the general conduct of the Indians tribes, from the beginning of the troubles in America, too sagacious and too faithful to the deluded or corrupted, they have observed the violated rights of the parental power they love, and burned to vindicate them. A few individuals alone, the refuse of a small tribe, at the first were led away, and the misrepresentations, the special allurements, the insidious promises and diversified [plots] in which the rebels are exercised, and all of which they employed for that effect, have served only in the end, to enhance the honour of the tribes in general for demonstrating to the world, how few and how contemptible are the apostates. It is a truth known to you all, that, these pitiful examples excepted (and

* This speech of Burgoyne to the Indians appears at the end of Digby's Journal, and is imperfect, the leaves which contained the concluding portion of it and the old chief's reply being lost. These I have been enabled to supply, J. P. B.

they probably have before this day hid their faces in shame), the collected voices and hands of the Indian tribes over their vast continent, are on the side of justice, of law and of the king.

[The restraint you have put upon your resentment in waiting the King, your father's call to arms, the hardest proof, I am persuaded, to which your affection could have been put, is another manifest and affecting mark of your adherence to that principle of connection to which you were always fond to allude, and which is the mutual joy and the duty of the parent to cherish.]

The clemency of your father has been abused, the offers of his mercy have been despised and his farther patience, would in his eyes become culpable in asmuch as it would withold redress from the most grievous oppressions in the provinces, that ever disgraced the history of mankind. It therefore remains for me the general of one of his majesties armies, and in this council his representative, to release you from those bonds [which] your obedience imposed. Warriors [you are free! Go] forth in the might of your valour [and your cause; strike at the common enemies of Great Britain and America — disturbers of public order, peace, and happiness — destroyers of commerce, parricides of the State."

Having reached this part of his speech General Burgoyne raised his hand and pointed to the British officers which surrounded him and then to their German allies and continued.

"The circle around you—the chiefs of His Majesty's European forces and of the Princes his allies, esteem you as brothers in the war: [emulous in glory and in friendship, we will endeavour reciprocally to give and to receive examples; we know how to value, and we will strive to imitate your preseverance in enterprise and your constancy, to resist hunger, weariness and pain.] Be it our task, from the dictates of our religion, the laws of our warfare, and the principles and interests of our policy, to regulate your passions when they overbear, to point out where it is nobler to spare than to revenge, to discriminate the degrees of guilt, to suspend the uplifted stroke, to chastise and not to destroy.

[This war to you my friends is new; upon all former occasions, in taking the field, you held yourselves authorized to destroy wherever you came, because every where you found an enemy. The case is now very different.

The King has many faithful subjects dispersed in the provinces consequently you have many brothers there, and these people are more to be pitied, that they are persecuted or imprisoned wherever they are discovered or suspected, and to dissemble, to a generous mind, is a yet more grievous punishment.

Persuaded that your magnanimity of character, joined to your principles of affection to the King, will give me fuller controul over your minds than the military rank with which I am invested, I enjoin your most serious attention to the rules which I hereby proclaim for your invariable observation during the campaign ".]

To this the Indians shouted vociferously *Etow! Etow! Etow!* to signify their approval and then listened with eager attention, to gather from the interpreter the General's instructions which were as follows:—

"I positively forbid bloodshed when you are not opposed in arms.

"Aged men, women, children, and prisoners must be held secure from the knife or hatchet, even in the time of actual conflict.

"You shall receive compensation for the prisoners you take, but you will be called to account for scalps.

"In conformity and indulgence to your customs, which have affixed an idea of honour to such badges of victory, you will be allowed to take the scalps of the dead when killed by your fire or in fair opposition, but on no account or pretence or subtilty or prevarication are they to be taken from the wounded or even from the dying, and still less pardonable will it be held to kill men in that condition [on purpose, and upon a supposition that this protection to the wounded would be thereby evaded. Base lurking assassins, incendiaries, ravagers and plunderers of the country, to whatever army they may belong, shall be treated with less reserve; but the latitude must be given you by order, and I must be the judge on the occasion.] Should the enemy on their part dare to countenance acts of barbarity towards those who fall into their hands, it shall be yours also to retaliate, but till this severity shall be thus compelled, bear immovable in your hearts this solid maxim: (it cannot be too deeply impressed) [that the great essential reward the worthy service of your alliance] the sincerity of your zeal to the King, your father and never-failing protector, will be examined and judged upon the test only of your steady and uniform adherence to the orders and counsels of those to whom His Majesty has entrusted the direction and the honour of his arms."]

At the conclusion they again shouted Etow! Etow! Etow! and after holding a consultation, an aged Iroquois chief gravely arose and replied as follows:

Reply of the Old Chief of the Iroquois to Burgoyne's speech of June 21st, 1777.

I stand up in the name of all the nations present, to assure our father that we have attentively listened to his discourse. We receive you as our father, because when you speak we have the voice of our great father beyond the great lake. We rejoice in the approbation you have expressed of our behaviour. We have been tried and tempted by the Bostonians; but we have loved our father, and our hatchets have been sharpened upon our affections. In proof of the sincerity of our professions, our whole villages able to go to war are come forth. The old and infirm, our infants and wives alone remain at home.

With one common assent we promise a constant obedience to all you have ordered, and all you shall order ; and may the Father of Days give you many and success."

When the Iroquois Chief had concluded his speech his hearers applauded as before with loud shouts of *Etow! Etow! Etow!*

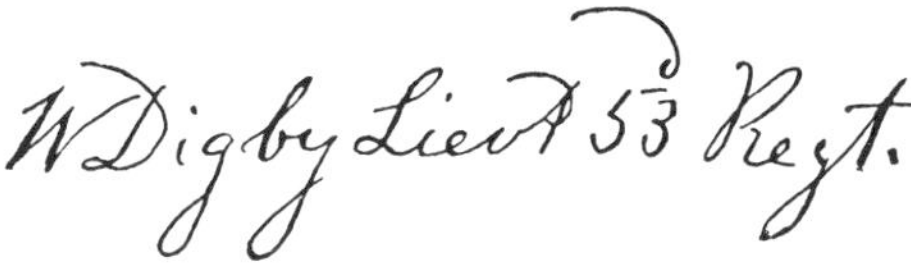

INDEX.

I am indebted to Mr. Edward Denham, of New Bedford, an expert in all matters relating to indexing, for his valuable services in compiling this index.